A Walk *in the* Woods

Also by Bill Bryson

THE LOST CONTINENT
MOTHER TONGUE
NEITHER HERE NOR THERE
MADE IN AMERICA
NOTES FROM A SMALL ISLAND

A WALK *in the* WOODS

BILL BRYSON

Illustrated by David Cook

TED SMART

Published 1997 by Doubleday
a division of Transworld Publishers Ltd
Copyright © 1997 by Bill Bryson

This edition produced for
The Book People Ltd,
Hall Wood Avenue,
Haydock,
St Helens WA11 9UL

Line illustrations © David Cook

The right of Bill Bryson to be identified
as the author of this work has been asserted
in accordance with sections 77 and 78 of the Copyright
Designs and Patents Act 1988.

Typeset 11/13½ Garamond by Falcon Oast Graphic Art
Printed in Great Britain
by Mackays of Chatham plc, Chatham, Kent

To Katz,
of course.

1. SPRINGER MOUNTAIN
2. HIAWASSEE
3. FRANKLIN
4. SMOKY MOUNTAINS NATIONAL PARK
5. ROANOKE
6. WAYNESBORO
7. ROCKFISH GAP
8. SHENANDOAH NATIONAL PARK
9. SKYLAND
10. FRONT ROYAL
11. HARPERS FERRY
12. CENTRALIA
13. DELAWARE WATER GAP
14. PITTSFIELD
15. WILLIAMSTOWN
16. MANCHESTER
17. MOUNT KILLINGTON
18. HANOVER
19. MOUNT WASHINGTON
20. MONSON
21. MOUNT KATAHDIN

Chapter 1

Not long after I moved with my family to a small town in New Hampshire I happened upon a path that vanished into a wood on the edge of town.

A sign announced that this was no ordinary footpath, but the celebrated Appalachian Trail. Running more than 2,100 miles along America's eastern seaboard, through the serene and beckoning Appalachian Mountains, the AT is the granddaddy of long hikes. The Virginia portion alone is twice the length of the Pennine Way. From Georgia to Maine, it wanders across fourteen states, through plump, comely hills whose very names – Blue Ridge, Smokies, Cumberlands, Catskills, Green Mountains, White Mountains – seem an invitation to amble. Who could say the words 'Great Smoky Mountains' or 'Shenandoah Valley' and not feel an urge, as the naturalist John Muir once put it, to 'throw a loaf of bread and a pound of tea in an old sack and jump over the back fence'?

And here it was, quite unexpectedly, meandering in a

dangerously beguiling fashion through the pleasant New England community in which I had just settled. It seemed such an extraordinary notion – the idea that I could set off from home and walk 1,800 miles through woods to Georgia, or turn the other way and clamber over the rough and stony White Mountains to the fabled prow of Mount Katahdin floating in forest 450 miles to the north in a wilderness few have seen. A little voice in my head said: 'Sounds neat! Let's do it!'

I formed a number of rationalizations. It would get me fit after years of waddlesome sloth. It would be useful – I wasn't quite sure in what way, but I was sure none the less – to learn to fend for myself in the wilderness. When guys in camouflage pants and hunting hats sat around in the Four Aces Diner talking about fearsome things done out of doors I would no longer have to feel like such a cupcake. I wanted a little of that swagger that comes with being able to gaze at a far horizon through eyes of chipped granite and say with a slow, manly sniff, 'Yeah, I've shit in the woods.'

And there was a more compelling reason to go. The Appalachians are the home of one of the world's great hardwood forests – a relic of the richest, most diversified sweep of woodland ever to grace the temperate world – and that forest is in trouble. If the global temperature rises by 4°C over the next fifty years, as is evidently possible, then the whole of the Appalachian wilderness below New England could become savannah. Already trees are dying in mysterious and frightening numbers. The elms and chestnuts are long gone, the stately hemlocks and flowery dogwoods are going, and the red spruces, Fraser firs, hickories, mountain ashes and sugar maples may be about to follow. Clearly if ever there was a time to experience this singular wilderness, it was now.

So I decided to do it. More rashly, I announced my intention – told friends and neighbours, confidently informed my publisher, made it common knowledge among those who knew me. Then I bought some books and talked to people who had done the trail in whole or in part and came gradually to realize that this was way beyond – *way* beyond – anything I had attempted before.

Nearly everyone I talked to had some gruesome story involving a guileless acquaintance who had gone off hiking the trail with high hopes and new boots and come stumbling back two days later with a bobcat attached to his head or dripping blood from an armless sleeve and whispering '*Bear!*' in a hoarse voice, before sinking into a troubled unconsciousness.

The woods were full of peril – rattlesnakes and water moccasins and nests of copperheads; bobcats, bears, coyotes, wolves, and wild boar; loony hillbillies destabilized by gross quantities of impure corn liquor and generations of profoundly unbiblical sex; rabies-crazed skunks, raccoons and squirrels; merciless fire ants and ravening blackfly; poison ivy, poison sumac, poison salamanders; even a scattering of moose lethally deranged by a parasitic worm that burrows a nest in their brains and befuddles them into chasing hapless hikers through remote, sunny meadows and into glacial lakes.

Literally unimaginable things could happen to you out there. I heard of a man who had stepped from his tent for a midnight pee and was swooped upon by a short-sighted hoot owl – the last he saw of his scalp it was dangling from talons prettily silhouetted against a harvest moon – and of a young woman who was woken by a sinuous tickle across her belly and peeked into her sleeping bag to find a copperhead bunking down in the warmth between her legs. I heard four separate stories (always related with a chuckle) of campers and bears sharing tents for a few confused and lively moments; of people abruptly vaporized ('tweren't nothing left of him but a scorch mark') by body-sized bolts of lightning when caught in sudden storms on high ridgelines; of tents crushed beneath falling trees, or eased off precipices on ballbearings of beaded rain and sent paragliding onto distant valley floors, or swept away by the watery wall of a flash flood; of hikers beyond counting whose

last experience was trembling earth and the befuddled thought
'Now what the f—?'

It required only a little light reading in adventure books and
almost no imagination to envision circumstances in which I
would find myself caught in a tightening circle of hunger-
emboldened wolves, staggering and shredding clothes under an
onslaught of pincered fire ants, or dumbly transfixed by the
sight of enlivened undergrowth advancing towards me, like a
torpedo through water, before being bowled backwards by
a sofa-sized boar with cold beady eyes, a piercing squeal, and a
slaverous, chomping appetite for pink, plump, city-softened
flesh.

Then there were all the diseases lurking in the woods –
Giardia lamblia, Eastern equine encephalitis, Rocky Mountain
spotted fever, Lyme disease, *Helicobacter pylori*, *Ehrlichia
chaffeenis*, schistosomiasis, brucellosis, and shigella, to offer but
a sampling. Eastern equine encephalitis, caused by the prick of
a mosquito, attacks the brain and central nervous system. If you
are very lucky you can hope to spend the rest of your life
propped in a chair with a bib round your neck, but generally it
will kill you. There is no known cure. No less arresting is Lyme
disease, which comes from the bite of a deer tick smaller than
a pinhead. If undetected, it can lie dormant in the human body
for years before erupting in a positive fiesta of maladies. This is
a disease for the person who wants to experience it all. The
symptoms begin with headaches, fatigue, fever, chills, shortness
of breath, dizziness, and shooting pains in the extremities, then
march on to cardiac irregularities, facial paralysis, muscle
spasms, severe mental impairment, loss of control of body func-
tions, and – not surprising in the circumstances – chronic
depression.

Then there is the little-known family of organisms called
hantaviruses, which swarm in the micro-haze above the faeces
of mice and rats, and are hoovered into the human respiratory
system by anyone unlucky enough to stick a breathing orifice

near them – by lying down, say, on a sleeping platform over which infected mice have recently scampered. In 1993 a single outbreak of hantavirus killed thirty-two people in the south-western United States, and the following year the disease claimed its first victim on the AT when a hiker contracted it after sleeping in a 'rodent-infested shelter'. (All AT shelters are rodent infested.) Among viruses, only rabies, Ebola and HIV are more certainly lethal. Again, there is no treatment.

Finally, this being America, there is the constant possibility of murder. At least nine hikers – the actual number depends on which source you consult and how you define a hiker – have been murdered along the trail since 1974. Two young women would die while I was out there.

For various practical reasons, principally to do with the long, punishing winters of northern New England, there are only so many available months to hike the trail each year. If you start at the northern end, at Mount Katahdin in Maine, you must wait for the snows to clear in late May or June. If, on the other hand, you start in Georgia and head north, you must time it to finish before mid-October when the snows blow back in. Most people hike from south to north with spring, ideally keeping one step ahead of the worst of the hot weather and the more irksome and infectious of insects. My intention was to start in the south in early March. I put aside six weeks for the first leg.

The precise length of the Appalachian Trail is a matter of interesting uncertainty. The US National Park Service, which constantly distinguishes itself in a variety of alarming ways, manages in a single leaflet to give the length of the trail as 2,155 miles and 2,200 miles. The official Appalachian Trail Guides, a set of eleven books each dealing with a particular state or section, variously give the length as 2,144 miles, 2,147 miles, 2,159 miles and 'more than 2,150 miles'. The Appalachian Trail Conference, the governing body, in 1993 put the trail length at exactly 2,146.7 miles, then changed for a couple of years to a hesitantly vague 'more than 2,150 miles', but has recently returned to confident precision with a length of 2,160.2 miles. In 1993, three people rolled a measuring wheel along its entire length and came up with a distance of 2,164.9 miles. At about the same time a careful measure based on a full set of US Geological Survey maps put the distance at 2,118.3 miles.

What is certain is that it is a long way, and from either end it is not easy. The peaks of the Appalachian Trail are not particularly formidable as mountains go – the highest, Clingmans Dome, in Tennessee, tops out at a little under 6,700 feet – but they are big enough and they go on and on. There are more than 350 peaks over 5,000 feet along the AT, and perhaps a thousand more in the vicinity. In a week you can cross fifty Snowdons. Altogether, it takes about five months, and five million steps, to walk the trail from end to end.

And of course on the AT you must lug on your back everything you need. It may seem obvious, but it came as a small shock to me to realize that this wasn't going to be even remotely like an amble through the Lake District, where you head off for the day with a haversack containing a packed lunch and a copy of Wainwright, and at day's end retire from the hills to a convivial inn. Here you sleep out of doors and cook your own food. Few people manage to carry less than 40 pounds and when you are hauling that kind of weight, believe me, never for a moment does it escape your notice. It is one thing to walk 2,000 miles; quite another to walk 2,000 miles with a wardrobe on your back.

My first inkling of just how daunting an undertaking it was to be came when I went to our local outfitters, the Dartmouth Co-Op, to purchase equipment. My son had just got an after-school job there, so I was under strict instructions of good behaviour. Specifically, I was not to say or do anything stupid, try on anything that would require me to expose my stomach, say 'Are you shitting me?' when informed of the price of a product, be conspicuously inattentive when a sales assistant was explaining the correct maintenance or aftercare of a product, and above all not to don anything inappropriate, like a woman's ski hat, in an attempt to amuse.

I was told to ask for Dave Mengle because he had walked large parts of the trail himself and was something of an encyclopedia of outdoor knowledge. A kindly and deferential sort of fellow, Mengle could talk for perhaps four days solid, with interest, about any aspect of hiking equipment.

I have never been so simultaneously impressed and bewildered. We spent a whole afternoon going through his stock. He would say things to me like: 'Now this has a 70-denier high-density abrasion-resistant fly with a ripstop weave. On the other hand, and I'll be frank with you here' – and he would lean towards me and reduce his voice to a low, candid tone, as if disclosing that it had once been arrested in a public toilet with a sailor – 'the seams are lap-felled rather than bias-taped and the vestibule is a little cramped.'

I think because I mentioned that I had done a bit of hiking in England, he assumed some measure of competence on my part. I didn't wish to alarm or disappoint him, so when he asked me questions like 'What's your view on carbon fibre stays?' I would shake my head with a rueful chuckle, in recognition of the famous variability of views on this perennially thorny issue, and say, 'You know, Dave, I've never been able to make up my mind on that one – what do you think?'

Together we discussed and gravely considered the relative merits of side compression straps, spindrift collars, crampon patches, load transfer differentials, airflow channels, webbing loops, and something called the occipital cutout ratio. We went through that with every item. Even an aluminium cookset offered considerations of weight, compactness, thermal dynamics, and general utility that could occupy a mind for hours. In between there was lots of discussion about hiking generally, mostly to do with hazards like rockfalls, bear encounters, cookstove explosions, and snakebites, which he described with a certain misty-eyed fondness, before coming back to the topic at hand.

With everything, he talked a lot about weight. It seemed to me a trifle overfastidious to choose one sleeping bag over another because it weighed three ounces less, but as equipment piled up around us I began to appreciate how ounces accumulate into pounds. I hadn't expected to buy so much – I already owned hiking boots, a Swiss army knife and a plastic map pouch that you wear round your neck on a piece of string, so I had felt I was pretty well there – but the more I talked to Dave the more I realized that I was shopping for an expedition.

The two big shocks were how expensive everything was – each time Dave dodged into the storeroom or went off to confirm a denier rating, I stole looks at price tags and was invariably appalled – and that every piece of equipment appeared to require some further piece of equipment. If you bought a sleeping bag, then you needed a stuff sack for it. The stuff sack cost $29. I found this an increasingly difficult concept to warm to.

When after much solemn consideration I settled on a backpack – a very expensive Gregory, top of the range, no-point-in-stinting-here sort of thing – he said, 'Now what kind of straps do you want with that?'

'I beg your pardon?' I said, and recognized at once that I was on the brink of a dangerous condition known as retail burnout. No more now would I blithely say, 'Better give me half a dozen of those, Dave. Oh, and I'll take eight of these – what the heck, make it a dozen. You only live once, eh?' The mound of provisions that a minute ago had looked so pleasingly abundant and exciting – all new! all mine! – suddenly seemed burdensome and extravagant.

'Straps,' Dave explained. 'You know, to tie on your sleeping bag and lash things down.'

'It doesn't come with straps?' I said in a new, level tone.

'Oh, no.' He surveyed a wall of products, and touched a

finger to his nose. 'You'll need a raincover too, of course.'

I blinked. 'A raincover? Why?'

'To keep out the rain.'

'The backpack's not rainproof?'

He grimaced as if making an exceptionally delicate distinction. 'Well, not a hundred per cent . . .'

This was extraordinary to me. 'Really? Did it not occur to the manufacturer that people might want to take their packs outdoors from time to time? Perhaps even go camping with them. How much is this pack anyway?'

'Two hundred and fifty dollars.'

'Two hundred and fifty dollars! Are you shi—' I paused and put on a new voice. 'Are you saying, Dave, that I pay two hundred and fifty dollars for a pack and it doesn't have straps and it isn't waterproof?'

He nodded.

'Does it have a bottom in it?'

Mengle smiled uneasily. It was not in his nature to grow critical or weary in the rich, promising world of camping equipment. 'The straps come in a choice of six colours,' he offered helpfully.

I ended up with enough equipment to bring full employment to a vale of sherpas – a three-season tent, self-inflating sleeping pad, nested pots and pans, folding cutlery, plastic dish and cup, complicated pump-action water purifier, stuff sacks in a rainbow of colours, seam sealer, patching kit, sleeping bag, bungee cords, water bottles, waterproof poncho, waterproof matches, pack cover, a rather nifty compass/thermometer keyring, a little collapsible stove that looked frankly like trouble, gas bottle and spare gas bottle, a hands-free torch that you wear on your head like a miner's lamp (this I liked very much), a big knife for killing bears and hillbillies, insulated long johns and vests, four bandannas, and lots of other stuff, some of which I had to go back again and ask what it was for exactly. I drew the line at buying a designer groundcloth for $59.95, knowing I could acquire a lawn tarp at K-mart for $5. I also said no to a first-aid kit, sewing kit, anti-snakebite kit, $12 emergency whistle and small orange plastic shovel for burying one's poop, on the grounds that these were unnecessary, too expensive or invited ridicule. The orange spade in particular seemed to shout: 'Greenhorn! Sissy! Make way for Mr Buttercup!'

Then, just to get it all over and done with at once, I went to the local bookshop and bought books – *The Thru-Hiker's Handbook, Walking the Appalachian Trail,* several books on wildlife and the natural sciences, a geological history of the Appalachian Trail by the exquisitely named V. Collins Chew, and the complete, aforementioned set of official Appalachian Trail Guides, consisting of eleven small paperback books and fifty-nine maps in different sizes, styles and scales covering the whole trail from Springer Mountain to Mount Katahdin, and ambitiously priced at $233.45 the set. On the way out I noticed a volume called *Bear Attacks: Their Causes and Avoidance,* opened it up at random, found the sentence 'This is a clear example of the general type of incident in which a black bear sees a person and decides to try to kill and eat him', and tossed that into the shopping basket, too.

I took all this home and carried it down to the basement in several trips. There was such a lot, nearly all of it techno-logically unfamiliar to me, which made it both exciting and daunting, but mostly daunting. I put the hands-free torch on my head, for the heck of it, and pulled the tent from its plastic packaging and erected it on the floor. I unfurled the self-inflating sleeping pad and pushed it inside and followed that with my fluffy new sleeping bag. Then I crawled in and lay there for quite a long time trying out for size the expensive, confined, strangely new-smelling, entirely novel space that was soon to be my home from home. I tried to imagine myself lying not in a basement beside the reassuring, cosily domesticated roar of the furnace, but rather outside, in a high mountain pass, listening to wind and tree noise, the lonely cry of doglike

creatures, the hoarse whisper of a Georgia mountain accent saying: 'Hey, Virgil, there's one over here. Y'all remember the
rope?' But I couldn't really.

I hadn't been in a space like this since I stopped making dens
with blankets and card tables at about the age of nine. It was
really quite snug and, once you got used to the smell, which I
naively presumed would dissipate over time, and the fact that
the fabric gave everything inside a sickly greenish pallor, like
the glow off a radar screen, it was not so bad. A little claustro-
phobic perhaps, a little odd-smelling, but cosy and sturdy even
so.

This wouldn't be so bad, I told myself. But secretly I knew
that I was quite wrong.

Chapter 2

On the afternoon of 5 July 1983, three adult supervisors and a group of youngsters set up camp at a popular spot beside Lake Canimina in the fragrant pine forests of western Quebec, about 80 miles north of Ottawa, in a park called La Vérendrye Provincial Reserve. They cooked dinner and afterwards, in the correct fashion, secured their food in a bag and carried it a hundred or so feet into the woods, where they suspended it above the ground between two trees, out of the reach of bears.

About midnight, a black bear came prowling around the margins of the camp, spied the bag and brought it down by climbing one of the trees and breaking a branch. He plundered the food and departed, but an hour later he was back, this time entering the camp itself, drawn by the lingering smell of cooked meat in the campers' clothes and hair, in their sleeping bags and tent fabric. It was to be a long night for the Canimina party. Three times between midnight and 3.30 a.m. the bear came to the camp.

Imagine, if you will, lying in the dark alone in a little tent, nothing but a few microns of trembling nylon between you and the chill night air, listening to a 400-pound bear moving around your campsite. Imagine its quiet grunts and mysterious snufflings, the clatter of upended cookware and sounds of moist gnawings, the pad of its feet and the heaviness of its breath, the singing brush of its haunch along your tent side. Imagine the hot flood of adrenalin, that unwelcome tingling in the back of your arms, at the sudden rough bump of its snout against the foot of your tent, the alarming wild wobble of your frail shell as it roots through the backpack that you left casually propped by the entrance – with, you suddenly recall, a Snickers bar in the pouch. Bears adore Snickers bars, you've heard.

And then the dull thought – oh, God – that perhaps you brought the Snickers bar in here with you, that it's somewhere in here, down by your feet or underneath you or – oh, shit, here it is. Another bump of grunting head against the tent, this time near your shoulders. More crazy wobble. Then silence, a very long silence, and – wait, shhhhh . . . yes! – the unutterable relief of realizing that the bear has withdrawn to the other side of the camp or shambled back into the woods. I tell you right now. I couldn't stand it.

So imagine then what it must have been like for poor little David Anderson, aged twelve, when at 3.30 a.m., on the third foray, his tent of all tents was abruptly rent with a swipe of claw and the bear, driven to distraction by the rich, unfixable, every-where aroma of hamburger, bit hard into a flinching limb and dragged him shouting and flailing through the camp and into the woods. In the few moments it took the boy's fellow campers to unzip themselves from their accoutrements – and imagine, if you will, trying to swim out of suddenly voluminous sleeping bags, take up flashlights and makeshift cudgels, undo tent zips with helplessly fumbling fingers, and give chase – in those few moments, poor little David Anderson was dead.

Now imagine reading a nonfiction book packed with stories

such as this – true tales soberly related – just before setting off alone on a camping trip of your own into the North American wilderness. The book to which I refer is *Bear Attacks: Their Causes and Avoidance* by a Canadian academic named Stephen Herrero. If it is not the last word on the subject, then I really, really, really do not wish to hear the last word. Through long winter nights in New Hampshire, while snow piled up outdoors and my wife slumbered peacefully beside me, I lay saucer-eyed in bed reading clinically precise accounts of people gnawed pulpy in their sleeping bags, plucked whimpering from trees, even noiselessly stalked (I didn't know this happened!) as they sauntered unawares down leafy paths or cooled their feet in mountain streams. People whose one fatal mistake was to smooth their hair with a dab of aromatic gel, or eat juicy meat, or tuck a Snickers bar in their shirt pocket for later, or have sex, or even, possibly, menstruate, or in some small, inadvertent way pique the olfactory properties of the hungry bear. Or, come to that, whose fatal failing was simply to be very, very un-fortunate – to round a bend and find a moody male blocking the path, head rocking appraisingly, or wander unwittingly into the territory of a bear too slowed by age or idleness to chase down fleeter prey.

Now it is important to establish right away that the possibility of a serious bear attack on the Appalachian Trail is remote. To begin with, the really terrifying American bear, the grizzly – *Ursus horribilis* as it is so vividly and correctly labelled – doesn't range east of the Mississippi, which is good news because griz-zlies are large, powerful and ferociously bad-tempered. When Lewis and Clark went into the wilderness, they found that noth-ing unnerved the native Indians more than the grizzly, and not surprisingly since you could riddle a grizzly with arrows – positively porcupine it – and it would still keep coming. Even Lewis and Clark with their big guns were astounded and un-settled by the ability of the grizzly to absorb volleys of lead with barely a wobble.

Herrero recounts an incident that nicely conveys the near indestructibility of the grizzly. It concerns a professional hunter in Alaska named Alexei Pitka, who stalked a big male through snow and finally felled it with a well-aimed shot to the heart from a large-bore rifle. Pitka should probably have carried a card with him that said: 'First make sure bear is dead. Then put gun down.' He advanced cautiously and spent a minute or two watching the bear for movement, but when there was none he set the gun against a tree – big mistake – and strode forward to claim his prize. Just as he arrived, the bear sprang up, clapped its expansive jaws around the front of Pitka's head, as if giving him a big kiss, and with a single jerk tore off his face.

Miraculously, Pitka survived. 'I don't know why I set that durn gun against the tree,' he said later. Actually what he said was, 'Mrffff mmmpg nnnmmm mffffffn,' on account of having no lips, teeth, nose, tongue or other vocal apparatus.

If I were to be pawed and chewed – and this seemed to me entirely possible, the more I read – it would be by a black bear, *Ursus americanus*. There are at least 500,000 black bears in North America, possibly as many as 700,000. They are notably common in the hills along the Appalachian Trail (indeed, they often *use* the trail, for convenience), and their numbers are growing. Grizzlies, by contrast, number no more than 35,000 in the whole of North America, and just 1,000 in the mainland United States principally in and around Yellowstone National Park. Of the two species, black bears are generally smaller (though this is a decidedly relative condition; a male black bear can still weigh up to 650 pounds) and unquestionably more retiring.

Black bears rarely attack. But here's the thing. Sometimes they do. All bears are agile, cunning and immensely strong, and they are always hungry. If they want to kill you and eat you, they can, and pretty much whenever they want. That doesn't happen often, but – and here is the absolutely salient point – once would be enough.

Herrero is at pains to stress that black bear attacks are infrequent, relative to their numbers. In the eight decades to 1980 he found just twenty-three confirmed black bear killings of humans (about half the number of killings by grizzlies), and most of these were out west or in Canada. In New Hampshire there has not been an unprovoked fatal attack on a human by a bear since 1784. In Vermont, there has never been one.

I wanted very much to be calmed by these assurances but could never quite manage the necessary leap of faith. After noting that just 500 people were attacked and hurt by black bears between 1960 and 1980 – twenty-five attacks a year from a resident population of at least half a million bears – Herrero adds that most of these injuries were not severe. 'The typical black bear-inflicted injury', he writes blandly, 'is minor and usually involves only a few scratches or light bites.'

Pardon me, but what exactly is a light bite? Are we talking a playful wrestle and gummy nips? I think not. And is 500 certified attacks really such a modest number, considering how few people go into the North American woods? And how foolish must one be to be reassured by the information that no bear has killed a human in Vermont or New Hampshire in 200 years? That's not because the bears have signed a treaty, you know. There's nothing to say that they won't start a modest rampage tomorrow.

So let us imagine that a bear does go for us out in the wilds. What are we to do? Interestingly, the advised stratagems are exactly opposite for grizzly and black bear. With a grizzly, you should make for a tall tree, since grizzlies aren't much for climbing. If a tree is not available, then you should back off slowly, avoiding direct eye contact. All the books tell you that if the grizzly comes for you on no account should you run. This is the sort of advice you get from someone who is sitting at a keyboard when he gives it. Take it from me, if you are in an open space with no weapons and a grizzly comes for you, run. You may as well. If nothing else, it will give you something to do with the last seven seconds of your life. However, when the grizzly overtakes you, as it most assuredly will, you should fall to the ground and play dead. A grizzly may chew on a limp form for a minute or two, but generally will lose interest and shuffle off. With black bears, however, playing dead is futile since they will continue chewing on you until you are considerably past caring. It is also foolish to climb a tree because black bears are adroit climbers and, as Herrero drily notes, you will simply end up fighting the bear in a tree.

To ward off an aggressive black bear, Herrero suggests making a lot of noise, banging pots and pans together, throwing sticks and rocks, and 'running at the bear'. (Yeah, right. You first, Professor.) On the other hand, he then adds judiciously, these tactics could 'merely provoke the bear'. Well, thanks. Elsewhere he suggests that hikers should consider making noises from time to time – singing a song, say – to alert bears to their presence, since a startled bear is more likely to be an angry bear, but then a few pages later cautions that 'there may be danger in making noise', since that can attract a hungry bear that might otherwise overlook you.

The fact is, no one can tell you what to do. Bears are unpredictable, and what works in one circumstance may not work in another. In 1973, two teenagers, Mark Seeley and Michael Whitten, were out for a hike in Yellowstone when they inadvertently crossed between a mother and her cubs. Nothing worries and antagonizes a female bear more than to have people between her and her brood. Furious, she turned and gave chase – despite the bear's lolloping gait it can move at up to 35 miles an hour – and the two boys scrambled up trees. The bear followed Whitten up his tree, clamped her mouth round his right foot, and slowly and patiently tugged him from his perch. (Is it me, or can you feel your fingernails scraping through the bark?) On the ground, she began mauling him extensively. In an attempt to distract the bear from his friend, Seeley shouted at it, whereupon the bear came and pulled him out of his tree, too. Both young men played dead – precisely the wrong thing to do, according to all the instruction manuals – and the bear left.

I won't say I became obsessed by all this, but it did occupy my thoughts a great deal in the months while I waited for spring to come. My particular dread – the vivid possibility that left me staring at tree shadows on the bedroom ceiling night after night – was having to lie in a small tent, alone in an inky wilderness, listening to a foraging bear outside, and wondering what its intentions were. I was especially riveted by an amateur photograph in Herrero's book, taken late at night by a camper with a flash at a campground out west. The photograph caught four black bears as they puzzled over a suspended food bag. The bears were clearly startled but not remotely alarmed by the flash. It was not the size or demeanour of the bears that troubled me – they looked almost comically unaggressive, like four guys who had got a Frisbee caught up a tree – but their numbers. Up to that moment it had not occurred to me that bears might prowl in parties. What on earth would I do if *four* bears came into my camp?

Why, I would die, of course. Literally shit myself lifeless. I would blow my sphincter out of my backside like one of those unrolling paper streamers you get at children's parties – I dare say it would even give a merry toot – and bleed to a messy death in my sleeping bag.

Herrero's book was written in 1985. Since that time, according to an article in the *New York Times*, bear attacks in North America have increased by 25 per cent. The *Times* article also noted that bears are far more likely to attack humans in the spring following a bad berry year. The previous year had been a very bad berry year. I didn't like the feel of any of this.

Then there were all the problems and particular dangers of solitude. I still have my appendix, and any number of other organs that might burst or sputter in the empty wilds. What would I do then? What if I fell from a ledge and broke my back?

What if I lost the trail in a blizzard or fog, or was seized at the throat by a venomous snake, or lost my footing on moss-slickened rocks crossing a stream and cracked my head a concussive blow? You could drown in three inches of water on your own. You could die from a twisted ankle. No, I didn't like the feel of this at all.

At Christmas, I put notes in lots of cards inviting people to come with me on the trail, if only part of the way. Nobody responded, of course. Then one day in late February, with departure nigh, I got a call. It was from an old school friend named Stephen Katz. Katz and I had grown up together in Iowa, but I had pretty well lost touch with him. Those of you who have read *Neither Here Nor There* may recall Katz as my youthful travelling companion round Europe. In the twenty-five years since, I had run into him three or four times on visits home, but hadn't seen him otherwise.

'I've been hesitating to call,' he said slowly. He seemed to be searching for words. 'But this Appalachian Trail deal – do you think maybe I could come with you?'

I couldn't believe it. 'You want to come with me?'

'If it's a problem, I understand.'

'No,' I said. 'No, no, no. You're very welcome. You are extremely welcome.'

'Really?' He seemed to brighten.

'Of course.' I really could not believe it. I wasn't going to have to walk alone. I did a little jig. *I wasn't going to have to walk alone.* 'I can't tell you how welcome you would be.'

'Oh, great,' he said in a flood of relief, then added in a confessional tone, 'I thought maybe you might not want me along.'

'Why ever not?'

'Because, you know, I still owe you six hundred dollars from Europe.'

'Hey, jeez, certainly not – you owe me six hundred dollars?'

'I still intend to pay you back.'

'Hey,' I said, 'hey.' I couldn't remember any $600. I had

never released anyone from a debt of this magnitude before and it took me a moment to get the words out. 'Listen, it's not a problem. Just come hiking with me. Are you sure you're up for this?'

'Absolutely.'

'What kind of shape are you in?'

'Real good. I walk everywhere these days.'

'Really?' This is most unusual in America.

'Well, they repossessed my car, you see.'

'Ah.'

We talked a little more about this and that – his mother, my mother, Des Moines. I told him what little I knew about the trail and the wilderness life that awaited us. We settled that he would fly to New Hampshire the next Wednesday, we would spend two days making preparations, and then hit the trail. For the first time in months I felt positively positive about this enterprise. He seemed remarkably upbeat, too, for someone who didn't have to do this at all.

My last words to him were, 'So, how are you with bears?'

'Hey, they haven't got me yet!'

That's the spirit, I thought. Good old Katz. Good old anyone with a pulse and a willingness to go walking with me. After he rang off, it occurred to me I hadn't asked him why he wanted to come. Katz was the one person I knew on earth who might be on the run from guys with names like Julio and Mr Big. Anyway, I didn't care. I wasn't going to have to walk alone.

I found my wife at the kitchen sink and told her the good news. She was more reserved in her enthusiasm than I had hoped.

'You're going into the woods for weeks and weeks with a person you have barely seen for twenty-five years. Have you really thought this through?' (As if I have ever thought anything through.) 'I thought you two ended up getting on each other's nerves in Europe.'

'No.' This was not quite correct. 'We started off on each

other's nerves. We ended up despising each other. But that was a long time ago.'

She gave me her pull-the-other-one look. 'You have nothing in common.'

'We have everything in common. We're forty-four years old. We'll talk about haemorrhoids and lower back pain and how we can't remember where we put anything, and the next night I'll say, "Hey, did I tell you about my back problems?" and he'll say, "No, I don't think so," and we'll do it all over again. It'll be great.'

'It'll be hell.'

'Yeah, I know,' I said.

And so I found myself, six days later, standing at our local airport watching a tin commuter plane containing Katz touch down and taxi to a halt on the tarmac twenty yards from the terminal. The hum of the propellers intensified for a moment, then gradually stuttered to a halt and the plane's door-cum-stairway fell open. I tried to remember the last time I had seen him. After our summer in Europe, Katz had gone back to Des Moines and devoted himself single-handedly to ensuring that Iowa had a thriving drug culture. He had partied for years, until there was no-one left to party with, then he had partied with himself, alone in small apartments, in T-shirt and boxer shorts, with a bottle and a baggie of pot and a TV with rabbit ears. I remembered now that the last time I had seen him was about five years before in a Denny's restaurant where I was taking my mother for breakfast. He was sitting in a booth with a haggard fellow who looked as if his name would be Virgil Starkweather, tucking into pancakes and taking occasional illicit nips from a bottle in a paper bag. It was eight in the morning and Katz looked very happy. He was always happy when he was drunk, and he was always drunk.

Two weeks after that, I later heard, police found him in an upside-down car in a field outside Mingo, hanging by his seatbelt, still clutching the steering wheel and saying, 'Well, what seems to be the problem, officers?' There was a small quantity of cocaine in the glovebox and he was despatched to a minimum security prison for eighteen months. While there, he started attending AA meetings. To everyone's surprise, not least his own, he had not touched alcohol or an illegal substance since.

After his release, he got a little job, went back to college part time and settled down for a while with a hairdresser named Patty. For the past three years he had devoted himself to rectitude and – I instantly saw now as he stooped out of the door of the plane – growing a stomach. Katz was arrestingly larger than when I had last seen him. He had always been kind of fleshy, but now he brought to mind Orson Welles after a very bad night. He was limping a little and breathing harder than one ought to after a walk of 20 yards.

'Man, I'm hungry,' he said without preamble, and let me take his carry-on bag, which instantly jerked my arm to the floor.

'What have you got in here?' I gasped.

'Ah, just some tapes and shit for the trail. There a Dunkin' Donuts anywhere around here? I haven't had anything to eat since Boston.'

'Boston? You've just come from Boston.'

'Yeah, I gotta eat something every hour or so or I have, whaddayacallit, seizures.'

'Seizures?' This wasn't quite the reunion scenario I had envisioned. I imagined him bouncing around on the Appalachian Trail like some wind-up toy that had fallen on its back.

'Ever since I took some contaminated phenylthiamines about ten years ago. If I eat a couple of doughnuts or something I'm usually OK.'

'Stephen, we're going to be in the wilderness in three days. There won't be doughnut stores.'

He beamed proudly. 'I thought of that.' He indicated his bag on the carousel – a green army surplus duffel – and let me pick it up. It weighed at least seventy-five pounds. He saw my look of wonder. 'Snickers,' he explained. 'Lots and lots of Snickers.'

We drove home by way of Dunkin' Donuts. My wife and I sat with him at the kitchen table and watched him eat five Boston cream doughnuts, which he washed down with two glasses of milk. Then he said he wanted to go and lie down awhile. It took him whole minutes to get up the stairs.

My wife turned to me with a look of perfect blankness.

'Please just don't say anything,' I said.

In the afternoon, after Katz had rested, he and I visited Dave Mengle and got him fitted with a backpack and a tent and sleeping bag and all the rest of it, and then went to K-mart for a groundsheet and thermal underwear and some other small things. After that he rested some more.

The following day we went to the supermarket to buy provisions for our first week on the trail. I knew nothing about cooking, but Katz had been looking after himself for years and had a repertoire of dishes, principally involving peanut butter, tuna and noodles stirred together in a pot, that he thought would transfer nicely to a camping milieu, but he also piled lots of other things into the trolley – four large pepperoni sausages, five pounds of rice, assorted packets of cookies, oatmeal, raisins, M&Ms, Spam, more Snickers, sunflower seeds, Graham crackers, instant mashed potatoes, two large bags of brown sugar – these, he said confidingly, were absolutely vital – several sticks of beef jerky, a couple of bricks of cheese, a tinned ham, and the full range of gooey and evidently imperishable cakes and doughnuts produced by a company called Little Debbie.

'You know, I don't think we'll be able to carry all this,' I suggested as he placed a horsecollar-shaped bologna in the trolley.

Katz surveyed the trolley grimly. 'Yeah, you're right,' he agreed. 'Let's start again.'

He abandoned the trolley there and went off for another one. We went round again, this time trying to be more intelligently selective, but we still ended up with clearly too much.

We took everything home, divided it up, and went off to pack – Katz to the bedroom where all his other stuff was, I to my basement HQ. I packed for two hours, but I couldn't begin to get everything in. I put aside books and notebooks and nearly all my spare clothes, and tried lots of different combinations, but every time I finished I would turn to find something large and important left over. Eventually I went upstairs to see how Katz was doing. He was lying on the bed, listening to his Walkman. Stuff was scattered everywhere. His backpack was limp and unattended. Little percussive hisses of music were leaking from his ears.

'Aren't you packing?' I said.

'Yeah.'

I waited a minute, thinking he would bound up, but he didn't move. 'Forgive me, Stephen, but you give the impression that you are lying down.'

'Yeah.'

'Can you actually hear what I'm saying?'

'Yeah, in a minute.'

I sighed and went back down to the basement.

Katz said little during dinner and afterwards returned to his room. We heard nothing more from him throughout the evening, but about midnight, as we lay in bed, noises began to float to us through the walls – clompings and mutterings, sounds like furniture being dragged across the floor, and brief enraged outbursts, interspersed with long periods of silence. I held my wife's hand and couldn't think of anything to say.

In the morning, I tapped on Katz's door and eventually put my head in. He was asleep, fully dressed, on top of a tumult of bedding. The mattress was partway off the bed, as if he had been engaged in the night in some scuffle with intruders. His pack was full, but unsecured, and personal effects were still liberally distributed around the room. I told him we had to leave in an hour to catch our plane.

'Yeah,' he said.

Twenty minutes later, he came downstairs, laboriously and with a great deal of soft cursing. Without even looking you could tell he was coming down sideways and with care, as if the steps were glazed with ice. He was wearing his pack. Things were tied to it all over – a pair of grubby sneakers and what looked like a pair of dress boots, his pots and pans, a Laura Ashley carrier bag evidently appropriated from my wife's wardrobe and filled now with God knows what. 'This is the best I could do,' he said. 'I had to leave a few things.'

I nodded. I'd left a few things, too – notably the oatmeal, which I didn't like anyway, and the more disgusting-looking of the Little Debbie cakes, which is to say all of them.

My wife drove us to the airport in Manchester, through blowing snow, in the kind of awkward silence that precedes a long separation. Katz sat in the back and ate doughnuts. At the airport, she presented me with a knobbly walking stick the children had bought me. It had a red bow on it. I wanted to burst into tears – or, better still, climb in the car and speed off while Katz was still frowning over his new, unfamiliar straps. She squeezed my arm, gave a weak smile and went.

I watched her go, then went into the terminal with Katz. The man at the check-in desk looked at our tickets to Atlanta and our packs and said – quite alertly, I thought, for a person wearing a short-sleeved shirt in winter – 'You fellows hiking the Appalachian Trail?'

'Sure are,' said Katz proudly.

'Lot of trouble with wolves down in Georgia, you know.'

'Really?' Katz was all ears.

'Oh, yeah. Coupla people been attacked recently. Pretty savagely, too, from what I hear.' He messed around with tickets and luggage tags for a minute. 'Hope you brought some long underwear.'

Katz screwed up his face. 'For *wolves*?'

'No, for the weather. There's gonna be record cold down

there over the next four or five days. Gonna be *well* below zero in Atlanta tonight.'

'Oh, great,' Katz said and gave a ruptured, disconsolate sigh. He looked challengingly at the man. 'Any other news for us? Hospital call to say we got cancer or anything?'

The man beamed and slapped the tickets down on the counter. 'No, that's about it, but you have a real good trip. And hey' – he was addressing Katz now, in a lower voice – 'you watch out for those wolves, son, because between you and me you look like pretty good eating.' He gave a wink.

'Jesus,' said Katz in a low voice, and looked deeply, deeply gloomy.

We took the escalator up to our gate. 'And they won't feed us on this plane either, you know,' he announced with a curious bitter finality.

Chapter 3

It started with Benton MacKaye, a mild, kindly, infinitely well-meaning visionary who in the summer of 1921 unveiled an ambitious plan for a hiking trail to his friend Charles Harris Whitaker, editor of a leading architectural journal. To say that MacKaye's life at this point was not going well would be to engage in heartless understatement. In the previous decade he had been fired from a job at Harvard, eased out of a position at the National Forest Service, and eventually, for want of a better place to stick him, given a desk at the Labor Department, a federal agency, with a vague assignment to come up with ideas to improve efficiency and morale. There, he dutifully produced ambitious, unworkable proposals which were received with amused tolerance and promptly binned. In April 1921 his wife, a well-known pacifist and suffragette named Jessie Hardy Stubbs, flung herself off a bridge over the East River in New York and drowned.

It was against this background, just ten weeks later, that he offered Whitaker his idea for an Appalachian Trail, and the proposal was published in the somewhat unlikely forum of Whitaker's *Journal of the American Institute of Architects* the following October. A hiking trail was only part of MacKaye's grand vision. He saw the AT as a thread connecting a network of mountaintop work camps where pale, depleted urban workers in their thousands would come and engage in healthful toil in a selfless spirit and refresh themselves on nature. There were to be hostels and inns and seasonal study centres, and eventually permanent woodland villages – 'self-owning' communities whose inhabitants would support themselves with co-operative 'non-industrial activity' based on forestry, farming and crafts. The whole would be, as MacKaye ecstatically described it, 'a retreat from profit' – a notion that others saw as 'smacking of Bolshevism', in the words of one biographer.

At the time of MacKaye's proposal there were already several hiking clubs in the eastern United States – the Green Mountain Club, the Dartmouth Outing Club, the venerable Appalachian Mountain Club, among others – and these mostly patrician organizations already owned and maintained hundreds of miles of mountain and woodland trails, mostly in New England. In 1925 representatives of the leading clubs met in Washington and founded the Appalachian Trail Conference with a view to constructing a 1,200-mile-long trail connecting the two highest peaks in the east: 6,684-foot Mount Mitchell in North Carolina and the slightly smaller (by 396 feet) Mount Washington in New Hampshire. In fact, however, for the next five years nothing happened, largely because MacKaye occupied himself with refining and expanding his vision until he and it were only tangentially connected to the real world.

Not until 1930, when a young admiralty lawyer in Washington and keen hiker named Myron Avery took over the development of the project, did work actually begin, but suddenly it moved on apace. Avery was not evidently a lovable fellow. As one contemporary put it, he left two trails from Maine to Georgia: 'One

was of hurt feelings and bruised egos. The other was the AT.'
He had no patience with MacKaye and his 'quasi-mystical epi-
grams', and the two never got along. In 1935, they had an
acrimonious falling out over the development of the trail
through Shenandoah National Park – Avery was willing to
accommodate the building of a scenic highway through the
mountains; MacKaye thought it a betrayal of founding principles
– and they never spoke again.

MacKaye always gets the credit for the trail, but largely this
was because he lived to be ninety-six and had a good head of
white hair; he was always available in later years to say a few
words at ceremonies on sunny hillsides. Avery on the other
hand died in 1952, a quarter-century before MacKaye and when
the trail was still little known. But it was really Avery's trail. He
mapped it out, bullied and cajoled clubs into producing volunteer crews, and personally superintended the construction of
hundreds of miles of path. He extended its planned length from
1,200 miles to well over 2,000, and before it was finished had
walked every inch of it. In under seven years, using volunteer
labour, he built a 2,000-mile trail through mountain wilderness.
Armies have done less.

The Appalachian Trail was formally completed on 14 August
1937 with the clearing of a two-mile stretch of woods in a
remote part of Maine. Remarkably, the building of the longest
footpath in the world attracted almost no attention. Avery was
not one for publicity and by this time MacKaye had retired in a
funk. No newspapers noted the achievement. There was no
formal celebration to mark the occasion.

The path they built had no historical basis. It didn't follow
any Indian trails or colonial post roads. It didn't even seek out
the best views, or highest hills or most notable landmarks. In
the end, it went nowhere near Mount Mitchell, though it did
take in Mount Washington and then carried on another 350
miles to Mount Katahdin in Maine. (Avery, who had grown up
in Maine and done his formative hiking there, was most

insistent on this.) Essentially it went where access could be gained, mostly high up on the hills, over lonely ridges and forgotten hollows that no-one had ever used or coveted, or sometimes even named. It fell short of the actual southern end of the Appalachian Mountain chain by 150 miles, and of the northern end by nearer 700. The work camps and chalets, the schools and study centres, were never built.

Still, quite a lot of the original impulse behind MacKaye's vision survives. All 2,100 miles of the trail, as well as side trails, footbridges, signs, blazes, and shelters, are impeccably maintained by volunteers – indeed, the Appalachian Trail is said to be the largest volunteer-run undertaking on the planet. It remains gloriously free of commercialism. The Appalachian Trail Conference didn't hire its first paid employee until 1968, and retains the air of a friendly, accessible, well-intentioned outfit. The AT is no longer the longest long-distance footpath in the world – the Pacific Crest and Continental Divide trails, both out west, are slightly longer – but it will always be the first and greatest. It has a lot of friends. It deserves them.

Almost from the day of its opening, the trail has had to be moved around. First, 118 miles in Virginia were rerouted to accommodate the construction of Skyline Drive through Shenandoah National Park. Then, in 1958, overdevelopment on and around Mount Oglethorpe in Georgia necessitated lopping 20 miles off the trail's southern end and moving the start to Springer Mountain, in the protected wilderness of the Chattahoochee National Forest. Ten years later, the Maine Appalachian Trail Club rerouted 263 miles of trail – half its total length across the state – removing the trail from logging roads and putting it back in the wilds. Even now the trail is never quite the same from one year to the next.

The hardest part about hiking the Appalachian Trail is getting onto it, nowhere more than at its ends. Springer Mountain, the launching-off point in the south, is seven miles from the nearest highway, at a place called Amicalola Falls State Park, which in turn is a good way from anywhere. From Atlanta, the near-est outlet to the wider world, you have a choice of one train or two buses a day to Gainesville, and then you are still 40 miles short of being 7 miles short of the start of the trail, as it were. (To and from Katahdin in Maine is even more problematic.) Fortunately, there are people who will pick you up at Atlanta and take you to Amicalola for a fee. Thus it was that Katz and I delivered ourselves into the hands of a large, friendly guy in a baseball cap named Wes Wisson, who had agreed to take us from the airport in Atlanta to Amicalola Falls Lodge, our setting-off point for Springer, for $60.

Every year between early March and late April, about 2,000 hikers set off from Springer, most of them intending to go all the way to Katahdin. Only about 10 per cent actually make it. Half don't make it past central Virginia, less than a third of the way. A quarter get no further than North Carolina, the next state. Ten per cent drop out the first week. Wisson has seen it all.

'Last year, I dropped a guy off at the trailhead,' he told us as we tooled north through darkening pine forests towards the rugged hills of north Georgia. 'Three days later he calls me from the payphone at Woody Gap – that's the first payphone you come to. Says he wants to go home, that the trail wasn't what he expected it to be. So I drive him back to the airport. Two days after that he's back in Atlanta. Says his wife made him come back because he'd spent all this money on equipment and she wasn't going to let him quit so easy. So I drop him off at the trailhead. Three days later he phones from Woody Gap again. He wants to go to the airport. "Well, what about your wife?" I says. And he says, "This time I'm not going home."'

'How far is it to Woody Gap?' I asked.

'Twenty-one miles from Springer. Doesn't seem much, does it? I mean, he'd come all the way from Ohio.'

'So why did he quit so soon?'

'He said it wasn't what he expected it to be. They all say that.

Just last week I had three ladies from California – middle-aged gals, real nice, kind of giggly but, you know, *nice* – I dropped them off and they were in real high spirits. About four hours later they called and said they wanted to go home. They'd come all the way from California, you understand, spent God knows how much on airfares and equipment – I mean, they had the nicest stuff you ever saw, all brand new and top of the range – and they'd walked maybe a mile and a half before quitting. Said it wasn't what they expected.'

'What do they expect?'

'Who knows? Escalators maybe. It's hills and rocks and woods and a trail. You don't got to do a whole lot of scientific research to work that out. But you'd be amazed how many people quit. Then again, I had a guy, oh about six weeks ago, who shoulda quit and didn't. He was coming off the trail. He'd walked from Maine on his own. It took him eight months, longer than it takes most people, and I don't think he'd seen anybody for the last several weeks. When he came off he was just a trembling wreck. I had his wife with me. She'd come to meet him, and he just fell into her arms and started weeping. Couldn't talk at all. He was like that all the way to the airport. I've never seen anybody so relieved to have anything done with, and I kept thinking, "Well, you know, sir, hiking the Appalachian Trail is a voluntary endeavour," but of course I didn't say anything.'

'So can you tell when you drop people off whether they're gonna make it?'

'Pretty generally.'

'And do you think we'll make it?' said Katz.

He looked at us each in turn. 'Oh, you'll make it all right,' he replied, but his expression said otherwise.

Amicalola Falls Lodge was an eyrie high on a mountainside, reached up a long, winding road through the woods. The man at the airport in Manchester had certainly seen the right weather forecast. It was piercingly, shockingly cold when we stepped from the car. There was a treacherous, icy wind that seemed to dart round from every angle and then zip up sleeves and trouser legs. 'Jee-zuss!' Katz cried in astonishment, as if somebody had just thrown a bucket of ice water over him, and scooted inside. I paid up and followed.

The lodge was modern, posh and very warm, with an open lobby dominated by a stone fireplace, and the sort of anonymously comfortable rooms you would find in a Holiday Inn. We parted for our rooms and agreed to rendezvous at seven. I got a Coke from a machine in the corridor, had a lavishly steamy shower involving many towels, inserted myself between crisp sheets – how long would it be till I enjoyed this kind of comfort again? – watched discouraging reports by happy, mindless people on the Weather Channel, and slept hardly at all.

I was up before daybreak and sat by the window watching as a pale dawn grudgingly exposed the surrounding landscape – a stark and seemingly boundless expanse of thick, rolling hills covered in ranks of bare trees and the meagrest dusting of snow. It didn't look terribly forbidding – these weren't the Himalayas – but it didn't look like anything you would particularly want to walk out into.

On my way to breakfast, the sun popped out, filling the world with encouraging brightness, and I stepped outside to check out the air. The cold was startling, like a slap to the face, and the wind was still bitter. Dry little pellets of snow, like tiny spheres of polystyrene, chased around in swirls. A big wall thermometer by the entrance read 11°F.

'Coldest ever for this date in Georgia,' a hotel employee said with a big pleased smile as she hurried in from the car park, then stopped and said: 'You hiking?'

'Yeah.'

'Well, better you'n me. Good luck to ya. Brrrrrr!' And she dodged inside.

To my surprise, I felt a certain springy keenness. I was ready to hike. I had waited months for this day, after all, even if it had been mostly with foreboding. I wanted to see what was out there. All over America today people would be dragging themselves to work, stuck in traffic jams, wreathed in exhaust smoke. I was going for a walk in the woods. I was more than ready for this.

I found Katz in the dining room and he was looking laudably perky, too. This was because he had made a friend – a waitress named Rayette, who was attending to his dining requirements in a distinctly coquettish way. Rayette was six feet tall and had a face that would frighten a baby, but she seemed good-natured and was diligent with the coffee. She could not have signalled her availability to Katz more clearly if she had thrown her skirt over her head and lain across his Hungry Man Breakfast Platter. Katz in consequence was pumping testosterone.

'Ooh, I like a man who appreciates pancakes,' Rayette cooed.

'Well, honey, I sure appreciate *these* pancakes,' Katz responded, face agleam with syrup and early-morning happiness. It wasn't exactly Hepburn and Tracy, but it was strangely touching none the less.

She went off to deal with a distant customer and Katz watched her go with something like paternal pride. 'She's pretty ugly, isn't she?' he said with a big incongruous beam.

I sought for tact. 'Well, only compared with other women.'

Katz nodded thoughtfully, then fixed me with a sudden fearful look. 'You know what I look for in a female these days? A heartbeat and a full set of limbs.'

'I made a sympathetic expression.'

'And that's just my starting point, you understand. I'm prepared to compromise on the limbs. You think she's available?'

'I believe you might have to take a number.'

He nodded soberly. 'Probably be an idea if we ate up and got out of here.'

I was very happy with that. I drained a cup of coffee and we went off to get our things. But when we met up outside ten minutes later, togged up and ready to go, Katz was looking miserable. 'Let's stay here another night,' he said.

'What? Are you kidding?' I was completely taken aback by this. 'Why?'

'Because it's warm in there and it's cold out here.'

'We've gotta do it.'

He looked to the woods. 'We'll freeze out there.'

I looked to the woods, too. 'Yeah, probably. We've still gotta do it.'

I hoisted my pack, and took a backward stagger under the weight – it would be days before I could do this with anything approaching aplomb – jerked tight the belt and trudged off. At the edge of the woods, I glanced back to make sure Katz was following. Ahead of me spread a vast, stark world of winter-dead trees. I stepped portentously onto the path, a fragment of the original Appalachian Trail from the days when it passed here en route from Mount Oglethorpe to Springer.

The date was 9 March. We were on our way.

The route led down into a wooded valley with a chuckling stream edged with brittle ice, which the path followed for per-haps half a mile before taking us steeply up into denser woods. This was, it quickly became evident, the base of the first big hill, Frosty Mountain, and it was immediately taxing. The sun was shining and the sky was a hearty blue, but everything at ground level was brown – brown trees, brown earth, frozen brown leaves – and the cold was unyielding. I trudged perhaps a hun-dred feet up the hill, then stopped, bug-eyed, breathing hard, heart kabooming alarmingly. Katz was already falling behind and panting even harder. I pressed on.

It was hell. First days on hiking trips always are. I was hope-lessly out of shape – hopelessly. The pack weighed way too much. Way too much. I had never encountered anything so hard, for which I was so ill prepared. Every step was a struggle.

The hardest part was coming to terms with the constant dispiriting discovery that there is always more hill. The thing about being on a hill, as opposed to standing back from it, is that you can almost never see exactly what's to come. Between the curtain of trees on every side, the ever-receding contour of rising slope before you, and your own plodding weariness, you gradually lose track of how far you have come. Each time you haul yourself up to what you think must surely be the crest, you find that there is in fact more hill beyond, sloped at an angle that kept it from view before, and that beyond that slope there is another, and beyond that another and another, and beyond each of those more still, until it seems impossible that any hill could run on this long. Eventually you reach a height where you can see the tops of the topmost trees, with nothing but clear sky beyond, and your faltering spirit stirs – nearly there now! – but this is a pitiless deception. The elusive summit continually retreats by whatever distance you press forward, so that each time the canopy parts enough to give a view you are dismayed to see that the topmost trees are as remote, as unattainable, as before. Still you stagger on. What else can you do?

When, after ages and ages, you finally reach the tell-tale world of truly high ground, where the chilled air smells of pine sap and the vegetation is gnarled and tough and wind-bent, and push through to the mountain's open pinnacle, you are, alas, past caring. You sprawl face down on a sloping pavement of gneiss, pressed to the rock by the weight of your pack, and lie there for some minutes, reflecting in a distant, out-of-body way that you have never before looked this closely at lichen, not in fact looked this closely at anything in the natural world since you were four years old and had your first magnifying glass. Finally, with a weary puff, you roll over, unhook yourself from your pack, struggle to your feet and realize – again in a remote, light-headed, curiously not-there way – that the view is sensational: a boundless vista of wooded mountains, unmarked by human hand, marching off in every direction. This really could be heaven. It's splendid, no question, but the thought you cannot escape is that you have to walk this view – and this is the barest fraction of what you will traverse before you've finished.

You compare your map with the immediate landscape and note that the path ahead descends into a steep valley – a gorge really, not unlike the gorges the coyote is forever plunging into in Roadrunner cartoons; gorges that have actual vanishing points – which will deliver you to the base of a hill even more steep and formidable than this, and that when you scale that preposterously taxing peak you will have done 1.7 miles since breakfast, while your schedule (blithely drawn up at a kitchen table and jotted down after perhaps three seconds' consideration) calls for 8.9 miles by lunch, 16.8 by teatime, and even greater distances tomorrow.

But perhaps it is also raining, a cold, slanting, merciless rain, with thunder and lightning playing on the neighbouring hills. Perhaps a troop of Eagle Scouts comes by at a depressing trot. Perhaps you are cold and hungry and smell so bad that you can no longer smell yourself. Perhaps you want to lie down and be as the lichen: not dead exactly but just very still for a long, long time.

But of course I had all this ahead of me. Today I had nothing to do but traverse four middling mountains over seven miles of well-marked trail in clear, dry weather. It didn't seem too much to ask. It was hell.

I don't know when I lost track of Katz, but it was in the first couple of hours. At first I would wait for him to catch up, bitching every step of the way and pausing after each three or four shuffling paces to wipe his brow and look sourly at his immediate future. It was painful to behold in every way. Eventually I waited to see him pull into view, just to confirm that he was still coming, hadn't fallen to the path palpitating or thrown down his pack in disgust and gone looking for Wes Wisson. I would wait and wait and eventually his shape would appear among the trees, breathing heavily, moving with incredible slowness, and talking in a loud, bitter voice to himself. Halfway up the third big hill, the 3,400-foot-high Black Mountain, I stood and waited a long while, and thought about going back, but eventually turned and struggled on. I had enough small agonies of my own.

Seven miles seems so little, but it's not, believe me. With a pack, even for fit people it is not. You know what it's like when you're at a zoo or amusement park with a small child who won't walk another step? You hoist him lightly onto your shoulders and for a while – for a couple of minutes – it's actually kind of fun to have him up there, pretending you're going to tip him off or cruising his head towards some low projection before veering off (all being well) at the last instant. But then it starts to get uncomfortable. You feel a twinge in your neck, a tightening between your shoulder blades, and the sensation seeps and spreads until it is quite decidedly uncomfortable, and you announce to little Jimmy that you're going to have to put him down for a bit.

Of course, Jimmy bawls and won't go another step, and your partner gives you that disdainful, I-should-have-married-the-quarterback look because you haven't gone 400 yards. But, hey, it hurts. Hurts a lot. Believe me, I understand.

OK, now imagine *two* little Jimmies in a pack on your back, or, better still, something inert but weighty, something that doesn't want to be lifted, that makes it abundantly clear to you as soon as you pick it up that what it wants is to sit heavily on the ground – say, a bag of cement or a box of medical textbooks, in any case 40 pounds of profound heaviness. Imagine the jerk of the pack going on, like the pull of a down elevator. Imagine walking with that weight for hours, for days, and not along level asphalt paths with benches and refreshment kiosks at thoughtful intervals, but over a rough trail, full of sharp rocks and unyielding roots and staggering ascents that transfer enormous amounts of strain to your pale, shaking thighs. Now tilt your head back – please, this is the last thing I'll ask of you –

until your neck is taut and fix your gaze on a point two miles away. That's your first climb. It's 4,682 steep feet to the top and there are lots more like it. Don't tell me that seven miles is not far.

Oh, and here's the other thing. You don't have to do this. You're not in the army. You can quit right now. Go home. See your family. Sleep in a bed. Or alternatively, you poor, sad schmuck, you can walk 2,169 miles through mountains and wilderness to Maine.

And so I trudged along for hours, in a private little world of weariness and woe, up and over imposing hills, through an endless cocktail party of trees, all the time thinking: 'I must have done seven miles by now, *surely.*' But always the wandering trail ran on.

At half past three, I climbed some steps carved into granite and found myself on a spacious rock overlook: the summit of Springer Mountain. I shed my pack and sat down heavily against a tree, astounded at how weary I was. The view was splendid – the rolling swell of the Cohutta Mountains, brushed with a bluish haze the colour of cigarette smoke, running away to a far-off horizon. The sun was already low in the sky. I rested for perhaps ten minutes, then got up and had a look around. There was a bronze plaque screwed into a boulder announcing the start of the Appalachian Trail and nearby on a post was a wooden box containing a Bic pen on a length of string and a standard spiral notebook, its pages curled from the damp air. The notebook was the trail register – I had somehow expected it to be leatherbound and funereal – and it was filled with eager entries, nearly all written in a youthful hand. There were per- haps twenty-five pages of entries since 1 January – eight entries on this day alone. Most were hurried and cheery – 'March 2nd. Well, here we are and man it's *cold*! See y'all on Katahdin! Jaimie and Spud' – but about a third were longer and more carefully reflective, with messages along the lines of 'So here I am at Springer at last. I don't know what the coming weeks hold for me, but my faith in the Lord is strong and I know I have the love and support of my family. Mom and Pookie, this trip is for you', and so on.

I waited for Katz for three-quarters of an hour, then went looking for him. The light was fading and the air was growing sharp. I walked and walked, down the hill and through the endless trees, back over ground that I had gratefully put behind me for ever, I thought. Several times I called his name and listened, but there was nothing. I walked on and on, over fallen trees I had struggled over hours ago, down slopes I could only dimly recall. My grandmother could have got this far, I kept thinking. Finally, I rounded a bend and there he was stumbling towards me, wild-haired and one-gloved, and nearer hysteria than I have ever seen a grown person.

It was hard to get the full story out of him in a coherent flow, because he was so furious, but I gathered he had thrown many items from his pack over a cliff in a temper. None of the things that had been dangling from the outside were there any longer, including his water bottle.

'What did you get rid of?' I asked, trying not to betray too much alarm.

'Heavy fucking shit, that's what. The pepperoni, the rice, the brown sugar, the Spam, I don't know what all. Lots. Fuck.' Katz was almost cataleptic with displeasure. He acted as if he had been deeply betrayed by the trail. It wasn't, I guess, what he had expected.

I saw his glove lying in the path 30 yards back and went to retrieve it.

'OK,' I said when I returned, 'you haven't got too far to go.'

'How far?'

'Maybe a mile.'

'Shit,' he said bitterly.

'I'll take your pack.' I lifted it onto my back. It wasn't exactly empty now, but it was decidedly moderate in weight. God knows what he had thrown out.

We trudged up the hill to the summit in the enveloping dusk. A few hundred yards beyond the summit was a campsite with a wooden shelter in a big grassy clearing against a backdrop of black trees. There were a lot of people there, far more than I'd expected this early in the season. The shelter – a basic, three-sided affair with a sloping roof – looked crowded and there were a dozen or so tents scattered around the open ground. Nearly everywhere there was the hiss of little campstoves, threads of rising food smoke and the movements of lanky young people.

I found us a site on the edge of the clearing, almost in the woods, off by ourselves.

'I don't know how to put up my tent,' Katz said in a petulant tone.

'Well, I'll put it up for you then.' You big soft flabby baby. Suddenly I was very tired.

He sat on a log and watched me put up his tent. When I finished, he pushed in his pad and sleeping bag and crawled in after. I busied myself with my tent, fussily made it into a little home. When I completed my work and straightened up I realized there was no sound or movement from within his.

'Have you gone to bed?' I said, aghast.

'Yump,' he replied in a kind of affirmative growl.

'That's it? You've retired? With no dinner?'

'Yump.'

I stood for a minute, speechless and flummoxed, too tired to be indignant. Too tired to be hungry either, come to that. I crawled into my tent, brought in a water bottle and book, laid out my knife and torch for purposes of nocturnal illumination and defence, and finally shimmied into the bag, more grateful than I have ever been to be horizontal. I was asleep in moments. I don't believe I have ever slept so well.

When I awoke it was daylight. The inside of my tent was coated in a curious flaky rime, which I realized after a moment was all my night-time snores, condensed and frozen and pasted to the fabric, as if into a scrapbook of respiratory memories. My water bottle was frozen solid. This seemed gratifyingly macho, and I examined it with interest, as if it were a rare mineral. I was surprisingly snug in my bag and in no hurry at all to put myself through the foolishness of climbing hills, so I just lay there as if under grave orders not to move. After a while I became aware that Katz was moving around outside, grunting softly as if from aches and doing something that sounded improbably industrious.

After a minute or two, he came and crouched by my tent, his form a dark shadow on the fabric. He didn't ask if I was awake or anything, but just said in a quiet voice: 'Was I, would you say, a complete asshole last night?'

'Yes you were, Stephen.'

He was quiet a moment. 'I'm making coffee.' I gathered this was his way of an apology.

'That's very nice.'

'Buggering cold out here.'

'And in here.'

'My water bottle froze.'

'Mine, too.'

I unzipped myself from my nylon womb and emerged on creaking joints. It seemed very strange – very novel – to be standing outdoors in long johns. Katz was crouched over the campstove, boiling a pan of water. We seemed to be the only campers awake. It was cold, but perhaps just a trifle warmer than the day before and a low dawn sun burning through the trees looked cautiously promising.

'How do you feel?' he said.

I flexed my legs experimentally. 'Not too bad, actually.'

'Me either.'

He poured water into the filter cone. 'I'm going to be good today,' he promised.

'Good.' I watched over his shoulder. 'Is there a reason', I

asked, 'why you are filtering the coffee with toilet paper?'

'I, oh . . . I threw out the filter papers.'

I gave a sound that wasn't quite a laugh. 'They couldn't have weighed two ounces.'

'I know, but they were great for throwing. Fluttered all over.' He dribbled on more water. 'The toilet paper seems to be working OK, though.'

We watched it drip through and were strangely proud. Our first refreshment in the wilderness. He handed me a cup of coffee. It was swimming in grounds and little flecks of pink tissue, but it was piping hot, which was the main thing.

He gave me an apologetic look. 'I threw out the brown sugar too, so there won't be any sugar for the oatmeal.'

Ah. 'Actually, there won't be any oatmeal for the oatmeal. I left it in New Hampshire.'

He looked at me. 'Really?' Then he added, as if for the record: 'I love oatmeal.'

'What about some of that cheese?'

He shook his head. 'Flung.'

'Peanuts?'

'Flung.'

'Spam?'

'Really flung.'

This was beginning to sound a trifle grave. 'What about the baloney?'

'Oh, I ate that at Amicalola,' he said, as if it had been weeks ago, then added in a tone of sudden magnanimous concession, 'Hey, I'm happy with a cup of coffee and a couple of Little Debbies.'

I gave a small grimace. 'I left the Little Debbies, too.'

His face expanded. 'You left the Little Debbies?'

I nodded apologetically.

'*All* of them?'

I nodded.

He breathed out hard. This really was grave – a serious

challenge, apart from anything else, to his promised equanimity. We decided we had better take inventory. We cleared a space on a groundsheet and pooled our commissary. It was startlingly austere – some dried noodles, one bag of rice, raisins, coffee, salt, a good supply of chocolate bars, and toilet paper. That was about it.

We breakfasted on a Snickers bar and coffee, packed up our camp, hoisted our packs with a sideways stagger and set off once again.

'I can't believe you left the Little Debbies,' Katz said, and immediately began to fall behind.

Chapter 4

Woods are not like other spaces. To begin with they are cubic. Their trees surround you, loom over you, press in from all sides. Woods choke off views, and leave you muddled and without bearings. They make you feel small and confused and vulnerable, like a small child lost in a crowd of strange legs. Stand in a desert or prairie and you know you are in a big space. Stand in a wood and you only sense it. They are a vast, featureless nowhere. And they are alive.

So woods are spooky. Quite apart from the thought that they may harbour wild beasts and armed, genetically challenged fellows named Zeke and Festus, there is something innately sinister about them – some ineffable thing that makes you sense an atmosphere of pregnant doom with every step and leaves you profoundly aware that you are out of your element and ought to keep your ears pricked. Though you tell yourself it's preposterous, you can't quite shake the feeling that you are being watched. You order yourself to be serene – it's just a wood for goodness' sake – but really you are jumpier than Don Knotts with pistol drawn. Every sudden noise – the crack of a falling limb, the crash of a bolting deer – makes you spin in alarm and stifle a plea for mercy. Whatever mechanism within you is responsible for adrenalin, it has never been so sleek and polished – so keenly poised to pump out a warming squirt of adrenal fluid. Even asleep you are a coiled spring.

The American woods have been unnerving people for 300 years. The inestimably priggish and tiresome Henry David Thoreau thought nature was splendid, splendid indeed, so long as he could stroll to town for cakes and barley wine, but when he experienced real wilderness, on a visit to Katahdin in 1846, he was unnerved to the core. This wasn't the tame world of overgrown orchards and sun-dappled paths that passed for wilderness in suburban Concord, Massachusetts, but a forbidding, oppressive, primeval country that was 'grim and wild . . . savage and dreary', fit only for 'men nearer of kin to the rocks and wild animals than we'. The experience left him, in the words of one biographer, 'near hysterical'.

But even men far tougher and more attuned to the wilderness than Thoreau were sobered by its strange and palpable menace. Daniel Boone, who not only wrestled bears but tried to date their sisters, described corners of the southern Appalachians as 'so wild and horrid that it is impossible to behold them without terror'. When Daniel Boone is uneasy, you know it is time to watch your step.

When the first Europeans arrived in the New World there were perhaps 950 million acres of woodland in what would become the lower forty-eight states. The Chattahoochee National Forest through which Katz and I now trudged was part of an immense unbroken canopy stretching from southern Alabama to Canada and beyond, and from the shores of the Atlantic to the distant grasslands of the Missouri River.

Most of that forest is now gone, but what survives is more impressive than you might expect. The Chattahoochee is part of four million acres – 6,000 square miles – of federally owned forest stretching up to the Great Smoky Mountains and beyond, and spreading sideways across four states. On a map of the United States it is an incidental smudge of green, but on foot the scale of it is colossal. It would be four days before Katz and I crossed a public highway, eight days till we came to a town.

And so we walked. We walked up mountains and through high, forgotten hollows, along lonesome ridges with long views of more ridges, over grassy balds and down rocky, twisting, jarring descents, and through mile after endless mile of dark, deep, silent woods, on a wandering trail eighteen inches wide and marked with rectangular white blazes (two inches wide, six long) slapped at intervals on the grey-barked trees. Walking is what we did.

Compared with most other places in the developed world, America is still to a remarkable extent a land of forests. One third of the landscape of the lower forty-eight states is covered in trees – 728 million acres in all. Maine alone has ten million uninhabited acres. That's 15,600 square miles – an area considerably bigger than Belgium – without a single permanent resident. Altogether just 2 per cent of the United States is classified as built up.

About 240 million acres of America's forests are owned by the government. The bulk of this – 191 million acres, spread over 155 parcels of land – is held by the US Forest Service under the designations of National Forests, National Grasslands, and National Recreation Areas. All this sounds soothingly un-trampled and ecological, but in fact a great deal of Forest Service land is designated 'multiple-use', which is generously interpreted to allow any number of boisterous activities – mining, oil and gas extraction, ski resorts (137 of them), condominium developments, snowmobiling, off-road vehicle scrambling, and lots and lots and lots of logging – that seem curiously incompatible with woodland serenity.

The Forest Service is truly an extraordinary institution. It was conceived a century ago as a kind of woodland bank, a permanent repository of American timber, when people grew alarmed at the rate at which American forests were falling. Its remit was to manage and protect these resources for the nation. These were not intended to be parks. Private companies would be granted leases to extract minerals and harvest timber, but they would be required to do so in a restrained, intelligent way.

That was the plan. In the event, mostly what the Forest Service did was build roads. I am not kidding. There are 378,000 miles of roads in America's national forests. That may seem a meaningless figure, so look at it this way. It is eight times the total mileage of America's interstate highway system. It is the largest road system in the world in the control of a single body. The Forest Service has the second highest number of road engineers of any government institution on the planet. To say that these guys like to build roads barely hints at their level of dedication. Show them a stand of trees anywhere and they will regard it thoughtfully for a long while, and say, 'You know, we could put a road here.' It is the avowed aim of the US Forest Service to construct 580,000 miles of additional forest road by the middle of the next century.

The reason the Forest Service builds these roads, quite apart from the deep pleasure of doing noisy things in the woods with big yellow machines, is to allow private timber companies to get to previously inaccessible stands of trees. Of the Forest Service's 150 million acres of loggable land, about two-thirds is held in store for the future. The remaining one-third – 49 million acres, or an area roughly twice the size of Ohio – is available for logging. It allows huge swathes of land to be clear cut, including (to take one recent example) 209 acres of thousand-year-old redwoods in Oregon's Umpqua National Forest.

In 1987, it casually announced that it would allow private timber interests to remove hundreds of acres of wood a year from the venerable and verdant Pisgah National Forest, next door to the Great Smoky Mountains National Park, and that 80 per cent of that would be through what it calls 'scientific forestry' – clear cutting – which is not only a brutal visual affront to any landscape, but brings huge, reckless washoffs that gully the soil, robbing it of nutrients and disrupting ecologies further downstream, sometimes for miles. This isn't science. It's rape.

And yet the Forest Service grinds on. By the late 1980s – this is so extraordinary I can hardly stand it – it was the only significant player in the American timber industry that was cutting down trees faster than it replaced them. Moreover it was doing this with the most sumptuous inefficiency. Eighty per cent of its leasing arrangements lost money, often vast amounts of it. In one typical deal, the Forest Service sold hundred-year-old lodgepole pines in the Targhee National Forest in Idaho for about $2 each after spending $4 per tree surveying the land, drawing up contracts and – of course – building roads. Between 1989 and 1997, it lost an average of $242 million a year – almost $2 billion all told, according to the Wilderness Society. This is all so discouraging that I think we'll leave it here and return to our two lonely heroes trudging through the lost world of the Chattahoochee.

In 1890, a railway man from Cincinnati named Henry C. Bagley came to this part of Georgia, saw the stately white pines and poplars, and was so moved by their towering majesty and abundance that he decided to chop them all down. They were worth a lot of money. Besides, freighting the timber to northern mills would keep his railway cars puffing. In consequence over the next thirty years nearly all the hills of north Georgia were turned into sunny groves of stumps. By 1920, foresters in the South were taking away 15.4 billion board feet of timber a year. It wasn't until the 1930s, when the Chattahoochee National Forest was officially formed, that nature was invited back in, so the forest we walked through now was really just a strapping adolescent.

There is a strange frozen violence in a forest out of season. Every glade and dale seemed to have just completed some

massive cataclysm. Downed trees lay across the path every fifty
or sixty yards, often with great bomb craters of dirt around their
splayed roots. Dozens more lay rotting on the slopes, and every
third or fourth tree, it seemed, was leaning steeply on a neighbour. It was as if the trees couldn't wait to fall over, as if their
purpose in the universal scheme of things was to grow big
enough to topple with a really good, splintering crash. I was
forever coming up to trees so precariously and weightily tipped
over the path that I would waver, then scoot under, fearing the
crush of really unfortunate timing and imagining Katz coming
along a few minutes later, regarding my wriggling legs and saying, 'Shit, Bryson, what're you doing under there?' But no trees
fell. Everywhere the woods were still and preternaturally quiet.
Except for the occasional gurgle of running water and the shuffle
of fallen leaves in the wind, there was almost never a sound.

The woods were silent because spring had not yet come. In
a normal year we would be walking into the zestful bounty of
a southern mountain spring, through a radiant, productive,
newborn world alive with the zip of insects and the fussy twitter
of birds; a world bursting with fresh wholesome air and that
rich, velvety, lung-filling smell of chlorophyll you get when you
push through low branches. Above all there would be wild
flowers in dazzling profusion, blossoming from every twig,
pushing valiantly through the fertile litter on the forest floor,
carpeting every sunny slope and stream bank – trillium and
trailing arbutus, Dutchmen's breeches, jack-in-the-pulpit, man-
drake, violets, snowy bluets, buttercups and bloodroot, dwarf
iris, columbine and wood sorrel, and other cheerful nodding
wonders almost beyond counting. There are 1,500 types of wild
flower in the southern Appalachians, forty rare types in the
north Georgia woods alone. They are a sight to lift the hardest
heart. Instead we trudged through a cold, silent world of bare
trees, beneath pewter skies, on ground like iron.

We fell into a simple routine. Each morning we rose at first
light, shivering and rubbing arms, made coffee, broke camp, ate

a couple of fistfuls of raisins, and set off into the silent woods. We would walk from about half past seven to four. We seldom walked together – our paces didn't match – but every couple of hours I would sit on a log (always surveying the surrounding undergrowth for the rustle of bear or boar) and wait for Katz to catch up, to make sure everything was OK. Sometimes other hikers would come along, and they would tell me where Katz was and how he was progressing, which was nearly always slowly but gamely. The trail was much harder for him than for me, and to his credit he tried not to bitch. It never escaped me for a moment that he didn't have to be there.

I had thought we would have a jump on the crowds, but there was a fair scattering of other hikers – three students from Rutgers University in New Jersey; an astoundingly fit older couple with tiny packs hiking to their daughter's wedding in far-off Virginia; a gawky kid from Florida named Jonathan; perhaps two dozen of us altogether in the same general neck of the woods, all heading north. Because everyone walks at different rates and rests at different times, three or four times a day you bump into some or all of your fellow hikers, especially on mountaintops with panoramic views or beside streams with good water, and above all at the wooden shelters that stand at distant intervals, ostensibly but not always actually, a day's hike apart in clearings just off the trail. In consequence you get to know your fellow hikers at least a little, quite well if you meet them nightly at the shelters. You become part of an informal clump, a loose and sympathetic affiliation of people from different age groups and walks of life but all experiencing the same weather, same discomforts, same landscapes, same eccentric impulse to hike to Maine.

Even at busy times, however, the woods are great providers of solitude, and I encountered long periods of perfect aloneness, when I didn't see another soul for hours, and many times when I would wait for Katz for a long spell and no other hiker would come along. When that happened, I would leave my pack and go back and find him, to see that he was all right, which always pleased him. Sometimes he would be proudly bearing my stick, which I had left by a tree when I had stopped to tie my laces or adjust my pack. We seemed to be looking out for each other. It was very nice. I can put it no other way.

Around four we would find a spot to camp, and pitch our tents. One of us would go off to fetch and filter water while the other prepared a sludge of steamy noodles. Sometimes we would talk, but mostly we existed in a kind of companionable silence. By six o'clock, dark and cold and weariness would force us to our tents. Katz went to sleep instantly, as far as I could tell. I would read for an hour or so with my curiously inefficient little miner's lamp, its beam throwing quirky, concentric circles of light onto the page, like the light of a bicycle lamp, until my shoulders and arms grew chilly out of the bag, and heavy from tilting the book at awkward angles to catch the nervous light. So I would put myself in darkness and lie there listening to the peculiarly clear, articulated noises of the forest at night, the sighs and fidgets of wind and leaves, the weary groan of boughs, the endless murmurings and stirrings, like the noises of a convalescent ward after lights out, until at last I fell heavily asleep. In the morning we would rise shivering and rubbing arms, wordlessly repeat our small chores, fill and hoist our packs and venture into the great entangling forest again.

On the fourth evening we made a friend. We were sitting in a nice little clearing beside the trail, our tents pitched, eating our noodles, savouring the exquisite pleasure of just sitting, when a plumpish, bespectacled young woman in a red jacket and the customary outsized pack came along. She regarded us with the crinkled squint of someone who is either chronically confused or can't see very well. We exchanged hellos and the usual banalities about the weather and where we were. Then she squinted at the gathering gloom and announced she would camp with us.

Her name was Mary Ellen. She was from Florida, and she

was, as Katz for ever after termed her in a special tone of awe, a piece of work. She talked nonstop, except when she was clearing out her Eustachian tubes, which she did frequently, by pinching her nose and blowing out with a series of violent and alarming snorts of a sort that would make a dog leave the sofa and get under a table in the next room. I have long known that it is part of God's plan for me to spend a little time with each of the most stupid people on earth, and Mary Ellen was proof that even in the Appalachian woods I would not be spared. It became evident from the first moment that she was a rarity.

'So what are you guys eating?' she said, plonking herself down on a spare log and lifting her head to peer into our bowls. 'Noodles? Big mistake. Noodles have got like no energy. I mean like zero.' She unblocked her ears. 'Is that a Starship tent?'

I looked at my tent. 'I don't know.'

'Big mistake. They must have seen you coming at the camping store. What did you pay for it?'

'I don't know.'

'Too much, that's how much. You should have got a three-season tent.'

'It is a three-season tent.'

'Pardon me saying so, but it is like seriously dumb to come out here in March without a three-season tent.' She unblocked her ears.

'It is a three-season tent.'

'You're lucky you haven't froze yet. You should go back and like punch out the guy that sold it to you because he's been like, you know, negligible selling you that.'

'Believe me, it is a three-season tent.'

She unblocked her ears and shook her head impatiently. 'That's a three-season tent.' She indicated Katz's tent.

'*That*'s exactly the same tent.'

She glanced at it again. 'Whatever. How many miles did you do today?'

'About ten.' Actually we had done eight point four – but this had included several formidable escarpments, including a notable wall of hell called Preaching Rock, the highest eminence since Springer Mountain, for which we had awarded ourselves bonus miles, for purposes of morale.

'Ten miles? Is that all? You guys must be like *really* out of shape. I did fourteen-two.'

'How many have your lips done?' said Katz, looking up from his noodles.

She fixed him with one of her more severe squints. 'Same as the rest of me, of course.' She gave me a private look as if to say, 'Is your friend like seriously *weird* or something?' She cleared her ears. 'I started at Gooch Gap.'

'So did we. That's only eight point four miles.'

She shook her head sharply, as if shooing a particularly tenacious fly. 'Fourteen-two.'

'No, really, it's only eight point four.'

'Excuse me, but I just *walked* it. I think I ought to know.' And then suddenly: 'God, are those Timberland boots? *Mega* mistake. How much did you pay for them?'

And so it went. Eventually I went off to swill out the bowls and hang the food bag. When I came back, she was fixing her own dinner, but still talking away at Katz.

'You know what your problem is?' she was saying. 'Pardon my French, but you're too fat.'

Katz looked at her in quiet wonder. 'Excuse me?'

'You're too fat. You should have lost weight before you came out here. Shoulda done some training, 'cause you could have like a serious, you know, heart thing out here.'

'Heart thing?'

'You know, when your heart stops and you like, you know, die.'

'Do you mean a heart attack?'

'That's it.'

Mary Ellen, it should be noted, was not short on flesh herself, and unwisely at that moment she leaned over to get something from her pack, displaying an expanse of backside on which you could have projected motion pictures for, let us say, an army base. It was an interesting test of Katz's forbearance. He said nothing, but rose to go for a pee and out of the side of his mouth as he passed me he rendered a certain convenient expletive as three low, dismayed syllables, like the call of a freight train in the night.

The next day, as always, we rose chilled and feeling wretched, and set about the business of attending to our small tasks, but this time with the additional strain of having our every move examined and rated. While we ate raisins and drank coffee with flecks of toilet paper in it, Mary Ellen gorged on a multi-course breakfast of oatmeal, Pop Tarts, trail mix and a dozen small squares of chocolate, which she lined up in a row on the log beside her. We watched like orphaned refugees while she plumped her jowls with food and enlightened us as to our shortcomings with regard to diet, equipment and general manliness.

And then, now a trio, we set off into the woods. Mary Ellen walked sometimes with me and sometimes with Katz, but always with one of us. It was apparent that for all her bluster she was majestically inexperienced and untrailworthy – she hadn't the faintest idea how to read a map, for one thing – and ill at ease on her own in the wilderness. I couldn't help feeling a little sorry for her. Besides, I began to find her strangely entertaining. She had the most extraordinarily redundant turn of phrase. She would say things like 'There's a stream of water over there', and 'It's nearly ten o'clock a.m.'. Once, in reference to winters in central Florida, she solemnly informed me, 'We usually get frosts once or twice a winter, but this year we had 'em a couple of times.' Katz for his part clearly dreaded her company and winced beneath her tireless urgings to smarten his pace.

For once, the weather was kindly – more autumnal than springlike in feel, but gratifyingly mild. By ten o'clock, the temperature was comfortably in the sixties. For the first time since Amicalola I took off my jacket, and realized with mild perplexity that I had absolutely no place to put it. I tied it to my pack with a strap and trudged on.

We laboured four miles up and over Blood Mountain, at 4,461 feet the highest and toughest eminence on the trail in Georgia, then began a steep and exciting two-mile descent towards Neels Gap. Exciting because there was a shop at Neels Gap, at a place called the Walasi-Yi Inn, where you could buy sandwiches and ice cream. At about half past one, we heard a novel sound – motor traffic – and a few minutes later we emerged from the woods onto US Highway 19 and 129, which despite having two numbers was really just a back road through a high pass between wooded nowheres. Directly across the road was the Walasi-Yi Inn, a splendid stone building constructed by the Civilian Conservation Corps, a kind of army of the unemployed, during the Great Depression in the 1930s, and now a combination of hiking outfitters, grocery, bookshop and youth hostel. We hastened across the road – positively scurried across – and went inside.

Now it may seem to stretch credibility to suggest that things like a paved highway, the whoosh of passing cars and a proper building could seem exciting and unfamiliar after a scant five days in the woods, but in fact it was so. Just passing through a door, being inside, surrounded by walls and a ceiling, was novel. And the Walasi-Yi's stuff was – well, I can't begin to describe how wonderful it was. There was a single modest-sized chilled cabinet filled with fresh sandwiches, soft drinks, cartons of juice and perishables like cheese, and Katz and I stared into it for ages, dumbly captivated. I was beginning to learn that the central feature of life on the Appalachian Trail is deprivation, that the whole point of the experience is to remove yourself so thoroughly from the conveniences of everyday life that the most ordinary things – processed cheese, a can of pop gorgeously beaded with condensation – fill you with wonder and gratitude. It is an intoxicating experience to taste Coca-Cola as if for the first time and to be conveyed to the very brink of orgasm by white bread. Makes all the discomfort worthwhile.

Katz and I bought two egg salad sandwiches each, some crisps, chocolate bars and soft drinks, and went with them to a picnic table outside, where we ate with greedy smackings and expressions of rapture, then returned to the chill cabinet to stare in wonder some more. The Walasi-Yi, we discovered, provided other services to bona fide hikers for a small fee – laundry centre, showers, towel hire – and we greedily availed ourselves of all those. The shower was a dribbly, antiquated affair, but the water was hot and I have never, and I mean never, enjoyed a grooming experience more. I watched with the profoundest satisfaction as five days of grime ran down my legs and into the drainhole, and noticed with astonished gratitude that my body had taken on a noticeably svelter profile. We did two loads of laundry, washed out our cups and food bowls and pots and pans, bought and sent postcards, phoned home, and stocked up liberally on fresh and packaged foods in the shop.

The Walasi-Yi was run by an Engishman named Justin and his American wife Peggy, and we fell into a running conversation with them as we drifted in and out through the afternoon. Peggy told me that already they had had a thousand hikers through since 1 January, with the real start of the hiking season still to come. They were a kindly couple, and I got the sense that Peggy in particular spends a lot of her time talking people into not quitting. Only the day before a young man from Surrey had asked them to call him a cab to take him to Atlanta. Peggy had almost persuaded him to persevere, to try for just another week, but in the end he had broken down and wept quietly and asked from the heart to be let go home.

My own feeling was that for the first time I really wanted to keep going. The sun was shining. I was clean and refreshed. There was ample food in our packs. I had spoken to my wife by phone and knew that all was well. Above all, I was starting

to feel fit. I was sure I had lost half a stone already. I was ready
to go. Katz, too, was aglow with cleanness and looking chipper.

We packed our purchases on the porch and realized together
in the same instant, with joy and amazement, that Mary Ellen
was no longer part of our retinue. I put my head in the door
and asked if they had seen her.

'Oh, I think she left about an hour ago,' Peggy said.

Things were getting better and better.

It was after four o'clock by the time we set off again. Justin
had said there was a natural meadow ideal for camping about
an hour's walk further on. The trail was warmly inviting in late
afternoon sunlight – there were long shadows from the trees
and expansive views across a river valley to stout, charcoal-
coloured mountains – and the meadow was indeed a perfect
place to camp. We pitched our tents and ate sandwiches, crisps
and soft drinks we had bought for dinner.

Then, with as much pride as if I had baked them myself, I
brought out a little surprise – two packets of Hostess cupcakes.

Katz's face lit up like the birthday boy in a Norman Rockwell
painting.

'Oh, wow!'

'They didn't have any Little Debbies,' I apologized.

'Hey,' he said, 'hey.' He was lost for greater eloquence. Katz
loved cakes.

We ate three of the cupcakes between us, and left the last one
on the log, where we could admire it, for later. We were lying
there, propped against logs, burping, smoking, feeling rested
and content, talking for once – in short, acting much as I had
envisioned it in my more optimistic moments back home –
when Katz let out a low groan. I followed his gaze to find Mary
Ellen striding briskly down the trail towards us from the wrong
direction.

'I *wondered* where you guys had got to,' she scolded. 'You
know, you are like *really* slow. We could've done another four
miles by now easy. I can see I'm going to have to keep my eyes

on you from now— Say, is that a Hostess cupcake?' Before I
could speak or Katz could seize a log with which to smite her
dead, she said, 'Well, I don't mind if I do,' and ate it in two
bites.

It would be some days before Katz smiled again.

Chapter 5

'So what's your star sign?' said Mary Ellen.

'Cunnilingus,' Katz answered and looked profoundly unhappy.

She looked at him. 'I don't know that one.' She made an I'll-be-darned frown and said, 'I thought I knew them all. Mine's Libra.' She turned to me. 'What's yours?'

'I don't know.' I tried to think of something. 'Necrophilia.'

'I don't know that one either. Say, are you guys having me on?'

'Yeah.'

It was two nights later. We were camped at a lofty spot called Indian Grave Gap, between two brooding summits, the one tiring to recollect, the other dispiriting to behold. We had hiked 22 miles in two days – a highly respectable distance for us – but a distinct listlessnesss and sense of anticlimax, a kind of mid-mountain lassitude, had set in. We spent our days doing precisely what we had done on previous days and would continue to do on future days, over the same sorts of hills, along the same wandering track, through the same endless woods. The trees were so thick that we hardly ever got views, and when we did get views it was of infinite hills covered in more trees. I was discouraged to note that I was grubby again already and barking for white bread. And then of course there was the constant, prattling, awesomely brainless presence of Mary Ellen.

'When's your birthday?' she said to me.

'December the eighth.'

'That's Virgo.'

'No, actually it's Sagittarius.'

'Whatever.' And then abruptly: 'Jeez, you guys stink.'

'Well, uh, we've been walking.'

'Me, I don't sweat. Never have. Don't dream either.'

'Everybody dreams,' Katz said.

'Well, I don't.'

'Except people of extremely low intelligence. It's a scientific fact.'

Mary Ellen regarded him expressionlessly for a moment, then said abruptly, to neither of us in particular: 'Do you ever have that dream where you're like at school and you look down and like you haven't got any clothes on?' She shuddered. 'I hate that one.'

'I thought you didn't dream,' said Katz.

She stared at him for a very long moment, as if trying to remember where she had encountered him before. 'And falling,' she went on, unperturbed. 'I hate that one, too. Like when you fall into a hole and just fall and fall.' She gave a brief shiver, and then noisily unblocked her ears.

Katz watched her with idle interest. 'I know a guy who did that once and one of his eyes popped out,' he said.

She looked at him doubtfully.

'It rolled right across the living room floor and his dog ate it. Isn't that right, Bryson?'

I nodded.

'You're making that up.'

'I'm not. It rolled right across the floor and before anybody could do anything, the dog gobbled it down in one bite.'

I confirmed it for her with another nod.

She considered this for a minute. 'So what'd your friend do about his eye hole? Did he have to get a glass eye or something?'

'Well, he wanted to, but his family was kind of poor, you know, so what he did was he got a ping-pong ball and painted an eye on it and he used that.'

'Ugh,' said Mary Ellen softly.

'So I wouldn't go blowing out your ear holes any more.'

She considered again. 'Yeah, maybe you're right,' she said at length, and blew out her ear holes.

In our few private moments, when Mary Ellen went off to tinkle in distant shrubs, Katz and I had formed a secret pact that we would hike 14 miles on the morrow to a place called Dicks Creek Gap, where there was a highway to the town of Hiawassee, 11 miles to the north. We would hike to the gap if it killed us, and then try to hitchhike into Hiawassee for dinner and a night in a motel. Plan B was that we would kill Mary Ellen and take her Pop Tarts.

And so the next day we hiked, really hiked, startling Mary Ellen with our thrusting strides. There was a motel in Hiawassee – clean sheets! shower! colour TV! – and a reputed choice of restaurants. We needed no more incentive than that to perk our step. Katz flagged in the first hour, and I felt tired too by afternoon, but we pushed determinedly on. Mary Ellen fell further and further off the pace, until she was behind even Katz. It was a kind of miracle in the hills.

At about four o'clock, tired and overheated and streaked about the face with rivulets of gritty sweat, I stepped from the woods onto the broad shoulder of US Highway 76, an asphalt river through the woods, pleased to note that the road was wide and reasonably important-looking. A half-mile down the road

there was a clearing in the trees and a drive – a hint of civilization – before the road curved away invitingly. Several cars
passed as I stood there.

Katz tumbled from the woods a few minutes later, looking
wild of hair and eye, and I hustled him across the road against
his voluble protests that he needed to sit down *immediately*,
but I wanted to try to get a lift before Mary Ellen came along
and screwed things up. I couldn't think how she might, but I
knew she would.

'Have you seen her?' I asked anxiously.

'Miles back, sitting on a rock with her boots off rubbing her
feet. She looked real tired.'

'Good.'

Katz sagged onto his pack, grubby and spent, and I stood
beside him on the shoulder with my thumb out, trying to
project an image of wholesomeness and respectability, making
private irked tutting noises at every car and pickup that passed.
I had not hitchhiked in twenty-five years, and it was a vaguely
humbling experience. Cars shot past very fast – unbelievably
fast to us who now resided in Foot World – and gave us scarcely
a glance. A very few approached more slowly, always occupied
by elderly people – little white heads, just above the window
line – who stared at us without sympathy or expression, as they
would at a field of cows. It seemed unlikely that anyone would
stop for us. I wouldn't have stopped for us.

'We're never going to get picked up,' Katz announced
despondently after cars had forsaken us for fifteen minutes.

He was right, of course, but it always exasperated me how
easily he gave up on things. 'Can't you try to be a little more
positive?' I said.

'OK, I'm positive we're never going to get picked up. I mean,
look at us.' He smelled his armpits with disgust. 'Jesus, I smell
like Jeffrey Dahmer's refrigerator.'

There is a phenomenon called Trail Magic, known and
spoken of with reverence by everyone who hikes the trail,

which holds that often when things look darkest some little piece of serendipity comes along to put you back on a heavenly plane. Ours was a baby-blue Pontiac TransAm, which flew past, then screeched to a stop on the shoulder a hundred yards or so down the road, in a cloud of gravelly dust. It was so far beyond where we stood that we didn't think it could possibly be for us, but then it jerked into reverse and came at us, half on the shoulder and half off, moving very fast and a little wildly. I stood transfixed. The day before we had been told by a pair of seasoned hikers that sometimes in the South drivers will swerve at AT hitchhikers, or run over their packs, for purposes of hilarity, and I supposed this was one of those moments. I was about to fly for cover, and even Katz was halfway to his feet, when it stopped just before us, with a rock and another cloud of dust, and a youthful female head popped out of the passenger side window.

'Yew boys wunna rod?' she called.

'Yes ma'am, we sure do,' we said, putting on our best behaviour.

We hastened to the car with our packs and bowed down at the window to find a very handsome, very happy, very drunk young couple, who didn't look to be more than eighteen or nineteen years old. The woman was carefully topping up two plastic cups from a three-quarters-empty bottle of Wild Turkey. 'Hi!' she said. 'Hop in.'

We hesitated. The car was packed nearly solid with stuff – suitcases, boxes, assorted black plastic bags, hangerloads of clothes. It was a small car to begin with and there was barely room for them.

'Darren, why'n't you make some room for these gentlemen,' the young woman ordered and then added for us: 'This yere's Darren.'

Darren got out, grinned a hello, opened the boot and stared blankly at it while the perception slowly spread through his brain that it was also packed solid. He was so drunk that I thought for a moment he might fall asleep on his feet, but he snapped to and found some rope and quite deftly tied our packs on the roof. Then, ignoring the vigorous advice and instructions of his partner, he tossed stuff around in the back until he had somehow created a small cavity into which Katz and I climbed, puffing out apologies and expressions of the sincerest gratitude.

Her name was Donna, and they were on their way to some desperate-sounding community – Turkey Balls Falls or Coon Slick or some place – another 50 miles up the road, but they were pleased to drop us in Hiawassee, if they didn't kill us all first. Darren drove at 127 miles an hour with one finger on the wheel, his head bouncing to the rhythm of some internal song, while she twirled in her seat to talk to us. She was stunningly pretty, entrancingly pretty.

'Y'all have to excuse us. We're celebrating.' She held up her plastic cup as if in toast.

'What're you celebrating?' asked Katz.

'We're gittin' married tomorrah,' she announced proudly.

'No kidding,' said Katz. 'Congratulations.'

'Yup. Darren yere's gonna make a honest woman outta me.' She tousled his hair, then impulsively lunged over and gave the side of his head a kiss, which became lingering, then probing, then frankly lascivious, and concluded, as a kind of bonus, by shooting her hand into a surprising place – or at least so we surmised because Darren abruptly banged his head on the roof and took us on a brief but exciting detour into a lane of oncoming traffic. Then she turned to us with a dreamy, unabashed leer, as if to say, 'Who's next?' It looked, we reflected later, as if Darren might have his hands full, though we additionally concluded that it would probably be worth it.

'Hey, have a drink,' she offered suddenly, seizing the bottle round the neck and looking for spare cups on the floor.

'Oh, no thanks,' Katz said, but looked tempted.

'G'*won*,' she encouraged.

Katz held up a palm. 'I'm reformed.'

'Yew *are*? Well, good for you. Have a drink then.'

'No really.'

'How 'bout *yew*?' she said to me.

'Oh, no thanks.' I couldn't have freed my pinned arms even if I had wanted a drink. They dangled before me like Tyrannosaurus limbs.

'*Yer* not reformed, are ya?'

'Well, kind of.' I had decided, for purposes of solidarity, to forswear alcohol for the duration.

She looked at us. 'You guys like Mormons or something?'

'No, just hikers.'

She nodded thoughtfully, satisfied with that, and had a drink. Then she made Darren jump again.

They dropped us at Mull's Motel in Hiawassee, an old-fashioned, nondescript, patently non-chain establishment on a bend in the road near the centre of town. We thanked them profusely, went through a little song-and-dance of trying to give them petrol money, which they stoutly refused, and watched as Darren returned to the busy road as if fired from a rocket launcher. I believe I saw him bang his head again as they disappeared over a small rise.

And then we were alone with our packs in an empty motel car park in a dusty, forgotten, queer-looking little town in north Georgia. The word that clings to every hiker's thoughts in north Georgia is *Deliverance*, the 1974 novel by James Dickey and subsequent film. It concerns, as you may recall, four middle-aged men from Atlanta who go on a weekend canoeing trip down the fictional Cahulawasee River (but based on the real, nearby Chattooga) and find themselves severely out of their element. 'Every family I've ever met up here has at least one relative in the penitentiary,' a character in the book remarks forebodingly as they drive up. 'Some of them are in for making liquor or running it, but most of them are in for murder. They don't think a whole lot about killing people up here.' And so of course it proves, as our urban foursome find themselves variously buggered, murdered and hunted by a brace of demented backwoodsmen.

Early in the book Dickey has his characters stop for directions in some 'sleepy and hookwormy and ugly' town, which for all I know could have been Hiawassee. What is certainly true is that the book was set in this part of the state, and the movie was filmed in the area. The famous banjo-plucking albino who played Dueling Banjos in the movie still apparently lives in Clayton, just down the road.

Dickey's book, as you might expect, attracted heated criticism in the state when it was published – one observer called it 'the most demeaning characterization of southern highlanders in modern literature', which if anything was an understatement – but in fact it must be said people have been appalled by north-ern Georgians for 150 years. One nineteenth-century chronicler described the region's inhabitants as 'tall, thin, cadaverous-looking animals, as melancholy and lazy as boiled cod-fish', and others freely employed words like 'depraved', 'rude', 'uncivi-lized' and 'backward' to describe the reclusive, underbred folk of Georgia's deep, dark woods and desperate townships. Dickey, who was himself a Georgian and knew the area well, swore that his book was a faithful description.

Perhaps it was the lingering influence of the book, perhaps simply the time of day, or maybe nothing more than the un-accustomedness of being in a town, but Hiawassee did feel palpably weird and unsettling – the kind of place where it wouldn't altogether surprise you to find your gasoline being pumped by a cyclops. We went into the motel reception, which was more like a small, untidy living room than a place of busi-ness, and found an aged woman with lively white hair and a bright cotton dress sitting on a sofa by the door. She looked happy to see us.

'Hi,' I said. 'We're looking for a room.'

The woman grinned and nodded.

'Actually, two rooms if you've got them.'

The woman grinned and nodded again. I waited for her to get up, but she didn't move.

'For tonight,' I said encouragingly. 'You do have rooms?' Her grin became a kind of beam and she grasped my hand, and held on tight; her fingers felt cold and bony. She just looked at me intently and eagerly, as if she thought – hoped – that I would throw a stick for her to fetch.

'Tell her we come from Reality Land,' Katz whispered in my ear.

At that moment a door swung open and a grey-haired woman swept in, wiping her hands on an apron.

'Oh, ain't no good talking to her,' she said in a friendly manner. 'She don't know nothing, don't say nothing. Mother, let go the man's hand.' Her mother beamed at her. 'Mother, let *go* the man's hand.'

My hand was released and we booked into two rooms. We went off with our keys and agreed to meet in half an hour. My room was basic and battered – there were cigarette burns on every possible surface, including the toilet seat and door lintels, and the walls and ceiling were covered in big stains that suggested a strange fight to the death involving lots of hot coffee – but it was very heaven to me. I called Katz, for the novelty of using a telephone, and learned that his room was even worse. We were very happy.

We showered, put on such clean clothes as we could muster and eagerly repaired to a popular nearby bistro called the Georgia Mountain Restaurant. The car park was crowded with pickup trucks and inside it was busy with meaty people in baseball caps. I had a feeling that if I'd said 'Phone call for you, Bubba', every man in the room would have risen. I won't say the Georgia Mountain had food I would travel for, even within Hiawassee, but it was certainly reasonably priced. For $5.50 each, we got 'meat and three' (three being the number of vegetables) as they call it here, a trip to the salad bar and dessert. I ordered fried chicken, black-eyed peas, roast potatoes and 'ruterbeggars', as the menu had it. I had never had them before, and can't say I will again. We ate noisily and with gusto, and ordered many refills of iced tea.

Dessert was of course the highlight. Everyone on the trail dreams of something, usually a sweet, and my sustaining vision had been an outsized slab of pie. It had occupied my thoughts for days and when the waitress came to take our order I asked her, with beseeching eyes and a hand on her forearm, to bring me the largest piece she could slice without losing her job. She brought me a vast, viscous, canary-yellow wedge of lemon pie. It was a monument to food technology, yellow enough to give you a headache, sweet enough to make your eyeballs roll up into your head – everything, in short, you could want in a pie so long as taste and quality didn't enter into your requirements. I was just plunging into it when Katz broke a long silence by saying, with a strange kind of nervousness, 'You know what I keep doing? I keep looking up to see if Mary Ellen's coming through the door.'

I paused, a forkful of shimmering goo halfway to my mouth, and noticed with passing disbelief that his dessert plate was already empty. 'You're not going to tell me you miss her, Stephen?' I said drily and pushed the food home.

'No,' he responded tartly, not taking this as a joke at all. He took on a frustrated look from trying to find words to express his complex emotions. 'We did kind of ditch her, you know,' he finally blurted.

I considered the charge. 'Actually, we didn't kind of ditch her. We ditched her.' I wasn't with him at all on this. 'So?'

'Well, I just, I just feel kind of bad – just *kind* of bad – that we left her out in the woods on her own.' Then he crossed his arms as if to say: 'There, I've said it.'

I put my fork down and considered the point. 'She came into the woods on her own,' I said. 'We're not actually responsible for her, you know. I mean, it's not as if we signed a contract to look after her.'

I said these things, but even as I said them I realized with a kind of horrible seeping awareness that he was right. We had ditched her, left her to the bears and wolves and chortling mountain men. I had been so completely preoccupied with my own savage lust for food and a real bed that I had not paused to consider what our abrupt departure would mean for her – a night alone among the whispering trees, swaddled in darkness, listening with involuntary keenness for the tell-tale crack of branch or stick under a heavy foot or paw. It wasn't something I would wish on anyone. My gaze fell on my pie, and I realized I didn't want it any longer. 'Maybe she'll have found somebody else to camp with,' I suggested lamely, and pushed the pie away.

'Did *you* see anybody today?'

He was right. We had seen hardly a soul.

'She's probably still walking right now,' Katz said with a hint of sudden heat. 'Wondering where the hell we got to. Scared out of her chubby little wits.'

'Oh, don't,' I half pleaded, and distractedly pushed the pie a half-inch further away.

He nodded an emphatic, busy, righteous little nod, and looked at me with a strange, glowing, accusatory expression that said, 'And if she dies let it be on your conscience.' And he was right; I was the ringleader here. This was my fault.

Then he leaned closer and said in a completely different tone of voice, 'If you're not going to eat that pie, can I have it?'

In the morning we breakfasted at a Hardee's across the street and paid for a taxi to take us back to the trail. We didn't speak about Mary Ellen or much of anything else. Returning to the trail after a night's comforts in a town always left us disinclined to talk.

We were confronted with an immediate steep climb, and walked slowly, almost gingerly. I always felt terrible on the trail the first day after a break. Katz, on the other hand, just always felt terrible. Whatever restorative effects a town visit offered always vanished with astounding swiftness on the trail. Within two minutes it was as if we had never been away – actually worse, because on a normal day I would not be labouring up a steep hill with a greasy, leaden Hardee's breakfast threatening at every moment to come up for air.

We had been walking for about half an hour when another hiker – a fit-looking middle-aged guy – came along from the other direction. We asked him if he had seen a girl named Mary Ellen in a red jacket with kind of a loud voice.

He made an expression of possible recognition and said: 'Does she – I'm not being rude here or anything – but does she do this a lot?' and he pinched his nose and made a series of horrible honking noises.

We nodded vigorously.

'Yeah, I stayed with her and two other guys in Plumorchard Gap Shelter last night.' He regarded us closely, dubiously. 'She a friend of yours?'

'Oh, no,' we said, disavowing her entirely, as any sensible person would. 'She just sort of latched on to us for a couple of days.'

He nodded in understanding, then grinned. 'She's a piece of work, isn't she?'

We grinned, too. 'Was it bad?' I said.

He made a look that showed genuine pain, then abruptly, as if putting two and two together, said, 'So you must be the guys she was talking about.'

'Really?' Katz said. 'What'd she say?'

'Oh, nothing,' he said, but he was suppressing a small smile in that way that makes you say:

'What?'

'Nothing. It was nothing.' But he was smiling.

'*What?*'

He wavered. 'Oh, all right. She said you guys were a couple of overweight wimps who didn't know the first thing about hiking and that she was tired of carrying you.'

'She said *that?*' Katz said, scandalized.

'Actually I think she called you pussies.'

'She called us *pussies?*' Katz said. 'Now I will kill her.'

'Well, I don't suppose you'll have any trouble finding people to hold her down for you,' the man said absently, scanning the sky, and added: 'Supposed to snow.'

I made a crestfallen noise. This was the last thing we wanted. 'Really? Bad?'

He nodded. 'Six to eight inches. More on the higher elevations.' He lifted his eyebrows stoically, agreeing with my dismayed expression. Snow wasn't just discouraging, it was dangerous.

He let the prospect hang there for a moment, then said, 'Well, better keep moving.' I nodded in understanding, for that was what we did in these hills. I watched him go, then turned to Katz, who was shaking his head.

'Imagine her saying that after all we did for her,' he said, then noticed me staring at him, and said in a kind of squirmy way, 'What?' and then, more squirmily, '*What?*'

'Don't you ever, *ever,* spoil a piece of pie for me again. Do you understand?'

He winced. 'Yeah, all right. Jeez,' he said and trudged on muttering.

Two days later we heard that Mary Ellen had dropped out with blisters after trying to do 35 miles in two days. Big mistake.

Chapter 6

Distance changes utterly when you take the world on foot. A mile becomes a long way, two miles literally considerable, ten miles whopping, 50 miles at the very limits of conception. The world, you realize, is enormous in a way that only you and a small community of fellow hikers know. Planetary scale is your little secret.

Life takes on a neat simplicity, too. Time ceases to have any meaning. When it is dark you go to bed and when it is light again you get up, and everything in between is just in between. It's quite wonderful, really.

You have no engagements, commitments, obligations or duties; no special ambitions and only the smallest, least complicated of wants; you exist in a tranquil tedium, serenely beyond the reach of exasperation, 'far removed from the seats of strife', as the early explorer and botanist William Bartram put it. All that is required of you is a willingness to trudge.

There is no point in hurrying because you are not actually

going anywhere. However far or long you plod, you are always in the same place: in the woods. It's where you were yesterday, where you will be tomorrow. The woods is one boundless singularity. Every bend in the path presents a prospect indistinguishable from every other, every glimpse into the trees the same tangled mass. For all you know, your route could describe a very large, pointless circle. In a way, it would hardly matter.

At times, you become almost certain that you slabbed this hillside three days ago, crossed this stream yesterday, clambered over this fallen tree at least twice today already. But most of the time you don't think. No point. Instead you exist in a kind of mobile zen mode, your brain like a balloon tethered with string, accompanying but not actually part of the body below. Walking for hours and miles becomes as automatic, as unremarkable, as breathing. At the end of the day you don't think, 'Hey, I did sixteen miles today,' any more than you think, 'Hey, I took 8,000 breaths today.' It's just what you do.

And so we walked, hour upon hour, over rollercoaster hills, along knife-edge ridges and over grassy balds, through depthless ranks of oak, ash, chinkapin and pine. The skies grew sullen and the air chillier, but it wasn't until the third day that the snow came. It began in the morning as thinly scattered flecks, hardly noticeable, but then the wind rose, then rose again, until it was blowing with an end-of-the-world fury that seemed to have even the trees in a panic, and with it came snow, great flying masses of it. By midday we found ourselves plodding into a stinging, cold, hard-blowing storm. Soon after, we came to a narrow ledge of path along a wall of rock called Big Butt Mountain.

Even in ideal circumstances the path round Big Butt would have required delicacy and care. It was like a window ledge on a skyscraper, no more than fourteen or sixteen inches wide, and crumbling in places, with a sharp drop on one side of perhaps 80 feet and long, looming stretches of vertical granite on the other. Once or twice I nudged foot-sized rocks over the side and watched with faint horror as they crashed and tumbled to improbably remote resting places. The trail was cobbled with rocks and threaded with wandering tree roots against which we constantly stubbed and stumbled, and veneered everywhere with polished ice under a thin layer of powdery snow. At exasperatingly frequent intervals, the path was broken by steep, thickly bouldered streams, frozen solid and ribbed with blue ice, which could only be negotiated in a crablike crouch. And all the time, as we crept along on this absurdly narrow, dangerous perch, we were half blinded by flying snow and jostled by gusts of wind, which roared through the dancing trees and shook us by our packs. This wasn't a blizzard; it was a tempest. We proceeded with painstaking deliberativeness, placing each foot solidly before lifting the one behind. Even so, twice Katz made horrified, heartfelt, comic-book noises as his footing went – 'AIEEEEE!' noises and 'EEEARGH!' noises – and I turned to find him hugging a tree, feet skating, his expression bug-eyed and fearful.

It was deeply unnerving. It took us over two hours to cover six-tenths of a mile of trail. By the time we reached solid ground at a place called Bearpen Gap, the snow was four or five inches deep and accumulating fast. The whole world was white, filled with dime-sized snowflakes that fell at a slant before being caught by the wind and hurled in a variety of directions. We couldn't see more than 15 or 20 feet ahead, often not that.

The trail crossed a logging road, then led straight up Albert Mountain, a bouldered summit 5,250 feet above sea level, where the winds were so wild and angry that they hit the mountain with an actual walloping sound, and forced us to shout to hear each other. We started up and hastily retreated. Hiking packs leave you with no recognizable centre of gravity at the best of times; here we were literally being blown over. Confounded, we stood at the bottom of the summit and looked at each other. This was really quite grave. We were caught between a mountain we couldn't climb and a ledge we had no intention of trying to renegotiate. Our only apparent option was to pitch our tents – if we could in this wind – crawl in and hope for the best. I don't wish to reach for melodrama, but people have died in less trying circumstances.

I dumped my pack and searched through it for my trail map. Appalachian Trail maps are so monumentally useless that I had long since given up using them. AT maps vary somewhat, but most are on an abysmal scale of 1:100,000, which ludicrously compresses every kilometre of real world into a mere centimetre of map. Imagine a square kilometre of physical landscape and all that it might contain – logging roads, streams, a mountaintop or two, perhaps a fire tower, a knob or grassy bald, the wandering AT and maybe a pair of important side trails – and imagine trying to convey all that information on an area the size of the nail on your little finger. That's an AT map.

Actually, it's far, far worse than that because AT maps – for reasons that bewilder me beyond speculation – provide less detail than even their meagre scale allows. For any ten miles of trail, the maps will name and identify perhaps only three of the dozen or more peaks you cross. Valleys, lakes, gaps, creeks and other important, possibly vital, topographical features are routinely left unnamed. Forest Service roads are often not included and, if included, inconsistently identified. Even side trails are frequently left off. There are no co-ordinates, no way of directing rescuers to a particular place, no pointers to towns just off the map's edge. These are, in short, seriously inadequate maps.

In normal circumstances, this is merely irksome. Now, in a blizzard, it seemed closer to negligence. I dragged the map from the pack and fought the wind to look at it. It showed the trail as a red line. Nearby was a heavy, wandering black line, which I presumed to be the Forest Service road we stood beside, though there was no actual telling. According to the map, the road – if a road is what it was – started in the middle of nowhere and finished half a dozen miles later equally in the middle of nowhere, which clearly made no sense – indeed wasn't even possible. (You can't start a road in the middle of forest; earth-moving equipment can't spontaneously appear among the trees. Anyway, even if you could build a road that didn't go anywhere, why would you?) There was, obviously, something deeply and infuriatingly wrong with this map.

'Cost me eleven bucks,' I said to Katz a little wildly, shaking the map at him and then crumpling it into an approximately flat shape and jabbing it into my pocket.

'So what're we going to do?' he said.

I sighed, unsure, then yanked the map out and examined it again. I looked from it to the logging road and back. 'Well, it looks as if this logging road curves around the mountain and comes back near the trail on the other side. If it does and we can find it, then there's a shelter we can get to. If we can't get through, I don't know, I guess we take the road back downhill to lower ground and see if we can find a place out of the wind to camp.' I shrugged a little helplessly. 'I don't know. What do you think?'

Katz was looking at the sky, watching the flying snow. 'Well, I think', he said thoughtfully, 'that I'd like to have a long hot soak in a Jacuzzi, a big steak dinner with a baked potato and lots of sour cream, and I mean lots of sour cream, and then sex with the Dallas Cowboys cheerleaders on a tigerskin rug in front of a roaring fire in one of those big stone fireplaces like you get in a lodge at a ski resort. You know the kind I mean?' He looked at me. I nodded. 'That's what *I'd* like. But I'm willing to try your plan if you think it will be more fun.' He flicked snow from his brow. 'Besides, it would be a shame to waste all this delightful snow.' He issued a single bitter guffaw, and returned to the hysterical snow. I hoisted my pack and followed.

We plodded up the road, bent steeply, buffeted by winds. Where it settled, the snow was wet and heavy and getting so deep that soon it would be impassable and we would have to take shelter whether we wanted to or not. There was no place to pitch a tent here, I noticed uneasily – only steep, wooded slope going up on one side and down on the other. For quite a distance – far longer than it seemed it ought to – the road stayed straight. Even if, further on, it did curve back near the trail, there was no certainty – or even perhaps much likelihood – that we would spot it. In these trees and this snow you could be ten feet from the trail and not see it. It would be madness to leave the logging road and try to find it. Then again, it was probably madness to be following a logging road to higher ground in a blizzard.

Gradually, and then more decidedly, the road began to hook round behind the mountain. After about an hour of dragging sluggishly through ever-deepening snow we came to a high, windy level spot where the trail – or at least a trail – emerged down the back of Albert Mountain and continued on into level woods. I regarded my map with bewildered exasperation. It didn't give any indication of this whatever, but Katz spotted a white blaze 20 yards into the woods, and we whooped with joy. We had refound the AT. A shelter was only a few hundred yards further on. It looked as if we would live to hike another day.

The snow was nearly knee-deep now and we were tired, but we all but pranced through it, and Katz whooped again when we reached an arrowed sign on a low limb that pointed down a side trail and said BIG SPRING SHELTER. The shelter, a simple wooden affair, open on one side, stood in a snowy glade – a little winter wonderland – 150 yards or so off the main trail. Even from a distance we could see that the open side faced into the wind and that the drifting snow was nearly up to the lip of the sleeping platform. Still, if nothing else it offered at least a sense of refuge.

We crossed the clearing, heaved our packs onto the platform and in the same instant discovered that there were two people there already – a man and a boy of about fourteen. They were Jim and Heath, father and son, they were from Chattanooga and they were cheerful, friendly, and not remotely daunted by the weather. They had come hiking for the weekend, they told us (I hadn't even realized it was a weekend), and knew the weather was likely to be bad, though not perhaps quite this bad, and so were well prepared. Jim had brought a big clear plastic sheet, of the sort decorators use to cover floors, and was trying to rig it across the open front of the shelter. Katz, uncharacteristically, leapt to his assistance. The plastic sheet didn't quite reach, but we found that with one of our groundcloths lashed alongside it we could cover the entire front. The wind walloped ferociously against the plastic and from time to time tore part of it loose, where it fluttered and snapped, with a retort like gunshot, until one of us leapt up and fought it back into place. The whole shelter was in any case incredibly leaky of air – the plank walls and floors were full of cracks through which icy wind and occasional blasts of snow shot – but we were infinitely snugger than we would have been outside.

So we made a little home of it for ourselves, spread out our sleeping pads and bags, put on all the extra clothes we could find, and fixed dinner from a reclining position. Darkness fell quickly and heavily, which made the wildness outside seem even more severe. Jim and Heath had some chocolate cake which they shared with us – a treat beyond heaven – and then the four of us settled down to a long, cold night on hard wood, listening to a banshee wind and the crash of angry branches.

When I awoke, all was stillness – the sort of stillness that makes you sit up and take your bearings. The plastic sheet before me was peeled back a foot or so and weak light filled the space beyond. Snow was over the top of the platform and lying an inch deep over the foot of my sleeping bag. I shooed it off with a toss of my legs. Jim and Heath were already stirring to life. Katz slumbered heavily on, an arm flung over his forehead, his mouth a great open hole. It was not quite six.

I decided to go out to reconnoitre and see how stranded we might be. I hesitated at the platform's edge, then jumped out into the drift – it came up over my waist and made my eyes fly

open where it slipped under my clothes and found bare skin –
and pushed through it into the clearing, where it was slightly
– but only slightly – shallower. Even in sheltered areas, under
an umbrella of conifers, the snow was nearly knee-deep and
tedious to churn through. But everywhere it was stunning.
Every tree wore a thick cloak of white, every stump and
boulder a jaunty snowy cap, and there was that perfect,
immense stillness that you get nowhere else but in a big wood
after a heavy snowfall. Here and there clumps of snow fell from
the branches, but otherwise there was no sound or movement.
I followed the side trail up and under heavily bowed limbs to
where it rejoined the AT. The AT was a plumped blanket of
snow, round and bluish, in a long, dim tunnel of overbent
rhododendrons. It looked deep and hard going. I walked a few
yards as a test. It was deep and hard going.

When I returned to the shelter, Katz was up, moving slowly
and going through his morning groans, and Jim was studying
his maps, which were vastly better than mine. I crouched beside
him and he made room to let me look with him. It was 6.1 miles
to Wallace Gap and a paved road, old US 64. A mile down the
road from there was Rainbow Springs Campground, a private
campsite with showers and a store. I didn't know how hard it
would be to walk seven miles through deep snow and had no
confidence that the campground would be open this early in
the year. Still, it was obvious this snow wasn't going to melt for
days and we would have to make a move sometime; it might as
well be now when at least it was pretty and calm. Who knew
when another storm might blow in and really strand us?

Jim had decided that he and Heath would accompany us for
the first couple of hours, then turn off on a side trail called Long
Branch, which descended steeply through a ravine for 2.3 miles
and emerged near a car park where they had left their car. He
had hiked the Long Branch trail many times and knew what to
expect. Even so, I didn't like the sound of it, and asked him
hesitantly if he thought it was a good idea to go off on a little-

used side trail, into goodness knows what conditions, where no-one would come across him and his son if they got in trouble. Katz, to my relief, agreed with me. 'At least there's always other people on the AT,' he said. 'You don't know what might happen to you on a side trail.' Jim considered the matter and said they would turn back if it looked bad.

Katz and I treated ourselves to two cups of coffee, for warmth, and Jim and Heath shared with us some of their oatmeal, which made Katz intensely happy. Then we all set off together. It was cold and hard going. The tunnels of bowed rhododendrons, which often ran on for great distances, were exceedingly pretty, but when our packs brushed against them they dumped volumes of snow onto our heads and down the back of our necks. The three adults took it in turns to walk in front because the lead person always received the heaviest dumping, as well as having all the hard work of dibbing holes in the snow.

The Long Branch trail, when we reached it, descended steeply through bowed pines – too steeply, it seemed to me, to come back up if the trail proved impassable, and it looked as if it might. Katz and I urged them to reconsider, but Jim said it was all downhill and well marked and he was sure it would be all right.

'Hey, you know what day it is?' said Jim suddenly and, seeing our blank faces, supplied the answer: 'March the twenty-first.'

Our faces stayed blank.

'First day of spring,' he said.

We smiled at the irony of it, shook hands all round, wished each other luck and parted.

Katz and I walked for three hours more, silently and slowly through the cold, white forest, taking it in turns to break snow. At about one o'clock we came at last to Old 64, a lonesome, superannuated two-lane road through the mountains. It hadn't been cleared and there were no tyre tracks through it. It was starting to snow again, steadily, prettily. We set off down the road for the campground, and had walked about a quarter of a mile when from behind there was the crunching sound of a motorized vehicle proceeding cautiously through snow. We turned to see a big jeep-type car rolling up beside us. The driver's window hummed down. It was Jim and Heath. They had come to let us know they had made it, and to make sure we had likewise. 'Thought you might like a lift to the campground,' Jim said.

We climbed gratefully in, filling their nice car with snow, and rode down to the campsite. Jim told us that they had passed it on the way up and it looked open, but that they would take us to Franklin, the nearest town, if it wasn't. They had heard a weather forecast. More snow was expected over the next couple of days.

They dropped us at the camp ground – it was open – and departed with waves. Rainbow Springs was a small private campsite with several small overnight cottages, a shower block, and a couple of other indeterminate buildings scattered around a big level open area clearly intended for camper vans and recreational vehicles. By the entrance, in an old white house, was the office, which was really a general store. We went in and found that every hiker for 20 miles was already there, several of them sitting round a wood stove eating chilli or ice cream and looking rosy-cheeked and warm and clean. Three or four of them we knew already. The campground was run by Buddy and Jensine Crossman, who seemed friendly and welcoming. If nothing else, it was probably not often that business was this good in March. I enquired about a cabin.

Jensine stubbed out a cigarette and laughed at my naivety, which caused her a small coughing attack. 'Honey, the cabins went two days ago. There's two places left in the bunkhouse. After that people are going to have to sleep on floors.'

Bunkhouse is not a word I particularly want to hear at my time of life, but we had no choice. We signed in, were given two very small, stiff towels for the shower, and trudged off across the grounds to see what we got for our $11 apiece. The answer was very little.

The bunkhouse was basic and awesomely unlovely. It was dominated by twelve narrow wood bunks stacked in tiers of three, each with a thin bare mattress and a grubby bare pillow lumpily filled with shreds of styrofoam. In one corner stood a potbellied stove, hissing softly, surrounded by a semicircle of limp boots and draped with wet woollen socks, which steamed foully. A small wooden table and a pair of broken-down easy chairs, both sprouting stuffing, completed the furnishings. Everywhere there was stuff – tents, clothes, backpacks, rain-covers – hanging out to dry, dripping sluggishly. The floor was bare concrete, the walls uninsulated plywood. It was singularly uninviting, like camping in a garage.

'Welcome to the Stalag,' said a man with an ironic smile and an English accent.

His name was Peter Fleming and he was a lecturer at a college in New Brunswick who had come south for a week's hiking but, like everyone else, had been driven in by the snow. He introduced us around – each person greeted us with a friendly but desultory nod – and indicated which were the spare bunks, one on the top level, nearly up at the ceiling, the other on the bottom on the opposite side of the room.

'Red Cross parcels come on the last Friday of the month, and there'll be a meeting of the escape committee at nineteen hundred hours this evening. I think that's about all you need to know.'

'And don't order the Philly cheese steak sandwich unless you want to puke all night,' said a wan but heartfelt voice from a shadowy bunk in the corner.

'That's Tex,' Fleming explained. We nodded.

Katz selected the topmost bunk and set about the long challenge of trying to get into it. I turned to my own bunk and examined it with a kind of appalled fascination. If the mattress stains were anything to go by, a previous user had not so much suffered from incontinence as rejoiced in it. He had evidently included the pillow in his celebrations. I lifted it and sniffed it, then wished I hadn't. I spread out my sleeping bag, draped some socks over the stove, hung up a few things to dry, then sat on the edge of the bed and passed a pleasant half-hour with the others watching Katz's dogged struggle to the summit, which mostly involved deep grunts, swimming legs, and invitations to all onlookers and well-wishers to go fuck themselves. From where I sat, all I could see was his expansive butt and homeless lower limbs. His posture brought to mind a shipwreck victim clinging to a square of floating wreckage on rough seas, or possibly someone who had been lifted unexpectedly into the sky by a weather balloon he was preparing to hoist – in any case, someone holding on for dear life in dangerous circumstances. I grabbed my pillow and climbed up alongside him to ask why he didn't just take the bottom bunk.

His face was wild and flushed; I'm not even sure he recognized me at that moment. 'Because heat rises, buddy,' he said, 'and when I get up here – if I fucking ever do – I'm going to be *toast*.' I nodded – there was seldom any point in trying to reason with Katz when he was puffed out and fixated – and used the opportunity to switch pillows on him.

Eventually, when it became unsustainably pathetic to watch, three of us pushed him home. He flopped heavily and with an alarming crack of wood which panicked the poor, quiet man in the bunk underneath, and announced he had no intention of leaving this spot until the snows had melted and spring had come to the mountains. Then he turned his back and went to sleep.

I trudged through the snow to the shower block for the pleasure of dancing through ice water, then went to the general store and hung out by the stove with half a dozen others. There was nothing else to do. I ate two bowls of chilli – the house speciality – and listened to the general conversation. This mostly involved Buddy and Jensine bitching about the previous day's customers, but it was nice to hear some voices other than Katz's.

'You shoulda seen 'em,' Jensine said with distaste, picking a fleck of tobacco off her tongue. 'Didn't say please, didn't say thank you. Not like you guys. You guys are a breath of fresh air in comparison, believe me. And they made a complete pigpen of the bunkhouse, didn't they, Buddy?' She passed the baton to Buddy.

'Took me an hour to clean it this morning,' he said grimly, which surprised me because the bunkhouse didn't look as if it had been cleaned this century. 'There were puddles all over the floor and somebody, I don't know who, left a filthy old flannel shirt, which was just disgusting. *And* they burned all the firewood. Three days' worth of firewood I took down there yesterday and they burned every stick of it.'

'We were real glad to see 'em go,' said Jensine. 'Real glad. Not like you guys. You guys are a breath of fresh air, believe me.' Then she went off to answer a ringing phone.

I was sitting next to one of the three kids from Rutgers University whom we had been running into off and on since the second day. They had a cabin now, but had been in the bunkhouse the night before. He leaned over and in a whisper said: 'She said the same thing yesterday about the people the day before. She'll be saying the same thing tomorrow about us. Do you know, there were fifteen of us in the bunkhouse last night.'

'Fifteen?' I repeated, in a tone of wonder. It was intolerable enough with twelve. 'Where on earth did the extra three sleep?'

'On the floor – and they were still charged eleven bucks for it. How's your chilli?'

I looked at it as if I hadn't thought about it, as in fact I hadn't. 'Pretty terrible, actually.'

He nodded. 'Wait till you've been eating it for two days.'

When I left to walk back to the bunkhouse, it was still snowing, but peacefully. Katz was awake and up on one elbow, smoking a cadged cigarette, and asking people to pass things up to him – scissors, a bandanna, matches – as the need arose and to take them away again as he finished with them. Three people stood at the window watching the snow. The talk was all of the weather. There was no telling when we would get out of here. It was impossible not to feel trapped.

We spent a wretched night in our bunks, faintly lit by the dancing glow of the stove, which the timid man (unable or reluctant to sleep with the restless mass of Katz bowing the slats just above his head) diligently kept stoked, and wrapped in a breathy, communal symphony of night-time noises – sighs, weary exhalations, dredging snores, a steady dying moan from the man who had eaten the Philly cheese steak sandwich, the monotone hiss of the stove, like the soundtrack of an old movie – and woke, stiff and unrested, to a gloomy dawn of falling snow and the dispiriting prospect of a long, long day with nothing to do but hang out at the camp store or lie on a bunkbed reading old Reader's Digests which filled a small shelf by the door. Then word came that an industrious youth named Zack from one of the cabins had somehow got to Franklin and rented a minivan, and was offering to take anyone to town for $5. There was a virtual stampede. To the dismay and disgust of Buddy and Jensine, practically everyone paid up and left. Fourteen of us packed into the minivan and started on the long descent to Franklin, in a snowless valley far below.

And so we had a little holiday in Franklin, which was small, dull and cautiously unattractive, but mostly dull – the sort of place where you find yourself, for want of anything better to do, strolling out to the lumberyard to watch guys on forklifts shunting wood about. There wasn't a thing in the way of diversions, nowhere to buy a book or even a magazine that didn't involve speedboats, customized cars or guns and ammo. The town was full of hikers like us who had been driven down from the hills and had nothing to do but hang out list-lessly in the diner or launderette, and two or three times a day make a pilgrimage to the far end of Main Street to stare forlornly at the distant, snow-draped, patently impassable peaks. The outlook was not good. There were rumours of seven-foot drifts in the Smokies. It could be days before the trail was passable again.

I was plunged into a restless depression by this, heightened by the realization that Katz was verily in heaven at the prospect of several days idling in a town, on vacation from purpose and exertion, trying out various attitudes of repose. To my intense vexation, he had even bought a *TV Guide*, to plan his viewing more effectively over the coming days.

I wanted to get back on the trail, to knock off miles. It was what we did. Besides, I was bored to a point somewhat beyond being bored out of my mind. I was reading restaurant place mats, then turning them over to see if there was anything on the back. At the lumberyard I talked to workmen through the fence. Late on the third afternoon I stood in a Burger King and studied, with absorption, the photographs of the manager and his executive crew (reflecting on the curious fact that people who go into hamburger management always look as if their mother slept with Goofy), then slid one pace to the right to examine the employee of the month awards. It was then I realized I had to get out of Franklin.

Twenty minutes later I announced to Katz that we were returning to the trail in the morning. He was of course astounded and dismayed. 'But it's *The X Files* on Friday,' he sputtered. 'I just bought cream soda.'

'The disappointment must be crushing,' I replied with a thin, heartless smile.

'But the snow. We'll never get through.'

I gave a shrug that was meant to look optimistic, but was probably closer to indifferent. 'We might,' I said.

'But what if we don't? What if there's another blizzard? We were very lucky, if you ask me, to escape with our lives last time.' He looked at me with desperate eyes. 'I've got eighteen cans of cream soda in my room,' he blurted and then wished he hadn't.

I arched an eyebrow. 'Eight*een*? Were you planning to settle here?'

'It was on special,' he muttered defensively and retreated into a sulk.

'Look, Stephen, I'm sorry to spoil your festive arrangements, but we didn't come all the way down here to drink pop and watch TV.'

'Didn't come down here to die either,' he said, but he argued no more.

So we went, and were lucky. The snow was deep, but passable. Some lone hiker, even more impatient than I, had pushed through ahead of us and compacted the snow a little, which helped. It was slick on the steep climbs – Katz was forever sliding back, falling down, cursing mightily – and occasionally on higher ground we had to detour round expansive drift fields, but there was never a place where we couldn't get through.

And the weather perked up. The sun came out; the air grew milder and heavier; the little mountain streams became lively with the tumble and gurgle of meltwater. I even heard the tentative twitter of birds. Above 4,500 feet, the snow lingered and the air felt refrigerated, but lower down the snow retreated in daily bounds until by the third day it was no more than scrappy patches on the darkest slopes. It really wasn't bad at all, though Katz refused to admit it. I didn't care. I just walked. I was *very* happy.

Chapter 7

For two days Katz barely spoke to me. On the second night, at
9 p.m. an unlikely noise came from his tent – the punctured-air
click of a beverage can being opened – and he said in a pug-
nacious tone, 'Do you know what that was, Bryson? Cream
soda. You know what else? I'm drinking it right now, and I'm
not giving you any. And you know what else? It's delicious.'
There was a slurpy, intentionally amplified drinking noise.
'Mmmm-mmmm. Dee-*light*-ful.' Another slurp. 'And do you
know why I'm drinking it now? Because it's nine p.m. – time for
The X Files, my favourite programme of all time.' There was a
long moment's drinking noise, the sound of a tent zip parting,
the *tink* of an empty can landing in undergrowth, the tent zip
closing. 'Man, that was so good. Now fuck you and good night.'

And that was the end of it. In the morning he was fine.

Katz never really did get into hiking, though goodness knows
he tried. From time to time, I believe, he glimpsed that there
was something – some elusive, elemental something – that

made being out in the woods almost gratifying. Occasionally, he would exclaim over a view or regard with admiration some passing marvel of nature, but mostly to him hiking was a tiring, dirty, pointless slog between distantly spaced comfort zones. I, meanwhile, was wholly, mindlessly, very contentedly absorbed with the business of just pushing forward. My congenital distraction sometimes fascinated him and sometimes amused him, but mostly it just drove him crazy.

Late on the morning of the fourth day after leaving Franklin, I was perched on a big green rock waiting for Katz after it dawned on me that I had not seen him for some time. When at last he came along, he was even more dishevelled than usual. There were twigs in his hair, an arresting new tear in his flannel shirt, and a trickle of dried blood on his forehead. He dropped his pack and sat heavily beside me with his water bottle, took a long swig, mopped his forehead, checked his hand for blood, and finally said, in a conversational tone: 'How did you get around that tree back there?'

'What tree?'

'The fallen tree, back there. The one across the ledge.'

I thought for a minute. 'I don't remember it.'

'What do you mean you don't remember it? It was blocking the path, for crying out loud.'

I thought again, harder, and shook my head with a look of feeble apology. I could see he was heading towards exasperation.

'Just back there four, five hundred yards.' He paused, waiting for a spark of recognition, and couldn't believe that it wasn't forthcoming. 'One side a sheer cliff, the other side a thicket of brambles with no way through, and in the middle a big fallen tree. You *had* to have noticed it.'

'Whereabouts was it exactly?' I asked, as if stalling for time.

Katz couldn't contain his irritation. 'Just back *there*, for Christ's sake. One side cliff, other side brambles, and in the middle a big fallen-down oak with about this much clearance.'

He held his hand about 14 inches off the ground, and was dumbfounded by my blank look. 'Bryson, I don't know what you're taking, but I gotta have some of it. The tree was too high to climb over and too low to crawl under and there wasn't any way round it. It took me a half-hour to get over it, and I cut myself all to shit in the process. How could you not remember it?'

'It might come to me after a bit,' I said hopefully. Katz shook his head sadly. I was never entirely certain why he found my mental absences so irritating – whether he thought I was being wilfully obtuse to annoy him or whether he felt I was unreasonably cheating hardship by failing to notice it – but I made a private pledge to remain alert and fully conscious for a while, so as not to exasperate him. This was a fortunate thing because two hours later we had one of those hallelujah moments that come but rarely on the trail. We were walking along the lofty breast of a mountain called High Top when the trees parted at a granite overlook and we were confronted with an arresting prospect – a sudden new world of big, muscular, comparatively craggy mountains, steeped in haze and nudged at the distant margins by moody-looking clouds, at once deeply beckoning and rather awesome.

We had found the Smokies.

Far below, squeezed into a narrow valley, was Fontana Lake, a long, fjord-like arm of pale green water. At the lake's western end, where the Little Tennessee River flows into it, stands a big hydroelectric dam, 480 feet high, built by the Tennessee Valley Authority in the 1930s. It is the biggest dam in America east of the Mississippi, and something of an attraction for people who like concrete in volume. We hastened down the trail to it as we had an inkling that there was a visitors' centre there, which meant the possibility of a cafeteria and other gratifying contacts with the developed world. At the very least, we speculated excitedly, there would be vending machines and rest rooms, where we could wash and get fresh water, look in a mirror – briefly be groomed and civilized.

There was indeed a visitors' centre, but it was shut. A peeling notice taped to the glass said it wouldn't open for another month. The vending machines were empty and unplugged, and to our dismay even the rest rooms were locked. Katz found a tap on an outside wall and turned it, but the water had been shut off. We sighed, exchanged stoic, long-suffering looks, and pushed on.

The trail crossed the lake on the top of the dam. The mountains before us didn't so much rise from the lake as rear from it, like startled beasts. It was clear at a glance that we were entering a new realm of magnificence and challenge. The far shore of the lake marked the southern boundary of Great Smoky Mountains National Park. Ahead lay 800 square miles of dense, steeply mountainous forest, with seven days and 71 miles of rigorous hiking before we came out the other end and could dream again of cheeseburgers, Cokes, flush toilets and running water. It would have been nice, at the very least, to have set off with clean hands and faces. I hadn't told Katz, but we were about to traverse sixteen peaks above 6,000 feet, including Clingmans Dome, the highest point on the AT at 6,643 feet (just 41 feet less than nearby Mount Mitchell, the highest mountain in the eastern United States). I was eager and excited – even Katz seemed cautiously keen – for there seemed a good deal to be excited about.

For one thing, we had just picked up our third state, Tennessee, which always brings a sense of achievement on the trail. For nearly its whole length through the Smokies, the AT marks the boundary between North Carolina and Tennessee. I liked this very much – the idea of being able to stand with my left foot in one state and my right foot in the other whenever I wanted, which was often, or to choose at rest breaks between sitting on a log in Tennessee and a rock in North Carolina, or to pee across state lines, or many other variations. Then there was the excitement of all the new things we might see in these rich, dark, storied mountains – giant salamanders and towering tulip trees and the famous jack-o'-lantern mushroom, which glows at night with a greenish phosphorescent light called fox-fire. Perhaps we would even see a bear (downwind, from a safe distance, oblivious of me, interested *exclusively* in Katz if either of us). Above all, there was the hope – the conviction – that spring could not be far off, that every passing day had to bring us closer to it, and that here in the natural Eden of the Smokies it would surely, at last, burst forth.

For the Smokies are indeed a very Eden. We were entering what botanists like to call 'the finest mixed mesophytic forest in the world'. The Smokies harbour an astonishing range of plant life – over 1,500 types of wild flower, 1,000 varieties of shrub, 530 mosses and lichen, 2,000 types of fungi. They are home to 130 native species of tree. The whole of Europe has just 85.

They owe this lavish abundance to the deep, loamy soils of their sheltered valleys, known locally as coves, to their warm, moist climate (which produces the natural bluish haze from which they get their name), and above all to the happy accident of the Appalachians' north–south orientation. During the last ice age, you see, as glaciers and ice sheets spread down from the Arctic, northern flora all over the world naturally fled south-wards. In Europe, untold numbers of native species were crushed against the impassable barrier of the Alps and its cousins, and fell into extinction. In eastern North America, there was no such impediment to retreat, so trees and other plants found their way through river valleys and over the mountains until they arrived at a congenial refuge in the Smokies, and there they have remained ever since. (When at last the ice sheets drew back, the native northern trees began the long process of returning to their former territories. Some, like the white cedar and rhododendron, are only now reaching home – a reminder that, geologically speaking, the ice sheets have only just gone.)

Rich plant life naturally brings rich animal life. The Smokies are home to 67 varieties of mammal, over 200 types of bird, and

80 species of reptile and amphibian – all larger numbers than are found in comparable-sized areas almost anywhere else in the temperate world. Above all, the Smokies are famous for their bears. There are an estimated 400 to 600 black bears in the park, not a large number, but they are a chronic problem because so many of them have lost their fear of people. Almost nine million people a year come to the Smokies, many of them to picnic. So bears have learned to associate people with food. Indeed, to them people are overweight creatures in baseball caps who spread lots and lots of food out on picnic tables and then shriek a little and waddle off to get their video cameras when old Mr Bear comes along and climbs onto the table and starts devouring their potato salad and chocolate cake. Since the bear doesn't mind being filmed and indeed seems indifferent to his audience, pretty generally some fool will come up to it and try to stroke it or feed it a cupcake or something. There is one recorded instance of a woman smearing honey on her toddler's fingers so that the bear would lick it off for the video camera. Failing to understand this, the bear ate the baby's hand.

When this sort of thing happens – and about a dozen people a year are injured, usually at picnic sites, usually by doing something dumb – or when a bear becomes persistent or aggressive, park rangers shoot it with a tranquillizer dart, truss it up and take it into the depths of the backcountry, far from roads and picnic sites, and let it loose. Of course by now the bear has become thoroughly habituated both to human beings and to human beings' food. And whom will they find to take food from out in the backcountry? Why, me and Katz, of course, and others like us. The annals of Appalachian Trail hikes are full of tales of hikers being mugged by bears in the backcountry of the Smokies. And so as we plunged into the steep, dense, covering woods of Shuckstack Mountain, I stayed closer than usual to Katz and carried my walking stick like a cosh. He thought I was a fool, of course.

The true creature of the Smokies, however, is the reclusive

and little-appreciated salamander. There are twenty-five varieties of salamander in the Smokies, more than anywhere else on earth. Salamanders are interesting, and don't let anyone tell you otherwise. To begin with, they are the oldest of all land vertebrates. When creatures first crawled from the seas, this is what came up, and they haven't changed a great deal since. Some varieties of Smokies salamander haven't even evolved lungs. (They breathe through their skin.) Most salamanders are tiny, only an inch or two long, but the rare and startlingly ugly hellbender salamander can attain lengths of over two feet. I ached to see a hellbender.

Even more varied and under-appreciated than the salamander is the freshwater mussel. Three hundred types of mussel, a third of the world's total, live in the Smokies. Smokies mussels have terrific names, like purple wartyback, shiny pigtoe and monkey-face pearlymussel. Unfortunately, that is where all interest in them ends. Because they are so little regarded, even by naturalists, mussels have vanished at an exceptional rate. Nearly half of all Smokies mussel species are endangered; twelve are thought to be extinct.

This ought to be a little surprising in a national park. I mean it's not as if mussels are flinging themselves under the wheels of passing cars. Still, the Smokies seem to be in the process of losing most of their mussels. The National Park Service actually has something of a tradition of making things extinct. Bryce Canyon National Park is perhaps the most interesting – certainly the most enthusiastic – example. It was founded in 1923, and in less than half a century under the Park Service's careful stewardship had lost seven species of mammal – the white-tailed jackrabbit, prairie dog, pronghorn antelope, flying squirrel, beaver, red fox and spotted skunk – quite an achievement. Altogether, forty-two species of mammal have disappeared from America's national parks this century.

Here in the Smokies, not far from where Katz and I now trod, the Park Service in 1957 decided to 'reclaim' Abrams Creek, a tributary of the Little Tennessee River, for rainbow trout. To that end, biologists dumped extravagant quantities of a poison called rotenone into 15 miles of creek. Within hours, tens of thousands of dead fish were floating on the surface like autumn leaves – what a proud moment that must be for a trained naturalist. Among the thirty-one species of Abrams Creek fish that were wiped out was one called the smoky madtom, which scientists had never seen before. Thus the Park Service biologists managed the wonderfully unusual accomplishment of discovering and eradicating a new species of fish in the same instant. (In 1980, another colony of smoky madtoms was found in a nearby stream.)

Of course, that was forty years ago and such foolishness would be unthinkable in these more enlightened times. Today the National Park Service employs a much more subtle approach to endangering wildlife: neglect. It spends almost nothing – less than 3 per cent of its budget – on research of any type, which is why no-one knows how many mussels are extinct or even why they are going extinct. Everywhere you look in the eastern forests, trees are dying in colossal numbers. In the Smokies, over 90 per cent of Fraser firs – a noble tree, unique to the southern Appalachian highlands – are sick or dying, from a combination of acid rain and the depredations of an insect called the balsam woolly adelgid. Ask a park official what they are doing about it and he will say, 'We are monitoring the situation closely.' For this read: 'We are watching them die.'

Or consider the grassy balds – treeless, meadowy expanses of mountaintop, up to 250 acres in extent, which are quite unique to the southern Appalachians. No-one knows why the balds are there, or how long they have existed, or why they appear on some mountains but not others. Some believe they are natural features, perhaps relics of lightning fires, and some that they are man-made, burned or cleared to provide land for summer grazing. What is certain is that they are central to the character of the Smokies. To climb for hours through cool, dark forest and emerge at last onto the liberating open space of a sunny bald, under a dome of blue sky, with views to every horizon, is an experience not to be forgotten. But they are far more than just grassy curiosities. According to the writer Hiram Rogers, grassy balds cover just 0.015 per cent of the Smokies landscape, but hold 29 per cent of its flora. For unknown numbers of years they were used first by Indians and then by European settlers for grazing summer livestock, but now, with graziers banished and the Park Service doing nothing, woody species like hawthorn and blackberry are steadily reclaiming the mountain-tops. Within twenty years, there may be no balds left in the Smokies. Ninety plant species have disappeared from the balds since the park was opened in the 1930s. At least twenty-five more are expected to go in the next few years. There is no plan to save them.

Now you might conclude from this that I don't much admire the Park Service and its people, and that's not exactly true. I never met a ranger who wasn't helpful and dedicated and generally well informed. Mind you, I hardly ever met a ranger because most of them have been let go, but the ones I en-countered were entirely all right. No, my problem is not with the people on the ground, it is with the Park Service itself. A lot of people point out in defence of the national parks that they have been starved of funds, and this is indubitably so. Adjusted for inflation, the Park Service budget today is $200 million a year less than it was a decade ago. In consequence, even as visitor numbers have soared – from 207 million in 1983 to nearly 300 million today – campsites and interpretation centres have been shut, warden numbers slashed, and essential main-tenance deferred to a positively ludicrous degree. By 1997, the repair backlog for the national parks had reached $6 billion. All quite scandalous.

But consider this. In 1991, as its trees were dying, its buildings crumbling, its visitors being turned away from campgrounds it could not afford to keep open, and its employees being laid off in record numbers, the National Park Service threw a seventy-fifth anniversary party for itself in Vail, Colorado. It spent $500,000 on the event. That may not be quite as moronically negligent as tipping hundreds of gallons of poison into a wilderness stream, but it is certainly in the right spirit.

But, hey, let's not lose our perspective here. The Smokies achieved their natural splendour without the guidance of a national park service and don't actually need it now. Indeed, given the Park Service's bizarre and erratic behaviour throughout its history (here's another one for you: in the 1960s it invited the Walt Disney Corporation to build an amusement complex in Sequoia National Park in California) it is perhaps not an altogether bad idea to starve it of funds. I am almost certain that if that $200 million a year were restored to the budget, nearly all of it would go into building more car parks and RV facilities, not into saving trees, and certainly not into restoring the precious, lovely grassy balds. It is actually Park Service policy to let the balds vanish. Having got everyone agitated by interfering with nature for years, it has decided now not to interfere with nature at all, even when that interference would be demonstrably beneficial. I tell you, these people are a wonder.

Dusk was settling in when we reached Birch Spring Gap Shelter, standing on a slope beside a muddy stream a couple of hundred feet downhill from the trail. In the silvery half-light it looked wonderful. In contrast to the utilitarian plywood structures found elsewhere on the trail, the shelters of the Smokies were solidly built of stone in an intentionally quaint, rustic style, so from a distance Birch Spring Gap Shelter had the snug, homey, inviting look of a cabin. Up close, however, it was somewhat less enthralling. The interior was dark and leaky, with a mud floor like chocolate pudding, a cramped and filthy sleeping platform, and scraps of wet litter everywhere. Water ran down the inside of the walls and trickled into pools on the sleeping ledge. Outside there was no picnic table, as at most other shelters, and no privy. Even by the austere standards of the Appalachian Trail, this was grim. But at least we had it to ourselves.

Like other AT shelters, it had an open front – I never really understood the thinking behind this – but this one was covered with a modern chain link fence. A sign on the fence said: BEARS ARE ACTIVE IN THIS AREA. DO NOT LEAVE DOOR OPEN. Interested to see just how active, I had a look at the shelter register while Katz boiled water for noodles. Every shelter has a register in which visitors make diary-like entries on the weather or their state of mind, if any, and note any unusual occurrences. This one mentioned only a couple of odd bearlike noises outside in the night, but what really caught the attention of the shelter's chroniclers was the unusual liveliness of its resident mice and even rats, and this, I can now attest, was so.

From the moment – the moment – we put our heads down that night there were the scurryings and scutterings of rodents. They were absolutely fearless and scampered freely over our bags and even across our heads. Cursing furiously, Katz banged around at them with his water bottle and whatever else came to hand. Once I turned on my headlamp to find a packmouse on top of my sleeping bag, high up on my chest, not six inches from my chin, sitting up on its haunches, and regarding me with a gimlet eye. Reflexively, I hit the bag from inside, flipping him into a startled oblivion.

'Got one!' cried Katz.

'Me, too,' I said, rather proudly.

Katz was scrabbling around on his hands and knees, as if trying to pass for a mouse himself, enlivening the dark with a flying flashlight beam and pausing from time to time to hurl a boot or bang down his water bottle. Then he would crawl back in his bag, be still for a time, curse abruptly, fling off encumbrances and repeat the process. I buried myself in my bag and pulled the drawstring tight over my head. And thus passed the

night, with repeated sequences of Katz being violent, followed
by silence, followed by scamperings, followed by Katz being
violent. I slept surprisingly well, all things considered.

I expected Katz to wake in a foul temper, but in fact he was
chipper.

'There's nothing like a good night's sleep and that was nothing like a good night's sleep,' he announced when he stirred,
and gave an appreciative snort. His happiness, it turned out,
was because he had killed seven mice, and was feeling very
proud – not to say pumped up and gladiatorial. Some fur and
a nubbin of something pink and pulpy still adhered to the
bottom of his water bottle, I noticed when he raised it to his
lips. Occasionally it troubled me – I presume it must trouble all
hikers from time to time – just how far one strays from the normal measures of civility on the trail. This was such a moment.

Outside, fog was stealing in, filling the spaces between the
trees. It was not an encouraging morning. A drizzle hung in
the air when we set off and before long it had turned into a
steady, merciless, deadfall rain.

Rain spoils everything. There is no pleasure in walking in
waterproofs. There is something deeply dispiriting about the
stiff rustle of nylon and the endless, curiously amplified patter
of rain on fabric. Worst of all you don't even stay dry; the waterproofs keep out the rain, but make you sweat so much that
soon you are clammily sodden. By afternoon, the trail was a
running stream. My boots gave up the will to stay dry. I was
soaked through and squelching with every step. It rains up to
120 inches a year in some parts of the Smokies. That's ten feet.
That's a lot of rain. We had a lot of it now.

We walked 9.7 miles to Spence Field Shelter, a modest distance even for us, but we were wet through and chilled, and
anyway it was too far to hike to the next one. The Park Service
– why does this seem so inevitable? – imposes a host of petty,
inflexible, exasperating rules on AT hikers, among them that
you must move smartly forward at all times, never stray from

the trail, and camp each night at a shelter. It means effectively not only that you must walk a prescribed distance each day, but then spend the night penned up with strangers. We peeled off the worst of our wet clothes and rooted for dry ones in our packs, but even stuff from deep in the middle felt damp. There was a stone fireplace built into the shelter wall, and some kindly soul had left a pile of twigs and small logs by the side. Katz tried to light a fire, but everything was so wet that it wouldn't burn. Even his matches wouldn't strike. Katz exhaled in disgust and gave up. I decided to make some coffee, to warm us up, and the stove proved equally temperamental.

As I fiddled with it, there was the singing rustle of nylon from without and two young women entered, blinking and bedraggled. They were from Boston and had hiked in on a side trail from Cades Cove. A minute or two later four guys on spring break from Wake Forest University came in, then a lone young hiker who proved to be our acquaintance Jonathan, and finally a couple of bearded middle-aged guys. After four or five days in which we had seen scarcely a soul, suddenly we were inundated with company.

Everyone was considerate and friendly, but there was no escaping the conclusion that we were hopelessly overcrowded. It occurred to me, not for the first time, how delightful, how truly delightful, it would be if MacKaye's original vision had been realized – if the shelters along the trail were proper hostels, with hot showers, individual bunks (with curtains for privacy and reading lights, please), and a resident caretaker/cook who would keep a cheery fire dancing in the grate and invite us, any minute now, to take our places at a long table for a dinner of stew and dumplings, cornbread and, oh, let us say, peach cobbler. Outside there would be a porch with rocking chairs, where you could sit and smoke your pipe and watch the sun sink into the lovely distant hills. What bliss it would be. I was perched on the edge of the sleeping platform lost in a little reverie along these lines and absorbed with trying to get a small volume of water to boil – quite happy really – when one of the middle-aged guys drifted over and introduced himself as Bob. I knew with a sinking heart that we were going to talk equipment. I could just see it coming. I hate talking equipment.

'So what made you buy a Gregory pack?' he said.

'Well, I thought it would be easier than carrying everything in my arms.'

He nodded thoughtfully, as if this were an answer worth considering, then said: 'I've got a Kelty.'

I wanted to say – ached to say – 'Well, here's an idea to try to get hold of, Bob. I don't remotely give a shit.' But talking equipment is one of those things you just have to do, like chatting to your mother's friends in the supermarket, so I said: 'Oh, yeah? You happy with it?'

'Oh, *yeah*,' was the deeply sincere reply. 'Tell you why.' He brought it over to show me its features – its snap pockets, its map pouch, its general miraculous ability to hold contents. He was particularly proud of a dropdown inner stowage pouch, bulging with little plastic bottles of vitamins and medicines, with a transparent window built into it. 'It lets you see what you've got in there, without having to undo the zipper,' he explained and looked at me with an expression that invited staggered admiration.

Just at that moment Katz stepped up. He was eating a carrot – nobody could cadge food like Katz – and was about to ask me something, but when his eye lit on Bob's transparent pouch, he said: 'Hey, look – a pouch with a window. Is that for people who are so stupid they can't figure out how to get it open?'

'Actually, it's a very useful feature,' said Bob in a carefully measured tone. 'It lets you check the contents without having to undo the zipper.'

Katz gave him a genuinely incredulous look. 'What – like you're so busy on the trail you can't spare the three seconds it takes to open a zipper and look inside?' He turned to me.

'These college kids are willing to trade Pop Tarts for Snickers. What do you think?'

'Well, I actually find it quite useful,' Bob said quietly, to himself, but he took his pack away and bothered us no more. I'm afraid my equipment conversations nearly always ended up like that somehow, with the talker retiring with hurt feelings and a piece of formerly prized equipment cradled to his chest. It was never my wish, believe me.

The Smokies went downhill from there. We walked for four days and the rain fell tirelessly, with an endless, typewriter patter. The trail everywhere became boggy and slick. Puddles filled every dip and trough. Mud became a feature of our lives. We trudged through it, stumbled and fell in it, knelt in it, set our packs down in it, left a streak of it on everything we touched. And always when you moved there was the maddening, monotonous sound of your nylon going *wiss, wiss, wiss* until you wanted to take a gun and shoot it. I didn't see a bear, didn't see a salamander, didn't see foxfire, didn't see anything actually – just perpetual dribbles and droplets of rain adhering to my glasses.

Each night we stopped in leaky byres, and cooked and lived with strangers – crowds of them, all cold and damp and shuffling, and gaunt and half mad from the ceaseless rain and the cheerlessness of wet hiking. It was awful. And the worse the weather got the more crowded the shelters grew. It was spring break – half term – at colleges all over the east, and scores and scores of young people had had the idea to come hiking in the Smokies. The Smokies shelters are supposed to be for thru-hikers, not casual drop-ins, and words were sometimes exchanged. It was not like the AT at all. It was worse than awful.

By the third day, Katz and I both had nothing dry and were shivering constantly. We slopped up to the summit of Clingmans Dome – a high point of the trip, by all accounts, with views in clear weather to make the heart take wing – and saw nothing, nothing whatever, but the dim shapes of dying trees in a sea of swirling fog.

We were soaked and filthy, desperately needed a launderette, clean, dry clothes, a square meal, and a Ripley's Believe It or Not Museum. It was time to go to Gatlinburg.

Chapter 8

But first we had to get there.

It was eight miles from Clingmans Dome to US 441, the first paved road since Fontana Dam four days before. Gatlinburg lay fifteen long, twisting, downhill miles to the north. It was too far to walk and it didn't seem likely that we would get a lift hitching in a national park, but in a parking area nearby I noticed three homeward bound youths loading packs into a large, fancy car with New Hampshire number plates, and impulsively I went and introduced myself to them as a fellow citizen of the Granite State and asked them if they could find it in their hearts to take two weary old guys into Gatlinburg. Before they could demur, which was clearly their instinct, we thanked them profusely and climbed into the back seat. And thus we secured a stylish but rather sullen passage to Gatlinburg.

Gatlinburg is a shock to the system from whichever angle you survey it, but never more so than when you descend upon it from a spell of moist, grubby isolation in the woods. It sits just outside the main entrance to Great Smoky Mountains National Park and specializes in providing all those things that the park does not, principally slurpy food, motels, gift shops and side-walks on which to waddle and dawdle, nearly all of it strewn along a single astoundingly ugly main street. For years it has prospered on the confident understanding that when Americans load up their cars and drive enormous distances to a setting of rare natural splendour what most of them want when they get there is to play a little crazy golf and eat dribbly food. Great Smoky Mountains National Park is the most popular national park in America, but Gatlinburg – this is so unbelievable – is more popular than the park.

So Gatlinburg is appalling. But that's OK. After eight days on the trail we were ready to be appalled, eager to be appalled. We checked into a motel, where we were received with a palpable lack of warmth, got honked at twice as we crossed the main street (one rather loses the knack of crossing roads on the trail) and finally presented ourselves at an establishment called Jersey Joe's Restaurant, where we ordered cheeseburgers and Cokes from a charmless, gum-popping waitress who declined to be heartened by our wholesome smiles. We were halfway through this simple, disappointing repast when the waitress dropped the bill on the table as she passed. It came to $20.74.

'You're joking,' I spluttered.

The waitress – let's call her Betty Slutz – stopped and looked at me, then slowly swaggered back to the table, staring at me with majestic disdain the while.

'You got a problem here?'

'Twenty dollars is a bit much for a couple of burgers, don't you think?' I squeaked in a strange, never-before-heard Bertie Wooster voice. She held her stare for another moment, then picked up the bill and read it through aloud for our benefit, smacking each item as she read.

'Two burgers. Two sodas. State sales tax. City sales tax. Beverage tax. Inclusive gratuity. Grand total: twenty dollars and seventy-four cents.' She let it fall back onto the table and graced us with a sneer. 'Welcome to Gatlinburg, gentlemen.'

Welcome, indeed.

And then we went out to see the town. I was particularly eager to have a look at Gatlinburg because I had read about it in a wonderful book called *The Lost Continent*. In it the author describes the scene on the main street thus: 'Walking in an un-hurried fashion up and down the street were more crowds of overweight tourists in boisterous clothes, with cameras boun-cing on their bellies, consuming ice-creams, cotton candy and corn dogs, sometimes simultaneously,' and so it was today. The same throngs of pear-shaped people in Reeboks wandered between food smells, clutching grotesque comestibles and bucket-sized soft drinks. It was still the same tacky, horrible place. Yet I would hardly have recognized it from just nine years before. Nearly every building I remembered had been torn down and replaced with something new, principally mini-malls and shopping courts, which stretched back from the main street and offered a whole new galaxy of shopping and eating opportunities.

In *The Lost Continent* I gave a specimen list of Gatlinburg's attractions as they were in 1987 – the Elvis Presley Hall of Fame, National Bible Museum, Stars Over Gatlinburg Wax Museum, Ripley's Believe It or Not Museum, American Historical Wax Museum, Gatlinburg Space Needle, Bonnie Lou and Buster Country Music Show, Carbo's Police Museum, Guinness Book of Records Exhibition Center, Irlene Mandrell Hall of Stars Museum and Shopping Mall, a pair of haunted houses, and three miscellaneous attractions, Hillbilly Village, Paradise Island, and World of Illusions. Of these fifteen diversions, just three appeared to be still in existence nine years later. They had of course been replaced by other things – a Mysterious Mansion, Hillbilly Golf, a Motion Master ride – and these in turn will no doubt be gone in another nine years, for that is the way of America.

I know the world is ever in motion, but the speed of change in the United States is simply dazzling. In 1951, the year I was born, Gatlinburg had just one retail business – a general store called Ogle's. Then, as the postwar boom years quickened, people began coming to the Smokies by car, and motels, restaurants, gas stations and gift shops popped up to serve them. By 1987, Gatlinburg had 60 motels and 200 gift shops. Today it has 100 motels and 400 gift shops. And the remarkable thing is that there is nothing remotely remarkable about that.

Consider this: half of all the offices and malls standing in America today have been built since 1980. Half of them. Eighty per cent of all the housing stock in the country dates from 1945. Of all the motel rooms in America, 230,000 have been built in the last fifteen years. Just up the road from Gatlinburg is the town of Pigeon Forge, which twenty years ago was a sleepy hamlet – nay, which *aspired* to be a sleepy hamlet – famous only as the hometown of Dolly Parton. Then the estimable Ms Parton built an amusement park called Dollywood. Now Pigeon Forge has 200 outlet shops stretched along three miles of highway. It is bigger and uglier than Gatlinburg, and has better parking, and so of course it gets more visitors.

Now compare all this with the Appalachian Trail. At the time of our hike, the Appalachian Trail was fifty-nine years old. That is, by American standards, incredibly venerable. The Oregon and Santa Fe trails didn't last as long. Route 66 didn't last as long. The old coast-to-coast Lincoln Highway, a road that brought transforming wealth and life to hundreds of little towns, so important and familiar that it became known as 'America's Main Street', didn't last as long. Nothing in America does. If a product or enterprise doesn't constantly reinvent itself it is superseded, cast aside, abandoned without sentiment in favour of something bigger, newer and, alas, always, always uglier. And then there is the good old AT, still quietly ticking along after six decades, unassuming, splendid, faithful to its founding principles, sweetly unaware that the world has quite moved on. It's a miracle really.

Katz needed bootlaces, so we went to an outfitter's and while he was off in the footwear section, I had an idle shuffle around. Pinned to a wall was a map showing the whole of the Appalachian Trail on its long march through fourteen states, but with the eastern seaboard rotated to give the AT the appearance of having a due north–south orientation, allowing the map-maker to fit the trail into an orderly rectangle, about six inches wide and four feet high. I looked at it with a polite, almost pro-prietorial interest – it was the first time since leaving New Hampshire that I had considered the trail in its entirety – and then inclined closer, with bigger eyes and slightly parted lips. Of the four feet of trail map before me, reaching approximately from my knees to the top of my head, we had done the bottom two inches.

I went and got Katz and brought him back with me, pulling on a pinch of shirtsleeve. 'What?' he said. 'What?'

I showed him the map. 'Yeah, what?' Katz didn't like mysteries.

'Look at the map, and then look at the part we've walked.'

He looked, then looked again. I watched closely as the ex-pression drained from his face. 'Jesus,' he breathed at last. He turned to me, full of astonishment. 'We've done *nothing*.'

We went and got a cup of coffee, and sat for some time in a kind of dumbfounded silence. All that we had experienced and done – all the effort and toil, the aches, the damp, the moun-tains, the horrible stodgy noodles, the blizzards, the dreary evenings with Mary Ellen, the endless, wearying, doggedly accumulated miles – all that came to two inches. My hair had grown more than that.

One thing was obvious. We were never going to walk to Maine.

In a way it was a liberation. If we couldn't walk the whole trail, we also didn't have to, which was a novel thought that grew more attractive the more we considered it. We had been released from our obligations. A whole dimension of drudgery – the tedious, mad, really quite pointless business of stepping over every inch of rocky ground between Georgia and Maine – had been removed. We could enjoy ourselves.

So the next morning, after breakfast, we spread maps out across my motel room bed and studied the possibilities. In the end we decided to return to the trail not at Newfound Gap, where we had left it, but a little further on at a place called Spivey Gap, near Ernestville. This would take us beyond the Smokies, with its crowded shelters and stifling regulations, and put us back in a world where we could please ourselves. I got out the Yellow Pages and looked up cab companies. There were three in Gatlinburg. I called the first one.

'How much would it be to take two of us to Ernestville?' I enquired.

'Dunno,' came the reply.

This threw me slightly. 'Well, how much do you think it would be?'

'Dunno.'

'But it's just down the road.'

There was a considerable silence and then the voice said: 'Yup.'

'Haven't you ever taken anybody there before?'

'Nope.'

'Well, it looks to me on my map like it's about twenty miles. Would you say that's about right?'

Another pause. 'Might be.'

'And how much would it be to take us twenty miles?'

'Dunno.'

I looked at the receiver. 'Excuse me, but I just have to say this. You are more stupid than a paramecium.'

Then I hung up.

'Maybe not my place to say,' Katz offered thoughtfully, 'but I'm not sure that's the best way to ensure prompt and cheerful service.'

I called up another cab company and asked how much it would be to Ernestville.

'Dunno,' said the voice.

Oh, for Christ's sake, I thought.

'What do you wanna go there for?' demanded the voice.

'Pardon?'

'What do you wanna go to Ernestville for? 'Tain't nothin there.'

'Well, actually we want to go to Spivey Gap. We're hiking the Appalachian Trail, you see.'

'Spivey Gap's another five miles.'

'Yeah, I was just trying to get an idea . . .'

'You shoulda said so 'cause Spivey Gap's another five miles.'

'Well, how much would it be to Spivey Gap then?'

'Dunno.'

'Excuse me, but is there some kind of gross stupidity require-ment to be a cab driver in Gatlinburg?'

'What?'

I hung up again and looked at Katz. 'What *is* it with this town? I've blown more intelligent life into a handker-chief.'

I called up the third and final company and asked how much it would be to Ernestville.

'How much you got?' barked a feisty voice.

Now here was a guy I could do business with. I grinned and said, 'I don't know. A dollar fifty?'

There was a snort. 'Well, it's gonna cost you more than that.' A pause and the creak of a chair going back. 'It's gonna go on what's on the meter, you understand, but I expect it'll be about twenty bucks, something like that. What do you wanna go to Ernestville for anyway?'

I explained about Spivey Gap and the AT.

'Appalachian Trail? You must be a danged fool. What time you wanna go?'

'I don't know. How about now?'

'Where y'at?'

I told him the name of the motel.

'I'll be there in ten minutes. Fifteen minutes at the outside. If I'm not there in twenty minutes, then go on ahead without me and I'll meet you at Ernestville.' He hung up. We had not only found a driver; we'd found a comedian.

While we waited on a bench outside the motel office, I bought a copy of the *Nashville Tennessean* newspaper out of a metal box, just to see what was happening in the world. The principal story indicated that the state legislature, in one of those moments of enlightenment with which the Southern states often distinguish themselves, was in the process of passing a law banning schools from teaching evolution. Instead they were to be required to instruct that the Earth was created by God, in seven days, sometime before the turn of the century. The article reminded us that this was not a new issue in Tennessee. The little town of Dayton – not far from where Katz and I now sat, as it happened – was the scene of the famous Scopes trial in 1925, when the state prosecuted a schoolteacher named John Thomas Scopes for rashly promulgating Darwinian hogwash. As nearly everyone knows, Clarence Darrow, for the defence, roundly humiliated William Jennings Bryan, for the prosecution, but what most people don't realize is that Darrow lost the case. Scopes was convicted and the law wasn't overturned in Tennessee until 1967. And now the state was about to bring the law back, proving conclusively that the danger for Tennesseans isn't so much that they may be descended from apes as that they may be overtaken by them.

Suddenly – I can't altogether explain it, but suddenly – I had a powerful urge not to be this far south any longer. I turned to Katz.

'Why don't we go to Virginia?'

'What?'

Somebody in a shelter a couple of days before had told us how delightful – how gorgeously amenable to hiking – the mountains of the Virginia Blue Ridge were. Once you got up into them, he had assured us, it was nearly all level walking with sumptuous views over the broad valley of the Shenandoah River. People routinely knocked off 25 miles a day up there. From the vantage of a dank, dripping Smokies shelter, this had sounded like Xanadu, and the idea had stuck. I explained my thinking to Katz.

He sat forward intently. 'Are you saying we leave out all the trail between here and Virginia? Not walk it? Skip it?' He seemed to want to make sure he understood this exactly.

I nodded.

'Well, shit yes.'

So when the cab driver pulled up a minute later and got out to look us over, I explained to him, hesitantly and a bit haplessly – for I had really not thought this through – that we didn't want to go to Ernestville at all now, but to Virginia.

'*Virginia?*' he said, as if I had asked him if there was anywhere local we could get a dose of syphilis. He was a little guy, short but built like iron, and at least seventy years old, but real bright, smarter than me and Katz put together, and he grasped the notion of the enterprise before I had halfway explained it.

'Well, then you want to go to Knoxville and rent a car and drive up to Roanoke. That's what you want to do.'

I nodded. 'How do we get to Knoxville?'

'How's a *cab* sound to you?' he barked at me as if I were three-quarters stupid. I think he might have been a bit hard of hearing, or else he just liked shouting at people. 'Probably cost you about fifty bucks,' he said speculatively.

Katz and I looked at each other. 'Yeah, OK,' I said and we got in.

And so, just like that, we found ourselves heading for Roanoke and the sweet green hills of old Virginny.

Chapter 9

In the summer of 1948, Earl V. Shaffer, a young man just out of the army, became the first person to hike the Appalachian Trail from end to end in a single summer. With no tent, and often navigating with nothing better than roadmaps, he walked for 123 days, from April to August, averaging 17 miles a day. Coincidentally, while he was hiking, the *Appalachian Trailway News*, the journal of the Appalachian Trail Conference, ran a long article by Myron Avery and the magazine's editor, Jean Stephenson, explaining why an end-to-end hike was probably not possible.

The trail Shaffer found was nothing like the groomed and orderly corridor that exists today. Though it was only eleven years since the trail's completion, by 1948 it was already subsiding into oblivion. Shaffer found that large parts of it were overgrown or erased by wholesale logging. Shelters were few, blazes often non-existent. He spent long periods bushwhacking over tangled mountains or following the wrong path when the trail forked. Occasionally he stepped onto a highway to find that he was miles from where he ought to be. Often he discovered that local people were not aware of the trail's existence or, if they knew of it, were amazed to be told that it ran all the way from Georgia to Maine. Frequently he was greeted with suspicion.

On the other hand, even the dustiest little hamlets nearly always had a store or café, unlike now, and generally when he left the trail he could count on a country bus to flag down for a lift to the nearest town. Although he saw almost no other hikers in the four months, there was other, real life along the trail. He often passed small farms and cabins, or found graziers tending herds on sunny balds. All those are long gone now. Today the AT is a wilderness by design – actually, by fiat, since many of the properties Shaffer passed were later compulsorily purchased and quietly returned to woodland. There were twice as many songbirds in the eastern United States in 1948 as now. Except for the chestnuts, the forest trees were healthy. Dogwood, elms, hemlocks, balsam firs and red spruces still thrived. Above all, he had 2,000 miles of trail almost entirely to himself.

When Shaffer completed the walk in early August, four months to the day after setting off, and reported his achievement to Conference headquarters, no-one there actually believed him. He had to show officials his photographs and trail journal, and undergo a 'charming but thorough cross-examination', as he put it in his later account of the journey, *Walking with Spring*, before his story was finally accepted.

When news of Shaffer's hike leaked out, it attracted a good deal of attention – newspapers came to interview him, the *National Geographic* ran a long article – and the AT underwent a modest revival. But hiking has always been a marginal pursuit in America, and within a few years the AT was once more largely forgotten except among a few diehards and eccentrics. In the early 1960s a plan was put forward to extend the Blue

Ridge Parkway, a scenic highway, south from the Smokies by building over the southern portion of the AT. That plan failed (on grounds of cost, not because of any particular outcry), but elsewhere the trail was nibbled away or reduced to a rutted, muddy track through zones of commerce. In 1958, as we've seen, 20 miles were lopped off the southern end from Mount Oglethorpe to Springer Mountain. By the mid-1960s it looked to any prudent observer as if the AT would survive only as scattered fragments – in the Smokies and Shenandoah National Park, from Vermont across to Maine, as forlorn relic strands in the odd state park, but otherwise buried under shopping malls and housing developments. Much of the trail crossed private land and new owners often revoked informal rights-of-way agreements, forcing confused and hasty relocations onto busy highways or other public roads – hardly the tranquil wilderness experience envisioned by Benton MacKaye. Once again, the AT looked doomed.

Then, in a timely piece of fortuitousness, America got a Secretary of the Interior, Stewart Udall, who actually liked hiking. Under his direction a National Trails System Act was passed in 1968. The law was ambitious and far-reaching – and largely never realized. It envisioned 25,000 miles of new hiking trails across America, most of which were never built. However, it did produce the Pacific Crest Trail and secured the future of the AT by making it a de facto national park. It also provided funds – $170 million since 1978 – for the purchase of private land to provide a wilderness buffer alongside it. Now nearly all the trail passes through protected wilderness. Just 21 miles of it – less than 1 per cent of the total – is on public roads, mostly on bridges and where it passes through towns.

In the half-century since Shaffer's hike, about 4,000 others have repeated the feat. There are two kinds of end-to-end hikers – those who do it in a single season, known as 'thru-hikers', and those who do it in chunks, known as 'section hikers'. The record for the longest section hike is forty-six years.

The Appalachian Trail Conference doesn't recognize speed records, on the grounds that that isn't in the spirit of the enterprise, but that doesn't stop people from trying. In the 1980s a man named Ward Leonard, carrying a full pack and with no support crew, hiked the trail in 60 days 16 hours – an incredible feat when you consider that it would take you about five days to drive an equivalent distance. In May 1991, an 'ultra-runner' named David Horton and an endurance hiker named Scott Grierson set off within two days of each other. Horton had a network of support crews waiting at road crossings and other strategic points, and so needed to carry nothing but a bottle of water. Each evening he was taken by car to a motel or private home. He averaged 38.3 miles a day with ten or eleven hours of running. Grierson, meanwhile, merely walked, but he did so for as much as eighteen hours a day. Horton finally overtook Grierson in New Hampshire on the thirty-ninth day, and reached his goal in 52 days 9 hours. Grierson came in a couple of days later.

All kinds of people have completed thru-hikes. One man hiked it in his eighties. Another did it on crutches. A blind man named Bill Irwin hiked the trail with a seeing-eye dog, and fell down an estimated 5,000 times in the process. Probably the most famous, certainly the most written about, of all thru-hikers was Emma 'Grandma' Gatewood, who successfully hiked the trail twice in her late sixties despite being eccentric, poorly equipped, a tad stupid (actually very stupid, but I don't want to seem unkind), and a danger to herself. (She was forever getting lost.) My own favourite, however, is a guy named Woodrow Murphy from Pepperell, Massachusetts, who did a thru-hike in the summer of 1995. I would have liked him anyway, just for being called Woodrow, but I especially admired him when I read that he weighed 350 pounds and was doing the hike to lose weight. In his first week on the trail, he managed just five miles a day, but he persevered and by August, when he reached his home state, he was up to a dozen miles a day. He had lost

53 pounds – a trifle, all things considered – and at last report was considering doing it all over again the following year.

A significant fraction of thru-hikers reach Katahdin, then turn around and start back to Georgia. They just can't stop walking, which kind of makes you wonder. In fact, the more you read about thru-hikers the more you end up being filled with a kind of wonder. Take Bill Irwin, the blind man. After his hike he said: 'I never enjoyed the hiking part. It was something I felt compelled to do. It wasn't my choice.' Or David Horton, the ultra-runner who set the speed record in 1991. Horton by his own account became 'a mental and emotional wreck' and spent most of the period crossing Maine weeping copiously. Well, then why do it, you stupid tit? Even good old Earl Shaffer ended up as a recluse in the backwoods of Pennsylvania. I don't mean to suggest that hiking the AT drives you potty, just that it takes a certain kind of person to do it.

And how did I feel about giving up the quest when a granny in plimsolls, a human beachball named Woodrow and over 3,990 others had made it to Katahdin? Well, pretty good, as a matter of fact. I was still going to hike the Appalachian Trail; I just wasn't going to hike all of it. Katz and I had already walked half a million steps, if you can believe it. It didn't seem altogether essential to do the other 4.5 million to get the idea of the thing.

So we rode to Knoxville with our comical cab driver, acquired a hire car at the airport, and found ourselves, shortly after midday, heading north out of Knoxville through a half-remembered world of busy roads, dangling traffic signals, vast intersections, huge signs, and acre upon acre of shopping malls, gas stations, discount stores, exhaust centres, car lots and all the rest. Even after a day in Gatlinburg, the transition was dazzling. I remember reading once how some Stone Age Indians from the Brazilian rainforest with no knowledge or expectation of a world beyond the jungle were taken to São Paulo or Rio, and when they saw the buildings and cars and passing aeroplanes they wet themselves, lavishly and in unison. I had some idea how they felt.

It is such a strange contrast. When you are on the AT, the forest is your universe, infinite and entire. It is all you experience day after day. Eventually it is about all you can imagine. You are aware, of course, that somewhere over the horizon there are mighty cities, busy factories, crowded freeways, but here in this part of the country, where woods drape the landscape for as far as the eye can see, the forest rules. Even the little towns like Franklin and Hiawassee and even Gatlinburg are just way stations scattered helpfully through the great cosmos of woods.

But come off the trail, properly off, and drive somewhere, as we did now, and you realize how magnificently deluded you have been. Here, the mountains and woods were just backdrop – familiar, known, nearby, but no more consequential or noticed than the clouds that scudded across their ridgelines. Here the real business was up close and on top of you: gas stations, Wal-Marts, K-marts, Dunkin' Donuts, Blockbuster Videos, a ceaseless unfolding pageant of commercial hideousness.

Even Katz was unnerved by it. 'Jeez, it's ugly,' he breathed in wonder, as if he had never witnessed such a thing before. I looked past him, along the line of his shoulder, to a vast shopping mall with a prairie-sized car park, and agreed. It was horrible. And then, lavishly and in unison, we wet ourselves.

Chapter 10

There is a painting by Asher Brown Durand called *Kindred Spirits*, which is often reproduced in books when the subject turns to the American landscape in the nineteenth century. Painted in 1849, it shows two men standing on a rock ledge in the Catskills in one of those sublime lost world settings that look as if they would take an expedition to reach, though the two figures in the painting are dressed, incongruously, as if for the office, in long coats and plump cravats. Below them, in a shadowy chasm, a stream dashes through a jumble of boulders. Beyond, glimpsed through a canopy of leaves, is a long view of gorgeously forbidding blue mountains. To right and left, jostling into frame, are disorderly ranks of trees which immediately vanish into consuming darkness.

I can't tell you how much I would like to step into that view. The scene is so manifestly untamed, so full of an impenetrable beyond, as to present a clearly foolhardy temptation. You would die out there for sure – shredded by a cougar or thudded with a tomahawk or just lost and wandering to a stumbling, confounded death. You can see that at a glance. But never mind. Already you are studying the foreground for a way down to the stream over the steep rocks and wondering if that notch ahead will get you through to the neighbouring valley. Farewell, my friends. Destiny calls. Don't wait supper.

Nothing like that view exists now, of course. Perhaps it never did. Who knows how much licence these romantic johnnies took with their stabbing brushes? Who after all is going to struggle with an easel and campstool and box of paints to some difficult overlook, on a hot July afternoon, in a wilderness filled with danger, and not paint something exquisite and grand?

But even if the pre-industrialized Appalachians were only half as wild and dramatic as in the paintings of Durand and others like him, they must have been something to behold. It is hard to imagine now how little known, how full of possibility, the world beyond the eastern seaboard once was. When Thomas Jefferson sent Lewis and Clark into the wilderness he confidently expected them to find woolly mammoths and mastodons. Had dinosaurs been known, he would almost certainly have asked them to bring him home a triceratops.

The first people to venture deep into the woods from the east (the Indians, of course, had got there perhaps as much as 20,000 years before them) weren't looking for prehistoric creatures or passages to the west or new lands to settle. They were looking for plants. America's botanical possibilities excited Europeans inordinately, and there was both glory and money to be made out in the woods. The eastern woods teemed with flora unknown to the old world and there was a huge eagerness, from scientists and amateur enthusiasts alike, to get a piece of it. Imagine if tomorrow a spaceship found a jungle growing beneath the gassy clouds of Venus. Think what Bill Gates, say, would pay for some tendrilled, purply-lobed piece of Venusian exotica to put in a pot in his greenhouse. That was the rhododendron in the eighteenth century – and the camellia, the hydrangea, the wild cherry, the rudbeckia, the azalea, the aster, the ostrich fern, the catalpa, the spice bush, the Venus fly-trap, the Virginia creeper, the euphorbia. These and hundreds more were collected in the American woods, shipped across the ocean to England and France and Russia, and received with greedy keenness and trembling fingers.

It started with John Bartram – actually, it started with tobacco, but in a scientific sense it started with John Bartram – a Pennsylvania Quaker, born in 1699, who grew interested in botany after reading a book on the subject, and began sending seeds and cuttings to a fellow Quaker in London. Encouraged to seek out more, he embarked on increasingly ambitious journeys into the wilderness, sometimes travelling over a thousand miles through the rugged mountains. Though he was entirely self-taught, never learned Latin, and had scant under-standing of Linnaean classifications, he was a prize plant collector, with an uncanny knack for finding and recognizing unknown species. Of the 800 plants discovered in America in the colonial period, Bartram was responsible for about a quarter. His son William found many more.

Before the century was out, the eastern woods were fairly crawling with botanists – Peter Kalm, Lars Yungstroem, Constantine Samuel Rafinesque-Schmaltz, John Fraser, André Michaux, Thomas Nuttall, John Lyon, and others pretty much beyond counting. There were so many people out there, hunt-ing so competitively, that it is often not possible to say with any precision who discovered what. Depending on which source you consult, Fraser found either forty-four new plants or 215, or something in between. One of his uncontested discoveries was the fragrant southern balsam, the Fraser fir, so characteristic of the high ranges of North Carolina and Tennessee, but it bears his name only because he scrambled to the top of Clingmans Dome just ahead of his keen rival Michaux.

These people covered astonishing sweeps, for considerable periods. One of the younger Bartram's expeditions lasted over five years and plunged him so deeply into the woods that he was long given up for lost; when he emerged he discovered that America had been at war with Britain for a year, and he had lost his patrons. Michaux's voyages took him from Florida to Hudson's Bay; the heroic Nuttall ventured as far as the shores of Lake Superior, going much of the way on foot for want of funds.

They often collected in prodigious, not to say rapacious, quantities. Lyon pulled 3,600 *Magnolia macrophylla* saplings from a single hillside, and thousands of plants more, including a pretty red thing which left him in a fevered delirium and covered 'almost in one continued blister all over my body'; he had found, it turned out, poison sumac. In 1765, John Bartram discovered a particularly lovely camellia, *Franklinia altamaha*; already rare, it was hunted to extinction in just twenty-five years. Today it survives only in cultivation – thanks entirely to Bartram. Rafinesque-Schmaltz, meanwhile, spent seven years wandering through the Appalachians, didn't discover much, but brought in 50,000 seeds and cuttings.

How they managed it is a wonder. Every plant had to be recorded and identified, its seeds collected or a cutting taken; if the latter, it had to be potted up in stiff paper or sailcloth, kept watered and tended, and somehow transported through a trackless wilderness to civilization. The privations and perils were constant and exhausting. Bears, snakes and panthers abounded. Michaux's son was severely mauled on one expedition when a bear charged him from the trees. (Black bears seem to have been notably more ferocious in former times; nearly every journal has accounts of sudden, unprovoked attacks. It seems altogether likely that eastern bears have become more retiring because they have learned to associate humans with guns.) Indians, too, were commonly hostile – though just as often bemused at finding European gentlemen carefully collecting and taking away plants that grew in natural abundance – and then there were all the diseases of the woods, like malaria and yellow fever. 'I can't find one [friend] that will bear the fatigue to accompany me in my peregrinations,' John Bartram complained wearily in a letter to his English patron. Hardly surprising.

But evidently it was worth it. A single, particularly valued seed could fetch up to five guineas. On one trip, John Lyon cleared £900 after expenses, a considerable fortune, then returned the next year and made nearly as much. Fraser made one long trip under the sponsorship of Catherine the Great of Russia and emerged from the wilderness only to find that there was a new czar who had no interest in plants, thought he was mad, and refused to honour his contract. So Fraser took everything to Chelsea, where he had a little nursery, and made a good living selling azaleas, rhododendrons and magnolias to the English gentry.

Others did it for the simple joy of finding something new – none more admirably than Thomas Nuttall, a bright but unschooled journeyman printer from Liverpool who came to America in 1808 and discovered an unexpected passion for plants. He undertook two long expeditions, which he paid for out of his own pocket, made many important discoveries, and generously gave to the Liverpool Botanic Gardens plants that might have made him rich. In just nine years, from a base of zero, he became the leading authority on American plants. In 1817, he produced (literally, for he not only wrote the text but set most of the type himself) the seminal *Genera of North American Plants*, which stood for the better part of a century as the principal encyclopedia of American botany. Four years later he was named curator of the Botanic Garden at Harvard University, a position he held with distinction for a dozen years, and somehow also found time to become a leading authority on birds, producing a celebrated text on American ornithology in 1832. He was, by all accounts, a kindly man who gained the esteem of everyone who met him. Stories don't get a great deal better than that.

Already in Nuttall's day the woods were being transformed. The panthers, elk and timberwolves were being driven to extinction, the beaver and bear nearly so. The great first-growth white pines of the north woods, some of them 220 feet high – that's the height of a twenty-storey building – had mostly been felled to make ship's masts or simply cleared away for farmland, and nearly all the rest would go before the century was out. Everywhere there was a kind of recklessness born of a sense that the American woods were effectively inexhaustible. Two-hundred-year-old pecan trees were commonly chopped down just to make it easier to harvest the nuts on their topmost branches. With each passing year the character of the woods changed perceptibly. But until quite recent times – painfully recent times – one thing remained in abundance that preserved the primeval super-Eden feel of the original forest: the massively graceful American chestnut.

There has never been a tree like it. Rising a hundred feet from the forest floor, its soaring boughs spread out in a canopy of incomparable lushness, an acre of leaves per tree, a million or so in all. Though only half the height of the tallest eastern pines, the chestnut had a weight and mass and symmetry that put it in another league. At ground level, a full-sized tree would be 10 feet through its bole, more than 20 feet around. I have seen a photograph, taken at the start of this century, of people picnicking in a grove of chestnuts not far from where Katz and I now hiked, in an area known as the Jefferson National Forest. It is a happy Sunday party, in heavy clothes, the ladies with clasped parasols, the men with bowler hats and walrus mous-taches, all handsomely arrayed on a blanket in a clearing, against a backdrop of steeply slanting shafts of light and trees of unbelievable grandeur. The people are so tiny, so preposter-ously out of scale to the trees around them, as to make you wonder for a moment if the picture has been manipulated as a kind of joke, like those old postcards that show watermelons as big as barns or an ear of corn that entirely fills a wagon under the droll legend A TYPICAL IOWA FARM SCENE. But this is simply the way it was – the way it was over tens of thousands of square miles of hill and cove, from the Carolinas to New England. And it is all gone now.

In 1904, a keeper at the Bronx Zoo in New York noticed that the zoo's handsome chestnuts had became covered in small orange cankers of an unfamiliar type. Within days they began to sicken and die. By the time scientists identified the source as an Asian fungus called *Endothia parasitica*, probably introduced with a shipment of trees or infected lumber from the Orient, the chestnuts were dead and the fungus had escaped into the great sprawl of the Appalachians, where one tree in every four was a chestnut.

For all its mass, a tree is a remarkably delicate thing. All of its internal life exists within three paper-thin layers of tissue, the phloem, xylem and cambium, just beneath the bark, which together form a moist sleeve around the dead heartwood. However tall it grows, a tree is just a few pounds of living cells thinly spread between roots and leaves. These three diligent layers of cells perform all the intricate science and engineering needed to keep a tree alive, and the efficiency with which they do it is one of the wonders of life. Without noise or fuss, every tree in a forest lifts massive volumes of water – several hundred gallons in the case of a large tree on a hot day – from its roots to its leaves, where it is returned to the atmosphere. Imagine the din and commotion, the clutter of machinery, that would be needed for a fire department to raise a similar volume of water to that of a single tree. And lifting water is just one of the many jobs that the phloem, xylem and cambium perform.

They also manufacture lignin and cellulose, regulate the storage and production of tannin, sap, gum, oils and resins, dole out minerals and nutrients, convert starches into sugars for future growth (which is where maple syrup comes into the picture), and goodness knows what else. But because all this is happening in such a thin layer, it also leaves the tree terribly vulnerable to invasive organisms. To combat this, trees have formed elaborate defence mechanisms. The reason a rubber tree seeps latex when cut is that this is its way of saying to insects and other organisms, 'Not tasty. Nothing here for you. Go away.' Trees can also deter destructive creatures like caterpillars by flooding their leaves with tannin, which makes the leaves less tasty and so inclines the caterpillars to look elsewhere. When infestations are particularly severe, some trees can even communicate the fact. Some species of oak release a chemical that tells other oaks in the vicinity that an attack is under way. In response, the neighbouring oaks step up their tannin production the better to withstand the coming onslaught.

By such means, of course, does nature tick along. The problem arises when a tree encounters an attacker for which evolution has left it unprepared, and seldom has a tree been more helpless against an invader than the American chestnut against *Endothia parasitica*. It enters a chestnut effortlessly, devours the cambium cells and positions itself for attack on the next tree before the tree has the faintest idea, chemically speaking, what hit it. It spreads by means of spores, which are produced in the hundreds of millions in each canker. A single woodpecker can transfer a billion spores on one flight between trees. At the height of the American chestnut blight, every woodland breeze would loose spores in uncountable trillions to drift in a pretty, lethal haze onto neighbouring hillsides. The mortality rate was 100 per cent. In just over thirty-five years the American chestnut became a memory. The Appalachians alone lost four billion trees, a quarter of its cover, in a generation.

A great tragedy, of course. But how lucky, when you think about it, that these diseases are at least species specific. Instead of a chestnut blight or Dutch elm disease or dogwood anthracnose, what if there was just a tree blight – something indiscriminate and unstoppable that swept through whole forests? In fact there is. It's called acid rain.

But let's stop there. I think we've both had enough science

for one chapter. But hold that thought, please, and bear it in mind when I tell you that there wasn't a day in the Appalachian woods when I didn't give passing thanks for what there was.

So the forest through which Katz and I passed now was nothing like the forest that was known even to people of my father's generation, but at least it was a forest. It was splendid in any case to be enveloped once more in our familiar surroundings. It was in every detectable respect the same forest that we had left in North Carolina – same violently slanted trees, same narrow brown path, same expansive silence, broken only by our tiny grunts and laboured breaths as we struggled up hills that proved to be as steep, if not quite as lofty, as those we had left behind. But, curiously, though we had come a couple of hundred miles north, spring seemed further advanced here. The trees, predominantly oak, were more fully in bud and there were occasional clumps of wild flowers – bloodroot and trillium and Dutchmen's breeches – rising through the carpet of last year's leaves. Sunlight filtered through the branches overhead, throwing spotlights on the path, and there was a certain distinctive, heady spring lightness in the air. We took off first our jackets and then our sweaters. The world seemed altogether a genial place.

Best of all, there were views, luscious and golden, to left and right. For 400 miles through Virginia, the Blue Ridge is essentially a single long fin, only a mile or two wide, notched here and there with deep, V-shaped passes called gaps, but otherwise holding generally steady at about 3,000 feet, with the broad green Valley of Virginia stretching off to the Allegheny Mountains to the west and lazy pastoral piedmont to the east. So here each time we hauled ourselves to a mountaintop and stepped onto a rocky overlook, instead of seeing nothing but endless tufted green mountains stretching to the horizon, we got airy views of a real, lived-in world: sunny farms, clustered hamlets, clumps of woodland and winding highways, all made exquisitely picturesque by distance. Even an interstate highway, with its cloverleaf interchanges and parallel carriageways, looked benign and thoughtful, like the illustrations you used to get in children's books in my boyhood, showing an America that was busy and on the move, but not too busy to be attractive.

We walked for a week and hardly saw a soul. One afternoon I met a man who had been section hiking for twenty-five years with a bicycle and a car. Each morning he would drop the bike at a finishing point ten miles or so down the trail, drive the car back to the start, hike between the two and cycle back to his car. He did this for two weeks every April and figured he had about another twenty years to go. Another day I followed an older man, lean and rangy, who looked to be well into his seventies. He had a small, old-fashioned day pack of tawny canvas and moved with extraordinary swiftness. Two or three times an hour I would sight him just ahead, 50 or 60 yards away, vanishing into the trees. Though he moved much faster than I did and never seemed to rest, he was always there. Wherever there was 50 or 60 yards of view, there he would be – just the back of him, just disappearing. It was like following a ghost. I tried to catch him up and couldn't. He never looked at me that I could see, but I was sure he was aware of me behind him. You get a kind of sixth sense for the presence of others in the woods, and when you realize people are near you always pause to let them catch up, just to exchange pleasantries and say hello and maybe find out if anyone has heard a weather forecast. But the man ahead never paused, never varied his pace, never looked back. In the late afternoon he vanished and I never saw him again.

In the evening, I told Katz about it.

'Jesus,' he muttered privately, 'now he's hallucinating on me.' But the next day Katz saw him all day – but behind him, following, always near but never overtaking. It was very weird. After that, neither of us saw him again. We didn't see anyone.

In consequence, we had shelters to ourselves each night,

which was a big treat. You know your life has grown pathetic when you are thrilled to have a covered wooden platform to call your own, but there you are – we were thrilled. The shelters along this section of trail were mostly new and spanking clean. Several were even provisioned with a broom – a cosy, domestic touch. Moreover, the brooms were used – we used them, and whistled while we did it – proving that if you give an AT hiker an appliance of comfort he will use it responsibly. Each shelter had a nearby privy, a good water source, and a picnic table, so we could prepare and eat our meals in a more or less normal posture instead of squatting on damp logs. All of these are great luxuries on the trail. On the fourth night, just as I was facing the dismal prospect of finishing my only book and thereafter having nothing to do in the evenings but lie in the half-light and listen to Katz snore, I was delighted, thrilled, sublimely gratified to find that some earlier user had left a Graham Greene paperback. If there is one thing the AT teaches, it is low-level ecstasy – something we could all do with more of in our lives.

So I was happy. We were doing 15 or 16 miles a day, nothing like the 25 miles we had been promised we would do, but still a perfectly respectable distance by our lights. I felt springy and fit and for the first time in years had a stomach that didn't look like a ball bag. I was still weary and stiff at the end of the day – that never stopped – but I had reached the point where aches and blisters were so central a feature of my existence that I ceased to notice them. Each time you leave the cosseted and hygienic world of towns and take yourself into the hills you go through a series of staged transformations – a kind of gentle descent into squalor – and each time it is as if you have never done it before. At the end of the first day, you feel mildly, self-consciously, grubby; by the second day disgustingly so; by the third you are beyond caring; by the fourth you have forgotten what it is like not to be like this. Hunger, too, follows a defined pattern. On the first night you are starving for your noodles; on the second night you are starving but wish it wasn't noodles;

on the third you don't want the noodles but know you had better eat something; by the fourth you have no appetite at all but just eat because that is what you do at this time of day. I can't explain it, but it's strangely agreeable.

And then something happens to make you realize how much – how immeasurably much – you want to revisit the real world. On our sixth night, after a long day in uncharacteristically dense woods, we emerged towards evening at a small grassy clearing on a high bluff with a long, sensational, unobstructed view to the north and west. The sun was just falling behind the distant blue-grey Allegheny ridge, and the country between – a plain of broad, orderly farms, each with a clump of trees and a farmhouse — was just at that point where it was beginning to drain of colour. But the feature that made us gawp was a town – a real town, the first we had seen in a week – that stood perhaps six or seven miles to the north. From where we stood we could just make out what were clearly the large, brightly lit, coloured signs of roadside restaurants and big motels. I don't think I have ever seen anything that looked half so beautiful, a quarter so tantalizing. I would almost swear to you I could smell the steaks grilling. We stared at it for ages, as if it were something we had read about in books but had never expected to see.

'Waynesboro,' I said to Katz at last.

He nodded solemnly. 'How far?'

I pulled out my map and had a look. 'About eight miles by trail.'

He nodded solemnly again. 'Good,' he said. It was, I realized, the longest conversation we had had in two or three days, but there was no need to say anything more. We had been a week on the trail and were going to town the next day. That was self-evident. We would hike eight miles, get a room, have a shower, phone home, do laundry, eat dinner, buy groceries, watch TV, sleep in a bed, eat breakfast, return to the trail. All this was known and obvious. Everything we did was known and obvious. It was wonderful really.

So we pitched our tents and fixed noodles with the last of our water, then sat side by side on a log, eating in silence, facing Waynesboro. A full moon rose in the pale evening sky, and glowed with a rich white inner light that brought to mind, but perfectly, the creamy inside of an Oreo cookie. (Eventually on the trail everything reminds you of food.) After a long period of silence, I turned to Katz and asked him abruptly, in a tone that was hopeful rather than accusatory, 'Do you know how to make anything besides noodles?' I had been thinking, I guess, about resupplying the next day.

He thought about this for a good while. 'French toast,' he said at last, and grew silent for a long period before inclining his head towards me very slightly and saying: 'You?'

'No,' I said at length. 'Nothing.'

Katz considered the implications of this, looked for a moment as if he might say something, then shook his head stoically, and returned to his dinner.

Chapter 11

Now here's a thought to consider. Every twenty minutes on the Appalachian Trail, Katz and I walked further than the average American walks in a week. For 93 per cent of all trips outside the home, for whatever distance or whatever purpose, Americans now get in a car. That's ridiculous. When we moved to the States one of the things we wanted was to live in a town, where we could walk to the shops and post office and library. We found such a place in Hanover, New Hampshire. It's a small, pleasant college town, with a big green, leafy residential streets, an old-fashioned main street. Nearly everyone in town is within an easy level walk of the centre, and yet almost no-one walks anywhere ever for anything. I have a neighbour who drives 800 yards to work. I know another – a perfectly fit woman – who will drive 100 yards to pick up her child from a friend's house. When school lets out here, virtually every child (except for four bitching kids with English accents) gets picked up and driven from a few hundred yards to three-quarters of a mile home.

(Those who live further away get a bus.) Most of the children sixteen years or older have their own cars. That's ridiculous, too. On average the total walking of an American these days – that's walking of all types: from car to office, from office to car, round the supermarket and shopping malls – adds up to 1.4 miles a week, barely 350 yards a day.

At least in Hanover we can walk. In many places in America now, it is not actually possible to be a pedestrian, even if you want to be. I had this brought home to me the next day in Waynesboro, after we had got a room and treated ourselves to an extravagant late breakfast. I left Katz at a launderette (he loved doing laundry, for some reason – loved to read the tattered magazines and experience the miracle of stiff, disgusting clothes emerging from big machines fluffed and sweet-smelling) and set off to find some insect repellent for us.

Waynesboro had a traditional, vaguely pleasant central business district covering five or six square blocks, but, as so often these days, most retail businesses had moved out to shopping centres on the periphery, leaving little but a sprinkling of banks, insurance offices and dusty thrift stores or secondhand shops in what presumably was once a thriving downtown. Lots of shops were dark and bare, and there was nowhere I could find to get insect repellent, but a man outside the post office suggested I try K-mart.

'Where's your car?' he said, preparatory to giving directions.

'I don't have a car.'

That stopped him. 'Really? It's over a mile, I'm afraid.'

'That's OK.'

He gave his head a little dubious shake, as if disowning responsibility for what he was about to tell me. 'Well, then what you want to do is go up Broad Street, take a right at the Burger King and keep on going. But, you know, when I think about it, it's *well* over a mile – maybe a mile and a half, mile and three-quarters. You walking back as well?'

'Yeah.'

Another shake. 'Long way.'

'I'll take emergency provisions.'

If he realized this was a joke he didn't show it. 'Well, good luck to you,' he said.

'Thank you.'

'You know, there's a cab company around the corner,' he offered helpfully as an afterthought.

'I actually prefer to walk,' I explained.

He nodded uncertainly. 'Well, good luck to you,' he said again.

So I walked. It was a warm afternoon, and it felt wonderful – you can't believe how wonderful – to be at large without a pack, bouncy and unburdened. With a pack you walk at a tilt, hunched and pressed forward, your eyes on the ground. You trudge; it is all you can do. Without, you are liberated. You walk erect. You look around. You spring. You saunter. You amble.

Or at least you do for four blocks. Then you come to a mad junction at Burger King and discover that the new six-lane road to K-mart is long, straight, very busy and entirely without facilities for pedestrians – no sidewalks, no zebra crossings, no central refuges, no buttons to push for a WALK signal at lively intersections. I walked through gas station and motel forecourts, across restaurant car parks, clambered over concrete barriers, crossed lawns, and pushed through neglected ranks of privet or honeysuckle at property boundaries. At bridges over creeks and culverts – and goodness me how developers love a culvert – I had no choice but to walk on the road, pressed against the dusty railings and causing less attentive cars to swerve to avoid me. Four times I was honked at for having the temerity to proceed through town without benefit of metal. One bridge was so patently dangerous that I hesitated at it. The creek it crossed was only a reedy trickle, narrow enough to step across, so I decided to go that way. I slid and scampered down the bank, found myself in a hidden zone of sucking grey mud, pitched over twice, hauled myself up the other side, pitched over again,

and emerged at length streaked and speckled with mud and
extravagantly decorated with burrs. When I finally reached the
K-mart Plaza I discovered that I was on the wrong side of
the road and had to dash through six lanes of hostile traffic. By
the time I crossed the car park and stepped into the air con-
ditioned, Muzak-happy world of K-mart I was as grubby as if I
had been on the trail and trembling all over.

The K-mart, it turned out, didn't stock insect repellent.

So I turned round and set off back to town, but this time, in
a burst of madness I don't even want to go into, I headed home
cross country, over farm fields and a zone of light industry. I
tore my jeans on barbed wire and got muddier still. When
finally I got back to town, I found Katz sitting in the sun on a
metal chair on the motel lawn, freshly showered, dressed in
newly laundered attire and looking intensely happy in a way
that only a hiker can look when he is in a town, at ease.
Technically, he was waxing his boots, but really he was just sitting watching the world go by and dreamily enjoying the
sunshine. He greeted me warmly. Katz was always a new man
in town.

'Good lord, look at you!' he cried, delighted at my grubbiness. 'What have you been doing – you're *filthy*.' He looked me
up and down admiringly, then said in a more solemn tone: 'You
haven't been screwing hogs again, have you, Bryson?'

'Ha ha ha.'

'They're not clean animals, you know, no matter how attractive they may look after a month on the trail. And don't forget
we're not in Tennessee any more. It's probably not even legal
here – at least without a note from the vet.' He patted the chair
beside him, beaming all over, happy with his quips. 'Come and
sit down and tell me all about it. So what was her name –
Bossy?' He leaned closely and confidentially. 'Did she squeal a
lot?'

I sat in the chair. 'You're only jealous.'

'Well, as a matter of fact, I'm not. I made a friend of my own today. At the laundromat. Her name's Beulah.'

'Beulah? You're joking.'

'I may wish I was, but it's a fact.'

'Nobody's named Beulah.'

'Well, she is. And real nice, too. Not real smart, but real nice, with cute little dimples just here.' He poked his cheeks to show me where. 'And she has a terrific body.'

'Oh, yes?'

He nodded. 'Of course,' he added judiciously, 'it's buried under two hundred and twenty pounds of wobbling fat. Fortunately I don't mind size in a woman as long as, you know, you don't have to remove a wall or anything to get her out of the house.' He gave his boot a thoughtful swipe.

'So how did you meet her?'

'As a matter of fact,' he said, sitting forward keenly, as if this was a story worth telling, 'she asked me to come and look at her panties.'

I nodded. 'Of course.'

'They'd got caught in the washing machine agitator,' he explained.

'And was she wearing them at the time? You said she wasn't real smart.'

'No, she was washing them and the elastic got stuck in the spindle thing and she asked me to come and help extract them. Big panties,' he added thoughtfully, and fell into a brief reverie at the memory of it, then continued: 'I got 'em out, but they were shredded all to hell, so I said, kind of droll like, "Well, miss, I sure hope you've got another pair, because these are shredded all to hell."'

'Oh, Stephen, the wit.'

'It'll do for Waynesboro, believe me. And *she* said – now here's the thing, my grubby, hog-humping friend – *she* said, "Well, wouldn't you like to know, honey."' He made his eyebrows bounce. 'I'm meeting her at seven outside the fire station.'

'What, she keeps her spare knickers there?'

He gave me an exasperated look. 'No, it's just a place to meet. We're going to Pappa John's Pizza for dinner. And then, with any luck, we'll do what you've been doing all day. Only I won't have to climb a fence and lure her with alfalfa. Well, I hope not anyway. Hey, look at this,' he said, and reached down to a paper bag at his feet. He brought out a pair of pink female knickers that could fairly be called capacious. 'I thought I'd give them to her. As a kind of joke, you understand.'

'In a restaurant? Are you sure that's a good idea?'

'Discreetly, you know.'

I held up the knickers with outstretched arms. They really were quite arrestingly jumbo-sized. 'If she doesn't like them, you can always use them as a groundsheet. Are these – I have to ask – are these this big as part of the joke, or—'

'Oh, she's a big woman,' Katz said and bounced his eyebrows again happily. He put them neatly, reverently back in the bag. '*Big* woman.'

So I dined alone at a place called the Coffee Mill Restaurant. It felt a little odd to be without Katz after so many days of constant companionship, but agreeable as well, for the same reason. I was eating a steak dinner, my book propped against a sugar shaker, entirely content, when I glanced up to find Katz stalking towards me across the restaurant, looking alarmed and furtive.

'Thank God I found you,' he said, and took a seat opposite me in the booth. He was sweating freely. 'There's some guy looking for me.'

'What're you talking about?'

'Beulah's husband.'

'Beulah has a husband?'

'I know. It's a miracle. There can't be more than two people on the planet who'd be willing to sleep with her and here we are both in the same town.'

This was all going too fast for me. 'I don't understand. What happened?'

'I was standing outside the fire station, you know, like we'd agreed, and a red pickup truck screeches to a stop and this guy gets out looking real angry and saying he's Beulah's old man and he wants to talk to me.'

'So what did you do?'

'I ran. What do you think?'

'And he didn't catch you?'

'He weighed about six hundred pounds. He wasn't exactly the sprinting type. More the shoot-your-balls-off type. He's been cruising round for a half-hour looking for me. I've been running through back yards and crashing into clothes lines and all kinds of shit. I ended up with some other guy chasing me because he thought I was a prowler. What the hell am I supposed to do now, Bryson?'

'OK, first you stop talking to fat ladies in laundromats.'

'Yeah yeah yeah yeah yeah.'

'Then I go out of here, see if the coast is clear, and give you a signal from the window.'

'Yeah? And then?'

'Then you walk very briskly back to the motel, with your hands over your balls, and hope this guy doesn't spot you.'

He was quiet a moment. 'That's it? That's your best plan? That's your very best plan?'

'Have you got a better one?'

'No, but I didn't go to college for four years.'

'Stephen, I didn't study how to save your ass in Waynesboro. I majored in political science. If your problem was to do with proportional representation in Switzerland, I might be able to help you.'

He sighed and sat back heavily with his arms crossed, bleakly considering his position and how he'd got himself into this fix. 'You don't let me talk to any women again, of any size, at least until we get out of the Confederacy. These guys have all got guns down here. You promise?'

'Oh, it's a promise.'

He sat in edgy silence while I finished my dinner, swivelling his head to check out all the windows, expecting to see a fat, angry face pressed against the glass. When I had finished and paid the bill, we went to the door.

'I could be dead in a minute,' he said grimly, then clutched my forearm. 'Look, if I get shot, do me a favour. Call my brother and tell him there's ten thousand dollars buried in a coffee can under his front lawn.'

'You buried ten thousand dollars under your brother's front lawn?'

'No, of course not, but he's a little prick and it would serve him right. Let's go.'

I stepped outside and the street was clear – completely empty of traffic. Waynesboro was at home, in front of the TV. I gave him a nod. His head came out, looked cautiously left and right, and he tore off down the street at a rate that was, all things considered, astounding. It took me two or three minutes to stroll to the motel. I didn't see anyone. At the motel, I knocked on his door.

Instantly a preposterously deep, authoritative voice said, 'Who is it?'

I sighed. 'Bubba T. Flubba. I wanna talk to yew, boy.'

'Bryson, don't fuck around. I can see you through the peep-hole.'

'Then why are you asking who it is?'

'Practising.'

I waited a minute. 'Are you going to let me in?'

'Can't. I got a chest of drawers in front of the door.'

'Are you serious?'

'Go to your room and I'll call you.'

My room was next door, but the phone was already ringing when I got there. Katz wanted every detail of my walk home, and had elaborate plans for his defence involving a heavy ceramic lamp base and, ultimately, escape out of the back window. My role was to create a diversion, ideally by setting the man's truck alight, then running in a contrary direction. Twice more in the night, once just after midnight, he called me to tell me that he had seen a red pickup truck cruising the streets. In the morning, he refused to go out for breakfast, so I went to the supermarket for groceries and brought us both a bag of food from Hardee's. He wouldn't leave the room until the cab was waiting by the motel office with the motor running. It was four miles back to the trail. He looked out of the back window the whole way.

The cab dropped us at Rockfish Gap, southern gateway to Shenandoah National Park. I was looking forward to the park because it is exceptionally beautiful – that is why it is a national park, of course – but filled with mild disquiet at the prospect of spending the next seven or eight nights and 101 miles under the yoke of National Park Service rules. At Rockfish Gap, there is a tollbooth manned by rangers where motorists have to pay an entrance fee and thru-hikers have to acquire a backcountry hiking permit. The permit doesn't cost anything – one of the noblest traditions of the Appalachian Trail is that every inch of it is free – but you have to complete a lengthy form giving your personal details, your itinerary through the park and where you plan to camp each night, which is a little ridiculous because you haven't seen the terrain and don't know what kind of mileage you might achieve. Appended to the form were the usual copious regulations and warnings of severe fines and immediate banishment for doing, well, pretty much anything. I filled out the form as best I could and handed it in at the window to a lady ranger.

'So you're hiking the trail?' she said brightly, if not terribly astutely, accepted the form without looking at it, banged it severely with rubber stamps and tore off the part that would serve as our licence to walk on land that, in theory, we owned anyway.

'Well, we're trying,' I said.

'I must get up there myself one of these days. I hear it's real nice.'

This took me aback. 'You've never been on the trail?' But you're a ranger, I wanted to say.

'No, afraid not,' she answered wistfully. 'Lived here all my life, but haven't got to it yet. One day I will.'

Katz, mindful of Beulah's husband, was practically dragging me towards the safety of the woods, but I was curious.

'How long have you been a ranger?' I called back.

'Twelve years in August,' she said proudly.

'You ought to give it a try sometime. It's real nice.'

'Might get some of that flab off your butt,' Katz muttered privately, and stepped into the woods. I looked at him with interest and surprise – it wasn't like Katz to be so uncharitable – and put it down to lack of sleep, profound sexual frustration and a surfeit of Hardee's sausage biscuits.

Shenandoah National Park is a park with problems. More even than the Smokies, it suffers from a chronic shortage (though a cynic might say a chronic misapplication) of funds. Several miles of side trails have been closed and others are deteriorating. If it weren't that volunteers from the Potomac Appalachian Trail Club maintain 80 per cent of the park's trails, including the whole of the AT through the park, the situation would be much worse. Mathews Arm Campground, one of the park's main recreational areas, was closed for lack of funds in 1993 and hasn't been open since. Several other recreation areas are closed for most of the year. For a time in the 1980s, even the trail shelters – or huts as they are known here – were shut. I don't know how they did it – I mean to say, how exactly do you close a wooden structure with a 15-foot-wide opening at the front? – and still less why, since forbidding hikers from resting for a few hours on a wooden sleeping platform is hardly going to transform the park's finances. But then making things difficult for hikers is something of a tradition in the eastern parks. A couple of months earlier, all the national parks, along with all other non-essential government departments, had been closed for a couple of weeks during a budget impasse between President Clinton and Congress. Yet Shenandoah, despite its perennial want of money, found the funds to post a warden at each AT access point to turn back all thru-hikers. In consequence, a couple of dozen harmless people had to make lengthy, pointless detours by road before they could resume their long hike. This vigilance couldn't have cost the Park Service less than $20,000, or the better part of $1,000 for each dangerous thru-hiker deflected.

On top of its self-generated shortcomings, Shenandoah has a lot of problems arising from factors largely beyond its control. Overcrowding is one. Although the park is over a hundred miles long, it is almost nowhere more than a mile or two wide, so all its two million annual visitors are crowded into a singularly narrow corridor along the ridgeline. Campgrounds, visitor centres, car parks, picnic sites, the AT, and Skyline Drive – the scenic road that runs down the spine of the park – all exist cheek by jowl. One of the most popular (non-AT) hiking routes in the park, up Old Rag Mountain, has become so much in demand that on summer weekends people sometimes have to queue to get on it.

Then there is the vexed matter of pollution. Thirty years ago it was still possible, on especially clear days, to see the Washington Monument, 75 miles away. Now, on hot, smoggy summer days, visibility can be as little as two miles and never more than 30. Acid rain in the streams has nearly wiped out the park's trout. Gypsy moths arrived in 1983 and have since ravaged considerable acreages of oaks and hickories. The Southern pine beetle has done similar work on conifers and the locust leaf miner has inflicted disfiguring (but mercifully usually non-fatal) damage on thousands of locust trees. In just seven years, the woolly adelgid has fatally damaged more than 90 per cent of the park's hemlocks. Nearly all the rest will be dying by the time you read this. An untreatable fungal disease called anthracnose is wiping out the lovely dogwoods not just here but everywhere in America. Before long, the dogwood, like the American chestnut and American elm, will effectively cease to exist. It would be hard, in short, to conceive a more stressed environment.

And yet here is the thing. Shenandoah National Park is lovely. It is possibly the most wonderful national park I have ever been in, and, considering the impossible and conflicting demands put on it, it is extremely well run. Almost at once it became my favourite part of the Appalachian Trail.

We hiked through deep-seeming woods, along gloriously untaxing terrain, climbing a gentle 500 feet in four miles. In the Smokies, you can climb 500 feet in, well, about 500 feet. This was more like it. The weather was kindly and there was a real sense of spring being on the turn. And there was life everywhere – zumming insects, squirrels scampering along boughs, birds twittering and hopping about, spiders' webs gleaming silver in the sun. Twice I flushed grouse – always a terrifying experience: an instantaneous explosion from the undergrowth at your feet, like balled socks fired from a gun, followed by drifting feathers and a lingering residue of fussy, bitching noise. I saw an owl, which watched me imperturbably from a near stout limb, and loads of deer, which raised their heads to stare, but otherwise seemed fearless, and casually returned to their browsing when I had passed. Sixty years ago, there were no deer in this neck of the Blue Ridge Mountains. They had been hunted out of existence. Then, after the park was created in 1936, thirteen white-tailed deer were introduced, and, with no-one to hunt them and few predators, they thrived. Today there are 5,000 deer in the park, all descended from those original thirteen, or others that migrated from nearby.

Surprisingly, considering its modest dimensions and how little room there is for real backcountry, the park is remarkably rich in wildlife. Bobcats, bears, red and grey foxes, beaver, skunks, raccoons, flying squirrels, and our friends the salamanders exist in admirable numbers, though you don't often see them, as most are nocturnal or wary of people. Shenandoah is said to have the highest density of black bears anywhere in the world – slightly over one per square mile. There have even been reported sightings – including by park rangers, who perhaps ought to know better – of mountain lions, even though mountain lions haven't been confirmed in the eastern woods for almost seventy years. There is the tiniest chance that they may exist in pockets in the northern woods – we shall get to that in due course and I think you'll be glad you waited – but not in an area as small and hemmed in as Shenandoah National Park.

We didn't see anything terribly exotic, or even remotely exotic, but it was nice just to see squirrels and deer, to feel that the forest was lived in. Late in the afternoon, I rounded a bend to find a wild turkey and her chicks crossing the trail ahead of me. The mother was regal and unflappable; her chicks were much too busy falling over and getting up again even to notice me. This was the way the woods were supposed to be. I couldn't have been more delighted.

We hiked till five and camped beside a tranquil spring in a small, grassy clearing in the trees just off the trail. Because it was our first day back on the trail, we were flush for food, including perishables like cheese and bread that had to be eaten before they went off or were shaken to bits in our packs, so we rather gorged ourselves, then sat around smoking and chatting idly until persistent and numerous midgelike creatures – no-see-ums, as they are universally known along the trail – drove us into our tents. It was perfect sleeping weather, cool enough to need a bag, but warm enough to sleep in your underwear, and I was looking forward to a long night's snooze – indeed was enjoying a long night's snooze when, at some indeterminate dark hour, there was a sound nearby that made my eyes fly open. Normally, I slept through everything – through thunderstorms, through Katz's snoring and noisy midnight pees – so something big enough or distinctive enough to wake me was unusual. There was a sound of undergrowth being disturbed – a click of breaking branches, a weighty pushing through low foliage – and then a kind of large, vaguely irritable snuffling noise.

Bear!

I sat bolt upright. Instantly every neuron in my brain was awake and dashing around frantically, like ants when you disturb their nest. I reached instinctively for my knife, then realized I had left it in my pack, just outside the tent. Nocturnal defence had ceased to be a concern after many successive nights of tranquil woodland repose.

There was another noise, quite near.

'Stephen, you awake?' I whispered.

'Yup,' he replied in a weary but normal voice.

'What was that?'

'How the hell should I know?'

'It sounded big.'

'Everything sounds big in the woods.'

This was true. Once a skunk had come plodding through our camp and it had sounded like a stegosaurus. There was another heavy rustle and then the sound of lapping at the spring. It was having a drink, whatever it was.

I shuffled on my knees to the foot of the tent, cautiously unzipped the mesh and peered out, but it was pitch black. As quietly as I could, I brought in my backpack and, with the light of a small torch, searched through it for my knife. When I found it and opened the blade I was appalled at how wimpy it looked. It was a perfectly respectable appliance for, say, buttering pancakes, but patently inadequate for defending oneself against 400 pounds of ravenous fur.

Carefully, very carefully, I climbed from the tent and put on the torch, which cast a distressingly feeble beam. Something about 15 or 20 feet away looked up at me. I couldn't see anything at all of its shape or size – only two shining eyes. It went silent, whatever it was, and stared back at me.

'Stephen,' I whispered at his tent, 'did you pack a knife?'

'No.'

'Have you got anything sharp at all?'

He thought for a moment. 'Nail clippers.'

I made a despairing face. 'Anything a little more vicious than that? Because, you see, there is definitely something out here.'

'It's probably just a skunk.'

'Then it's one big skunk. Its eyes are three feet off the ground.'

'A deer then.'

I nervously threw a stick at the animal, and it didn't move, whatever it was. A deer would have bolted. This thing just blinked once and kept staring.

I reported this to Katz.

'Probably a buck. They're not so timid. Trying shouting at it.'

I cautiously shouted at it: 'Hey! You there! Scat!' The creature blinked again, singularly unmoved. 'You shout,' I said.

'Oh, you brute, go away, do!' Katz shouted in merciless imitation. 'Please withdraw at once, you horrid creature.'

'Fuck you,' I said and lugged my tent right over to his. I didn't know what this would achieve exactly, but it brought me a tiny measure of comfort to be nearer to him.

'What are you doing?'

'I'm moving my tent.'

'Oh, good plan. That'll really confuse it.'

I peered and peered, but I couldn't see anything but those two wide-set eyes staring from the near distance like eyes in a cartoon. I couldn't decide whether I wanted to be outside and dead or inside and waiting to be dead. I was barefoot and in my underwear and shivering. What I really wanted – really, really wanted – was for the animal to withdraw. I picked up a small stone and tossed it at it. I think it may have hit it because the animal made a sudden noisy start, which scared the bejesus out of me and brought a whimper to my lips, and then it emitted a noise – not quite a growl, but near enough. It occurred to me that perhaps I oughtn't to provoke it.

'What are you doing, Bryson? Just leave it alone and it will go away.'

'How can you be so calm?'

'What do you want me to do? You're hysterical enough for both of us.'

'I think I have a right to be a trifle alarmed, pardon me. I'm in the woods, in the middle of nowhere, in the dark, staring at a bear, with a guy who has nothing to defend himself with but a pair of nail clippers. Let me ask you this. If it is a bear and it comes for you, what are you going to do – give it a pedicure?'

'I'll cross that bridge when I come to it,' Katz said implacably.

'What do you mean you'll cross that bridge? We're *on* the bridge, you moron. There's a bear out here, for Christ's sake. He's looking at us. He smells noodles and Snickers and – oh, shit.'

'What?'

'Oh. Shit.'

'What?'

'There's two of them. I can see another pair of eyes.' Just then, the torch battery started to go. The light flickered and then vanished. I scampered into my tent, stabbing myself lightly but hysterically in the thigh as I went, and began a quietly frantic search for spare batteries. If I were a bear, this would be the moment I would choose to lunge.

'Well, I'm going to sleep,' Katz announced.

'What are you talking about? You can't go to sleep.'

'Sure I can. I've done it lots of times.' There was the sound of him rolling over and a series of snuffling noises, not unlike those of the creature outside.

'Stephen, you can't go to sleep,' I ordered. But he could and he did, with amazing rapidity.

The creature – creatures, now – resumed drinking, with heavy lapping noises. I couldn't find any replacement batteries, so I flung the torch aside and put my miner's lamp on my head, made sure it worked, then switched it off. Then I sat for ages on my knees, facing the front of the tent, listening keenly, gripping my walking stick like a club, ready to beat back an attack, and with my knife open and at hand as a last line of defence. The bears – animals, whatever they were – drank for perhaps twenty minutes more, then quietly departed the way they had come. It was a joyous moment – but I knew from my reading that they would be likely to return. I listened and listened, but the forest returned to silence and stayed there.

Eventually I loosened my grip on the walking stick and put on a sweater – pausing twice to examine the tiniest noises, dreading the sound of a revisit – and after a very long time got back into my sleeping bag for warmth. I lay there staring at total blackness, and knew that never again would I sleep in the woods with a light heart.

And then, irresistibly and by degrees, I fell asleep.

Chapter 12

I'd expected Katz to be insufferable in the morning, but in fact he was surprisingly gracious. He called me for coffee and when I emerged, feeling wretched and cheated of sleep, he said to me: 'You OK? You look like shit.'

'Didn't get enough sleep.'

He nodded. 'So you think it really was a bear?'

'Who knows?' I suddenly thought of the food bag – that's what bears normally go for – and spun my head to see, but it was still suspended a dozen or so feet from the ground from a branch about twenty yards away. Probably a determined bear could have got it down. Actually, my grandmother could have got it down. 'Maybe not,' I said, disappointed.

'Well, you know what I've got in here, just in case?' Katz said and tapped his shirt pocket significantly. 'Toenail clippers – because you just never know when danger might arise. I've learned *my* lesson, believe me, buddy.' Then he guffawed.

And so we returned to the woods. For virtually the length of

Shenandoah National Park, the AT closely parallels and often crosses Skyline Drive, though most of the time you would scarcely guess it. Often you will be plodding through the sanctuary of woods when suddenly a car will sail past through the trees only 40 or 50 feet away – a perennially startling sight.

In the early 1930s, the Potomac Appalachian Trail Club – which was Myron Avery's baby and for a time was virtually indistinguishable from the Appalachian Trail Conference itself – came under attack from other hiking groups, particularly the patrician Appalachian Mountain Club in Boston, for not resisting the building of Skyline Drive through the park. Stung by these rebukes, Avery sent MacKaye a deeply insulting letter in December 1935, which effectively terminated MacKaye's official – but even then peripheral – relationship with the trail. The two men never spoke again, though to his credit MacKaye paid Avery a warm tribute on his death in 1952 and generously noted that the trail could not have been built without him. A lot of people still dislike the highway, but Katz and I quite warmed to it. Frequently we would leave the trail and hike on the road for an hour or two. This early in the season – it was still early April – there were hardly any cars on the road, so we treated Skyline Drive as a kind of broad, paved, alternative footpath. It was novel to have something firm underfoot and exceedingly agreeable to be out in the open, in warm sunshine, after weeks in impenetrable woods. Motorists certainly had a more cosseted, looked-after existence than we did. There were frequent expansive overlooks, with splendid views (though even now, in clear spring weather, blanketed with a dirty haze beyond about six or seven miles), information boards giving helpful facts on the park's wildlife and flora, and even litter bins. We could do with some of this on the trail, we agreed. And then, when the sun got too hot or our feet grew sore (for asphalt is surprisingly hard on the feet) or we just fancied a change, we would return to the familiar, cool, embracing woods. It was very agreeable – almost rakish – to have options.

At one of the Skyline Drive lay-bys we came to, an information board was angled to direct the reader's attention to a nearby slope handsomely spread with hemlocks, a very dark, almost black native conifer particularly characteristic of the Blue Ridge. All these hemlocks, and all the hemlocks everywhere along the trail and far beyond, are being killed by an aphid introduced accidentally from Asia in 1924. The National Park Service, the board noted sadly, could not afford to treat the trees. There were too many of them over too wide an area to make a spraying programme practicable. Well, here's an idea. Why not treat *some* of the trees? Why not treat *a* tree? The good news, according to the board, was that the National Park Service hoped that some of the trees would stage a natural recovery over time. Well, whew! for that.

Sixty years ago, there were almost no trees on the Blue Ridge Mountains. All this was farmland. Often in the woods now the trail would follow the relics of old stone field walls and once we passed a small, remote cemetery – reminders that this was one of the few mountaintop areas in the entire Appalachian chain where people once actually lived. Unluckily for them, they were the wrong kind of people. In the 1920s, sociologists and other academics from the cities ventured into the hills, and they were invariably appalled at what they found. Poverty and deprivation were universal. The land was ridiculously poor. Many people were farming slopes that were practically perpendicular. Three-quarters of the people in the hills couldn't read. Most had barely gone to school. Illegitimacy was 90 per cent. Sanitation was practically unknown; only 10 per cent of households had even a basic privy. On top of that, the Blue Ridge Mountains were sensationally beautiful and conveniently sited for the benefit of a new class of motoring tourist. The obvious solution was to move the people off the mountaintops and into the valleys, where they could be poor lower down, build a scenic highway for people to cruise up and down on Sundays, and turn the whole thing into a great mountaintop fun zone, with commercial campgrounds, restaurants, ice cream parlours, crazy golf, helter-skelters, and whatever else might turn a snappy dollar.

Unfortunately for the entrepreneurs, then came the Great Depression and the commercial impulse withered. Instead, under that dizzying socialist impulse (though you must never use that term) that marked the presidency of Franklin Roosevelt, the land was bought for the nation. The people were moved out, and the Civilian Conservation Corps was put to work building pretty stone bridges, picnic shelters, visitor centres, and much else, and the whole was opened to the public in July 1936. It is the quality of craftsmanship that accounts substantially for the glory of Shenandoah National Park. Indeed, it is one of the very few examples of human handiwork – Hoover Dam is another, and Mount Rushmore, I would submit, is a third – anywhere in the United States that complements, even enhances, a natural landscape. I suppose that, too, is one reason I liked walking along Skyline Drive, with its broad, lawn-like grass verges and stone retaining walls, its clusters of artfully planted birches, its gentle curves leading to arresting, thoughtfully composed panoramas. This is the way all highways should be. For a time it looked as if all highways *would* be like this. It is no accident that the first highways in America were called parkways. That's what they were envisioned to be – parks you could drive through.

Almost none of this spirit of craftsmanship is evident on the AT in the park – you wouldn't expect it to be on a trail devoted to wilderness – but it is agreeably encountered in the park's shelters, or huts, which have something of the picturesque rusticity of the Smokies shelters but are airier, cleaner, and better designed, and without those horrible, depressing chain-link fences across their fronts.

Though Katz thought I was preposterous, I insisted on sleeping at shelters after our night at the spring – I somehow felt I could defend a shelter against marauding bears – and in any case the Shenandoah shelters were too nice not to use. Every one of them was attractive, thoughtfully sited, had a good water source, and a picnic table and privy. For two nights we had shelters to ourselves, and on the third were just exchanging congratulations on this remarkable string of luck when we heard a cacophony of voices approaching through the woods. We peeked round the corner and found a Boy Scout troop marching into the clearing. They said hello and we said hello, and then we sat with our legs dangling from the sleeping platform and watched them fill the clearing with their tents and abundant gear, pleased to have something to look at other than each other. There were three adult supervisors and seventeen Boy Scouts, all charmingly incompetent. Tents went up, then swiftly collapsed or keeled over. One of the adults went off to filter water and fell in the creek. Even Katz agreed that this was better than TV. For the first time since we had left New Hampshire, we felt like masters of the trail.

A few minutes later, a cheerful lone hiker arrived. His name was John Connolly, and he was a high school teacher from upstate New York. He had been hiking the trail, evidently only a couple of miles behind us, for four days, and had been camping alone in the open each night, which struck me now as awfully brave. He hadn't seen any bears – indeed, had been section hiking the trail for years and had seen a bear only once, briefly, rump end and fleeing, deep in the Maine woods. He was followed shortly by two men about our age from Louisville – Jim and Chuck, both real nice fellows, self-effacing and funny. We hadn't seen more than three or four hikers since leaving Waynesboro, and now suddenly we were inundated.

'What day is it?' I asked, and everyone had to stop and think.

'Friday,' someone said. 'Yeah, Friday.' That explained it – the start of a weekend.

We all sat around the picnic table, cooking and eating. It was wonderfully convivial. The three others had hiked a great deal and told us all about the trail ahead as far as Maine, which still seemed as distant as the next cosmos. Then the conversation turned to a perennial favourite among hikers – how crowded the trail had become. Connolly talked about how he had hiked nearly half the trail in 1987, at the height of summer, and had gone days without seeing anyone, and Jim and Chuck heartily seconded this.

This is something you hear a lot, and it is certainly true that more people are hiking than ever before. Until the 1970s, fewer than fifty people a year thru-hiked the AT. As recently as 1984, the number was just 100. By 1990, it had pushed past 200, and today it is approaching 300. These are big increases, but they are also still tiny, tiny numbers. Just before we set off, my local newspaper in New Hampshire had an interview with a trail maintainer who noted that twenty years ago the three campsites in his section averaged about a dozen visitors a week in July and August and that now they sometimes got as many as a hundred in a week. The amazing thing about that, if you ask me, is that they got so few for so long. Anyway, a hundred visitors a week for three campsites at the height of summer hardly seems overwhelming.

Perhaps I was coming at this from the wrong direction, having hiked in crowded little England for so long, but what never ceased to astonish me throughout our long summer was how empty the trail was. Nobody knows how many people hike the Appalachian Trail, but most estimates put the number at around three or four million a year. If four million is right, and we assume that probably three-quarters of that hiking is done during the six warmest months, that means an average of 16,500 people on the trail a day in season, or 7.5 people for each mile of trail, one person every 700 feet. In fact, few sections will experience anything like that high a density. A very high proportion of those four million annual hikers will be concentrated in certain popular places for a day or a weekend – the Presidential Range in New Hampshire, Baxter State Park in Maine, Mount Greylock in Massachusetts, in the Smokies and

Shenandoah National Park. That four million will also include a high proportion of what you might call Reebok hikers – people who park their car, walk 400 yards, get back in their car and drive off, and never do anything as breathtaking as that again. Believe me, no matter what anyone tells you the Appalachian Trail is not crowded.

When people bleat on about the trail being too crowded, what they mean is that the shelters are too crowded, and this is indubitably sometimes so. The problem, however, is not that there are too many hikers for the shelters, but too few shelters for the hikers. Shenandoah National Park has just eight huts, each able to accommodate no more than eight people in comfort, ten at a pinch, in 101 miles of national park. That's about average for the trail overall. Although the distances between shelters can vary enormously, there is on average an AT shelter, cabin, hut or lean-to (240 of them altogether) about every ten miles. That means adequate covered sleeping space for just 2,500 hikers over 2,200 miles of trail. When you consider that more than 100 million Americans live within a day's drive of the Appalachian Trail, it is hardly surprising that 2,500 sleeping spaces is sometimes not enough. Yet, perversely, pressure is growing in some quarters to reduce the number of shelters to discourage what is seen – amazingly to me – as overuse of the trail.

So, as always when the conversation turned to the crowdedness of the trail and the fact that you now sometimes see a dozen people in a day when formerly you would have been lucky to see two, I listened politely and said, 'You guys ought to try hiking in England.'

Jim turned to me and said, in a kindly, patient way, 'But you see, Bill, we're not *in* England.' Perhaps he had a point.

Now here is another reason I am very, very fond of Shenandoah National Park, and why I am probably not cut out to be a proper American trail hiker – cheeseburgers. You can get cheeseburgers quite regularly in Shenandoah National Park, and Coca-Cola with ice and French fries and ice cream, and a good deal else. Although the rampant commercialization I spoke of a moment ago never happened – and thank goodness, of course – something of that *esprit de commerce* lives on in Shenandoah. The park is liberally sprinkled with public campgrounds and rest stops with restaurants and shops – and the AT, God bless it, pays nearly every one of them a call. It is entirely against the spirit of the AT to have restaurant breaks along the trail, but I never met a hiker who didn't appreciate it to bits.

Katz, Connolly and I had our first experience of it the next morning, after we had said farewell to Jim and Chuck and the Boy Scouts, who were all headed south, when we arrived about lunchtime at a lively commercial sprawl called Big Meadows.

Big Meadows had a campground, a lodge, a restaurant, a gift shop/general store, and lots and lots of people spread around a big sunny grassy space. (Although it is a big meadow, it was actually named for a guy named Meadows, which pleased me very much for some reason.) We dropped our packs on the grass outside and hastened into the busy restaurant where we greedily partook of everything greasy, then repaired to the lawn to smoke and burp and enjoy a spell of tranquil digestion. As we lay there propped against our packs, a tourist in an unfortunate straw hat, clutching an ice cream, came up and looked us over in a friendly manner. 'So you fellas hiking?' he said.

We said we were.

'And you carry those packs?'

'Until we find someone to carry them for us,' said Katz cheerfully.

'How far you come this morning?'

'Oh, about eight miles.'

'Eight miles! Lord. And how far'll you go this afternoon?'

'Oh, maybe another eight miles.'

'No kidding! Sixteen miles on foot? With those things on your back? *Man* – ain't that a kick.' He called across the lawn:

'Bernice, come here a minute. You gotta see this.' He looked at us again. 'So whaddaya got in there? Clothes and stuff, I suppose?'

'And food,' said Connolly.

'You carry your own food, huh?'

'Have to.'

'Well, ain't that a kick.'

Bernice arrived and he explained to her that we were using our legs to proceed across the landscape. 'Ain't that something? They got all their food and everything in those packs.'

'Is that a fact?' Bernice said with admiration and interest. 'So, you're like *walkin'* everywhere?' We nodded. 'You walked here? All the way up here?'

'We walk everywhere,' said Katz solemnly.

'You never walked all the way up here!'

'Well, we did,' said Katz, for whom this was becoming one of the proudest moments of his life.

I went off to call home from a payphone and use the gents. When I returned a few minutes later, Katz had accumulated a small, appreciative crowd and was demonstrating the use and theory of various straps and toggles on his backpack. Then, at someone's behest, he put the pack on and posed for pictures. I had never seen him so happy.

While he was still occupied, Connolly and I went into the little grocery part of the complex to have a look around, and I realized just how little regarded and incidental hikers are to the real business of the park. Only 3 per cent of Shenandoah's two million annual visitors go more than a few yards into what is generously termed the backcountry. Ninety per cent of visitors arrive in cars or motor homes. This was a store for them. Nearly everything in the store required microwaving or oven heating or scrupulous refrigeration or came in large, family-sized quantities. (It's a rare hiker who wants twenty-four hamburger buns, I find.) There was not a single item of conventional trail food – raisins or peanuts or small, portable quantities of packets or tinned goods – which was a little dispiriting in a national park.

With no choice, and desperate not to eat noodles again if we could possibly help it (Connolly, I was delighted to learn, was also a noodles man), we bought twenty-four hot dogs and matching buns, a two-litre bottle of Coke, and a couple of large packets of cookies. Then we collected Katz, who announced regretfully to his adoring audience that he had to go – there were mountains still to climb – and stepped valiantly back into the woods.

We stopped for the night at a lovely, secluded spot called Rock Spring Hut, perched on a steep hillside with a long view over the Shenandoah Valley far below. The shelter even had a swing – a two-seater that hung on chains from the shelter over-hang, put there in memory of one Theresa Affronti, who had loved the trail, according to a plaque on its back – which I thought was rather splendid. Earlier visitors to the shelter had left behind an assortment of tinned foods – beans, corn, Spam, baby carrots – which were lined up carefully along one of the support rafters. You find this sort of thing quite a lot on the trail. In some places, friends of the trail will hike up to shelters with home-made cookies or platters of fried chicken. It's quite won-derful.

While we were cooking dinner, a young southbound thru-hiker – the first of the season – arrived. He had hiked 26 miles that day and thought he had died and gone to heaven when he learned that hot dogs were on the menu. Six hot dogs apiece was more than Katz and Connolly and I could eat, so we ate four, and a quantity of cookies, and saved the rest for breakfast. But the young southbounder ate as if he had never eaten before. He downed six hot dogs, then a tin of baby carrots, and gratefully accepted a dozen or so Oreos, one after the other, and ate them with great savour and particularity. He told us he had started in Maine in deep snow, had been endlessly caught in blizzards, but was still averaging 25 miles a day. He was only about five foot six and his pack was enormous. No wonder he had an appetite. He was trying to hike the trail in three months, mostly by putting in very long days. When we woke in the morning, dawn was only just leaking in, but he had already gone. Where he had slept there was a brief note thanking us for the food and wishing us luck. We never did learn his name.

Late the next morning, when I realized that I had considerably outstripped Katz and Connolly, who were talking and not making very good time, I stopped to wait for them in a spacious, sun-dappled dell tucked into a bowl of small hills, which gave it an enchanting, secretive feel. Everything you might ask of a woodland scene was there – musical brook, carpet of lush ferns, elegant, well-spaced trees – and it struck me in passing what a nice place this would be to camp.

Just over a month later, two young women, Lollie Winans and Julianne Williams, evidently had the same thought. They pitched their tents somewhere in this tranquil, airy grove, then hiked the short way through the woods to Skyland Lodge, another commercial complex, to eat in its restaurant. No-one knows exactly what happened, but some person at Skyland presumably watched them dine, then followed them back to their campsite. They were found three days later in their tents with their hands bound and their throats cut. There was no apparent motive. There has never been a suspect. Their deaths will almost certainly for ever be a mystery. Of course I had no idea of this at the time, so when Katz and Connolly caught up I simply observed to them what a lovely spot it was. They looked at it and agreed, and then we moved on.

We had lunch with Connolly at Skyland, and then he left us to hitchhike back to his car at Rockfish Gap and return home. Katz and I bade him farewell and then pushed on, for that was what we did. We walked for three days more, stopping at restaurants when we came to them, and camping in shelters, which once again we had mostly to ourselves.

On our next to last day in the park, our sixth since setting off
from Rockfish Gap, we awoke to chill, gloomy weather. The
wind freshened and then it began to rain, steadily and heavily,
a really cold, penetrating rain. It turned out to be an awful day
in nearly every way. In the early afternoon, I discovered that I
had lost my backpack raincover – which, may I just say here,
was a completely useless, ill-designed piece of crap anyway, for
which I had paid $25 – and that nearly everything in my pack
now ranged from sodden to damp. I had, fortunately, taken to
wrapping my sleeping bag in a double thickness of trash bags
(cost 35 cents), so it at least was dry. Twenty minutes later, as I
sheltered under a bough waiting for Katz, he arrived and immediately said, 'Hey, where's your stick?' I had lost my beloved
walking stick – I suddenly remembered propping it against a
tree when I had stopped to tie a lace – and was filled with
despair. That stick had seen me through six and a half weeks of
mountains, had become all but part of me. It was a link with
my children, whom I missed more than I can tell you. I felt like
weeping. I told Katz where I thought I'd left it, at a place called
Elkwallow Gap, about four miles back.

'I'll get it for you,' he said without hesitation and started to
drop his pack. I could have wept again – he really meant it –
but I wouldn't let him go. It was too far and besides Elkwallow
Gap was a public place. Someone would have taken it as a
souvenir by now.

So we pressed on to a spot called Gravel Springs Hut. It was
only half past two when we got there. We had planned to go at
least six miles further, but we were so soaked and the rain was
so unrelenting that we decided to stop. I had no dry clothes, so
I stripped to my boxer shorts and climbed into my sleeping bag.
We spent the longest afternoon I can ever remember listlessly
reading and staring out at the pattering rain.

At about five o'clock, just to make our day complete, a group
of six noisy people arrived, three men and three women,
dressed in the most preposterously Ralph Lauren-style hiking

clothes – safari jackets and broad-brimmed canvas hats and
suede hiking boots. These were clothes for sauntering along the
veranda at Mackinac or perhaps going on a jeep safari, but
patently not for hiking. One of the women, arriving a few paces
behind the others and walking through the mud as if it were
radioactive, peered into the shelter at me and Katz and said
with undisguised distaste, 'Ooh, do we have to *share?*'

They were, to a degree that would have been fascinating in
less trying circumstances, stupid, obnoxious, cheerfully but
astonishingly self-absorbed, and not remotely acquainted with
trail etiquette. Katz and I found ourselves carelessly bumped
and jostled into the darkest corners, sprayed with water from
clothes being shaken out, and knocked on the head with
casually discarded equipment. In astonishment we watched as
clothes we had hung up to dry on a small clothes line were
pushed and bunched to one side to make abundant room for
their stuff. I sat sullenly, unable to concentrate on my book,
while two of the men crouched beside me, in my light, and had
the following conversation:

'I've never done this before.'

'What – camp in a shelter?'

'No, look through binoculars with my glasses on.'

'Oh, I thought you meant camp in a shelter – ha! ha! ha!'

'No, I meant look through binoculars with my glasses on –
ha! ha! ha!'

After about a half an hour of this Katz came over, knelt beside
me and said in a whisper, 'One of these guys just called me
"Sport". I'm getting the fuck out of here.'

'What're you going to do?'

'Pitch my tent in the clearing. You coming?'

'I'm in my underpants,' I said pathetically.

Katz nodded in understanding and stood up. 'Ladies and
gentlemen,' he announced, 'can I have your attention for a
minute? Excuse me, Sport, can I have your attention? We're
going to go out and pitch our tents in the rain, so you can have

all the space in here, but my friend here is in his boxer shorts, and is afraid of offending the ladies – and maybe exciting the gentlemen,' he added with a brief, sweet leer, 'so could you turn your heads for a minute while he puts his wet clothes back on? Meanwhile, I'll say goodbye and thank you for allowing us to share a few inches of your space for a little while. It's been a slice.'

Then he jumped down into the rain. I dressed hastily, surrounded by silence and self-consciously averted gazes, then bounded down with a small, wimpily neutral goodbye. We pitched our tents about 30 yards away – not an easy or enjoyable process in the driving rain, believe me – and climbed in. Before we had finished, voices from the shelter had resumed and were succeeded by peals of triumphant laughter. They were noisy until dark, then drunkenly noisy until the small hours. I wondered if at any point they would experience some twinge of charity or remorse and send over a peace offering – a brownie, perhaps, or a hot dog – but they did not.

When we woke in the morning, the rain had stopped, though the world was still insipid and drear, and water was dripping from the trees. We didn't bother with coffee. We just wanted to get out of there. We broke down our tents and packed away our stuff. Katz went to get a shirt from the line, and reported that our six friends were sleeping heavily. There were two empty bourbon bottles, he reported in a tone of disdain.

We hefted our packs and set off down the trail. We had walked perhaps 400 yards, out of sight of the camp, when Katz stopped me.

'You know that woman who said "Ooh, do we have to share?" and shoved our clothes to the end of the clothes line?' he asked.

I nodded. Of course I remembered her.

'Well, I'm not real proud of this. I want you to understand that. But when I went to get my shirt, I noticed her boots were

right by the edge of the platform and, well, I did something
kind of bad.'

'What?' I tried to imagine, but couldn't.

He opened his hand and there were two suede shoelaces.
Then he beamed – a big, winning beam – and stuck them in his
pocket and walked on.

Chapter 13

And that was about it for the start of our great adventure. We walked 18 miles to Front Royal, where my wife was to pick us up in two days if she managed to find her way by car from New Hampshire in an unfamiliar country.

I had to go off for a month to do other things – principally, try to persuade Americans to buy a book of mine even though it had nothing to do with effortless weight loss, running with the wolves, thriving in an age of anxiety, or the O.J. Simpson trial. (Even so, it sold over sixty copies.) Katz was going back to Des Moines, where he had the offer of a job for the summer building houses, though he promised to come back in August and hike the famous and forbidding Hundred Mile Wilderness in Maine with me.

At one point, very early in the trip, he had talked earnestly of doing the whole trail, pushing on alone until I was able to rejoin him in June, but when I mentioned this now he just gave a hollow laugh and invited me to join him in the real world when I felt up to it.

'To tell you the truth, I'm amazed we've come this far,' he said, and he was right. We had hiked 500 miles, a million and a quarter steps, since setting off from Amicalola. We had grounds to be proud. We were real hikers now. We had shit in the woods and slept with bears. We had become, we would for ever be, mountain men.

We reached Front Royal about seven, dead tired, and went to the first motel we came to. It was arrestingly dire, but cheap. The bed sagged, the TV picture jumped as if it were being mercilessly goosed by an electronic component, and my door didn't lock. It pretended to lock, but if you pushed on it from outside with a finger, it popped open. This perplexed me for a moment until I realized that no-one could possibly want any of my possessions, so I just pulled it shut and went off to find Katz and go to dinner. We ate at a steakhouse down the street and retired happily to our televisions and beds.

In the morning, I went early to K-mart and bought two complete new sets of clothes – socks, underwear, blue jeans, sneakers, handkerchiefs, and the two liveliest shirts I could find (one with boats and anchors, the other with a famous-monuments-of-Europe motif). I returned to the motel, presented Katz with half – he couldn't have been more thrilled – then went to my room and put on my new attire. We met in the motel car park ten minutes later, looking crisp and stylish, and exchanged many flattering comments. With a day to kill, we went for breakfast, had an idle, contented saunter through the modest central business district, poked around in thrift shops for something to do, found a camping store where I bought a replacement hiking stick exactly like the one I had lost, had lunch, and in the afternoon decided naturally to go for a walk. It was, after all, what we did.

We found some railroad tracks, which followed the stately curves of the Shenandoah River. There is nothing more agreeable, more pleasantly summery, than to stroll along railroad tracks in a new shirt. We walked without haste or particular purpose, mountain men on holiday, chatting seamlessly about nothing in particular, stepping aside from time to time to let a freight train lumber past, and generally enjoying the abundant sunshine, the beckoning infinite gleam of silver track, and the simple pleasure of moving forward on legs that felt tireless. We walked almost till sunset. It was a happy way to conclude the trip.

In the morning we went to breakfast and then there was the three hours of fidgety torture of standing at the edge of a motel drive watching traffic for a particular car filled with beaming, much-missed faces. Well, you can imagine the reunion scene, I'm sure – the exuberant hugs, the tumble of information about the confusion of finding the right turnoff and motel, the impressed appraisal of dad's new body, the less impressed appraisal of his new shirt, the sudden remembering to include Katz (bashfully grinning on the margins) in the celebrations, the tousling of hair, the whole transcendently happy business of being back together.

We took Katz to National Airport in Washington, where he was booked on a late afternoon flight to Des Moines. At the airport, I realized we were already in different universes – he in a 'Where do I go to check in?' sort of distraction, I in the distraction of knowing that my family waited, that the car was badly parked, that it was nearly rush hour in Washington – so we parted awkwardly, almost absently, with hasty wishes for a good flight and promises to meet again in August. When he was gone I felt bad, but then I turned to the car, saw my family, and didn't think about him again for weeks.

It was the end of May, almost June, before I got back on the trail. I went for a walk in the woods near our home, with a day pack containing a bottle of water, two peanut butter sandwiches, a map (for form's sake), and nothing else. It was summer now, so the woods were alive with green and heavy with birdsong and swarming mosquitoes and blackfly. I walked five miles over low hills through the woods to the town of Etna, where I sat beside an old cemetery and ate my sandwiches, then packed up and walked home. I was back before lunch. It didn't feel right at all.

The next day I drove to Mount Moosilauke, 50 miles from my home on the southern edge of the White Mountains. Moosilauke is a wonderful mountain, one of the most beautiful in New England, with a certain leonine grandeur and weighty majesty, but it is rather in the middle of nowhere so it doesn't attract a great deal of attention. It belongs to Dartmouth College, of Hanover, whose famous Outing Club has been look-ing after it in a commendably low-key way since the early years of this century. Dartmouth introduced the sport of downhill ski-ing to America on Moosilauke, and the first national championships were held there in 1933. But it was too remote, and soon the sport in New England moved to other mountains nearer main highways, and Moosilauke returned to a splendid obscurity. Today you would never guess that it had ever known fame.

I parked in a small dirt car park, the only car that day, and set off into the woods. This time I had water, peanut butter sandwiches, a map, and insect repellent. Mount Moosilauke is 4,802 feet high, and steep. Without a full pack, I walked straight up it without stopping – a novel and gratifying experience. The view from the top was gorgeously panoramic, but it still didn't feel right without Katz, without a full pack. I was home by 4 p.m. This didn't feel right at all. You don't hike the Appalachian Trail and then go home and cut the grass.

So I decided to return to the trail properly, far away from home. The problem was that it is almost impossible nearly everywhere along the AT to get on and off the trail without assistance. I could fly to Washington or Newark or Scranton or Wilkes-Barre, or any of several other places in the *region* of the trail, but in each case I would still be scores of miles short of the trail itself. I couldn't ask my wife to drive me back to Virginia or Pennsylvania, any more than you could ask your wife to drop you in Düsseldorf. So I decided to drive myself. I would, I figured, park at a likely-looking spot, hike for a day or two into the hills, hike back and drive on a bit. I suspected this would turn out to be fairly unsatisfying, possibly even imbecilic, and I was right on both counts, but I didn't have a better alternative.

And thus I was to be found in the first week of June standing on the banks of the Shenandoah again, in Harpers Ferry, West Virginia.

Harpers Ferry is an interesting place and for a number of reasons. First, it is quite pretty. This is because it is a National Historical Park, which means it is owned by the nation as a treasured monument, so there are no Pizza Huts, McDonald's, Burger Kings or even residents, at least in the lower, older part of town. Instead, you get restored or recreated buildings with plaques and interpretation boards, so it doesn't have much, or indeed any, real life, but it still has a kind of polished prettiness. You can see that it would be a truly nice place to live if only people could be trusted to reside there without succumbing to the urge to have Pizza Huts and Taco Bells (and personally I believe they could, for up to eighteen months), so instead you get a pretend town, attractively tucked between steep hills at the confluence of the Shenandoah and Potomac Rivers.

It is a National Historical Park because, of course, it is a historic place. It was at Harpers Ferry that the abolitionist John Brown decided to liberate America's slaves and set up a new nation of his own in northwestern Virginia, which was a pretty ambitious undertaking considering that he had an army of just twenty-one people. To that end, on 16 October 1859, he and his little group stole into town under cover of darkness, captured the federal armoury without resistance (it was guarded by a single nightwatchman), yet still managed to kill a hapless passer-by – who was, ironically, a freed black slave. When news got out that a federal armoury with 100,000 rifles and a great deal of ammunition was in the hands of a small band of lunatics, the President, James Buchanan, despatched Lieutenant-Colonel Robert E. Lee – at that time still a loyal Union soldier – to sort things out. It took Lee and his men less than three minutes of fighting to overcome the hapless rebellion. Brown was captured alive, swiftly tried and sentenced to be hanged a month hence.

One of the soldiers sent to oversee the hanging was Thomas J. Jackson – soon to become famous as Stonewall Jackson – and one of the eager onlookers in the crowd was John Wilkes Booth. So the capture of the federal armoury at Harpers Ferry served as quite a neat overture for all that followed.

Meanwhile, in the wake of Brown's little adventure, all hell was breaking loose. Northern abolitionists like Ralph Waldo Emerson made Brown a martyr, and Southern loyalists got up in arms, quite literally, at the idea that this might be the start of a trend. Before you knew it, the nation was at war.

Harpers Ferry remained at the centre of things throughout the wildly bloody conflict that followed. Gettysburg was just 30 miles to the north, Manassas a similar distance to the south, and Antietam (where, it is worth noting, twice as many men died in one day as the total American losses in the War of 1812, Mexican War and Spanish–American War combined) was just ten miles away. Harpers Ferry itself changed hands eight times during the war, though the record in this regard belongs to Winchester, Virginia, a few miles south, which managed to be captured and recaptured seventy-five times.

These days Harpers Ferry passes its time accommodating tourists and cleaning up after floods. With two temperamental rivers at its feet and a natural funnel of bluffs before and behind, it is forever being inundated. There had been a bad flood in the town six months before, and the park's staff were still busy mopping out, repainting and carrying furnishings, artefacts and displays down from upstairs storage rooms. (Three months after my visit, they would have to take everything back up again.) At one of the houses, two of the rangers came out of the door and down the walk, and nodded smiles at me as they passed. Both of them, I noticed, were packing sidearms. Goodness knows what the world is coming to when park rangers carry service revolvers.

I had a poke around the town, but nearly every building I went to had a locked door and a notice saying CLOSED FOR FLOOD REPAIRS. Then I went and looked at the spot where the two rivers flow together. There was an Appalachian Trail noticeboard there. Although it had been only about ten days since the two women were murdered in Shenandoah National Park, there was already a small poster appealing for information. It had colour photographs of them both. They were clearly photos taken by the women themselves along the trail, in hiking gear, looking happy and healthy, radiant even. It was hard to look at them, knowing their doom. It occurred to me, with a small inward start, that had the two women lived they would very probably be arriving in Harpers Ferry just about now, that instead of standing here looking at a poster of them I could be chatting with them – or indeed, given a slight alteration of luck and fate, that it could be they looking at a poster of me and Katz looking trail-happy and confident.

In one of the few houses open I found a friendly, well-informed, happily unarmed ranger named David Fox, who seemed surprised and pleased to have a visitor. He bobbed up instantly from his stool when I came in and was clearly eager to answer any questions. We got to talking about preservation, and he mentioned how hard it was for the Park Service with so few funds to do a proper job. When the park had been formed, there had been money enough to buy only about half of the Schoolhouse Ridge Battlefield above town – one of the most important if least celebrated of Civil War battle sites – and now a developer was in the process of building houses and shops on what Fox clearly saw as hallowed ground. The developer had even started running pipes across National Park land in the confident – but, as it happened, mistaken – presumption that the Park Service wouldn't have the will or money to stop him. Fox told me I should go up and look at it. I said I would.

But first I had a more important pilgrimage to make. Harpers Ferry is the headquarters of the Appalachian Trail Conference, overseers of the noble footpath to which I had dedicated my summer. The ATC occupies a modest white house on a steep hill above the old part of town. I trudged up and went in. The HQ was half office/half shop – the office portion commendably busy-looking, the shop half arrayed with AT guides and keepsakes. At one end of the public area was a large-scale model of the entire trail, which, had I seen it before I started, would very possibly have dissuaded me from attempting such an undertaking. It was perhaps 15 feet long and conveyed instantly and arrestingly what a hard hike the AT is. The rest of the public area was filled with AT goods – T-shirts, postcards, bandannas, books, miscellaneous publications. I chose a couple of books and some postcards, and was served at the counter by a friendly young woman named Laurie Potteiger, whose label described her as an Information Specialist, and they seem to have chosen the right person for she was a mine of information.

She told me that the previous year 1,500 prospective thru-hikers had started the trail, 1,200 had made it to Neels Gap (that's a drop-out rate of 20 per cent in the first week, from a corps of people who had intended to hike for five or six months!), about a third had made it to Harpers Ferry, roughly halfway, and about 300 had reached Katahdin, a higher success rate than usual. Sixty or so people had successfully hiked the trail from north to south. This year's crop of thru-hikers had been passing through for the past month. It was too early to say what the final figure for the year would be, but it would certainly be higher. It rose, in any case, almost every year.

I asked her about the dangers of the trail, and she told me that in the eight years she had worked for the ATC, there had been just two confirmed cases of snakebite, neither fatal, and one person killed by lightning.

I asked her about the recent murders.

She gave a grimace. 'It's awful. Everyone's really upset about it, because trust is such a kind of bedrock part of hiking the AT, you know? I thru-hiked myself in 1987, so I know how much you come to rely on the goodness of strangers. The trail is really all about that, isn't it? And to have that taken away, well . . .' Then, remembering her position, she gave me a little bit of the official line – a brief, practised, articulate spiel to the effect that one should never forget that the trail is not insulated from the larger ills of society but that statistically it remains extremely safe compared with most places in America. 'It's had nine murders since 1937 – about the same as you would get in many small towns.' This was correct, but a wee bit disingenuous. The AT had no murders in its first thirty-six years and nine in the past twenty-two. Still her larger point was unarguable. You are more likely to be murdered in your bed in America than on the AT. Or as an American friend put it to me much later: 'Look, if you draw a two-thousand-mile-long line across the United States at any angle, it's going to pass through nine murder victims.'

'If you're interested, there's a book about one of the murders,' she said and reached below the counter. She rooted for a moment in a box and brought out a paperback called *Eight Bullets*, which she passed to me for examination. It was about two women who were shot in Pennsylvania in 1988. 'We don't keep it out because, you know, it's kind of upsetting, especially now,' she said apologetically.

I bought it, and as she handed me my change I mentioned to her the thought that if the women had survived they would be passing through about now. 'Yeah,' she said, 'I'd thought about that.'

It was drizzling when I stepped back outside. I went up to Schoolhouse Ridge to have a look at the battlefield. It was a

large, park-like hilltop with a wandering path lined at intervals
with information boards describing charges and last-ditch stands
and other confused, noisy action. The battle for Harpers Ferry
was the finest moment for Stonewall Jackson – he who had last
come to town to hang John Brown – because it was here,
through some deft manoeuvring and a bit of luck, that he
managed to capture 12,500 Union troops, more American
soldiers than would be captured in a single action until Bataan
and Corregidor in the Second World War.

Now Stonewall Jackson is a man worth taking an interest in.
Few people in history have achieved greater fame in a shorter
period with less useful activity in the brainbox than General
Thomas J. Jackson. His idiosyncrasies were legendary. He was
hopelessly, but inventively, hypochondriacal. One of his more
engaging physiological beliefs was that one arm was bigger
than the other, and in consequence he always walked and rode
with that arm held straight up, so that his blood would drain
into his body. He was a champion sleeper. More than once he
fell asleep at the dinner table with food in his mouth. At the
Battle of White Oak Swamp, his lieutenants found it all but
impossible to rouse him and lifted him, insensible, onto his
horse where he continued to slumber while shells exploded
around him. His obtuseness was famed. Once when a celebrated singer sang 'Dixie' for him and his officers, then asked if
he had any special requests, he told her he had just one –
would she sing 'Dixie' for him? He showed excessive zeal in
recording captured goods, and would defend them at all costs.
His list of materiel liberated from the Union Army during the
1862 Shenandoah campaign included 'six handkerchiefs, two
and three-quarter dozen neckties, and one bottle of red ink'. He
constantly drove his superiors, fellow commanders and junior
officers to enraged frustration, partly by repeatedly disobeying
instructions and partly by his paranoid habit of refusing to
divulge his strategies, such as they were, to anyone. One officer
under his command was ordered to withdraw from the town of

Gordonsville, where he was on the brink of a signal victory, and march at the double to Staunton. Arriving in Staunton, he found fresh orders to go at once to Mount Crawford. There he was told to return to Gordonsville.

It was largely because of his habit of marching troops all over the Shenandoah Valley in an illogical and inexplicable fashion that Jackson earned a reputation among bewildered enemy offi-cers for wiliness. His ineradicable fame rests almost entirely on the fact that he had a couple of small victories when other Southern troops were being slaughtered and routed, and by dint of having the best nickname any soldier has ever enjoyed. He was unquestionably brave, but in fact it is altogether possi-ble that he was given that nickname not for gallantry and daring, but for standing inert, like a stone wall, when a charge was called for. General Barnard Bee, who gave him the name at the First Battle of Manassas, was killed before the day was out, so the matter will remain forever unresolvable.

His victory at Harpers Ferry, the greatest triumph for the Confederacy in the Civil War, was almost entirely because for once he followed the instructions of Robert E. Lee. It sealed his fame. A few months later he was accidentally shot by his own troops at the Battle of Chancellorsville, and died eight days later. The war was barely half over. He was just thirty-nine.

Jackson spent much of the war in and around the Blue Ridge Mountains, camping in and marching through the very woods and high gaps through which Katz and I had lately passed, so I was interested to see the scene of his greatest triumph, and followed the path around the undulating field reading the information boards with dutiful attention and peering unsuc-cessfully through the trees for a sign of the new housing development. It was late and the light was going, and anyway, to be perfectly frank, I have never been much good at battle-fields. It was, I suppose, theoretically interesting to know that Captain Poague's battery stood just here and Colonel Grigsby's troops were arrayed in a thin, wavery line over there, but really there is no getting round the fact that today it is just a pleasant grassy field on a West Virginia hill.

I was hungry and had driven a long way, so I didn't have the necessary energy to imagine the noise and smoke and carnage. Besides, I had had enough death for one day. So I tramped back to the car and continued on.

Chapter 14

In the morning, I drove on to Pennsylvania, 30 miles or so to the north. The Appalachian Trail runs for 230 miles in a north-easterly arc across the state, like the broad end of a slice of pie. I never met a hiker with a good word to say about the trail in Pennsylvania. It is, as someone told a *National Geographic* reporter in 1987, the place 'where boots go to die'. During the last ice age it experienced what geologists call a periglacial climate – a zone at the edge of an ice sheet characterized by frequent freeze–thaw cycles that fractured the rock. The result is mile upon mile of jagged, oddly angled slabs of stone strewn about in wobbly piles known to science as *Felsenmeer* (literally, 'sea of rocks'). These require constant attentiveness if you are not to twist an ankle or sprawl on your face – not a pleasant experience with 50 pounds of momentum on your back. Lots of people leave Pennsylvania limping and bruised. Pennsylvania also has what are reputed to be the meanest rattlesnakes any-where along the trail, and the most unreliable water sources, particularly in high summer. The AT in the state passes through no national parks or forests, traverses no notable eminences, offers no particularly memorable vistas, is untouched by history. It is essentially just the central part of a very long, taxing haul between the South and New England. It is little wonder that most people dislike it.

Oh, and it also has the very worst maps ever produced for hikers anywhere. The six sheets – maps is really much too strong a word for them – produced for Pennsylvania by a body called the Keystone Trails Association are small, monochrome, appallingly printed, inadequately keyed, and astoundingly vague – in short, completely useless: comically useless, heart-breakingly useless, dangerously useless. No-one should be sent into a wilderness with maps this bad.

I had this brought home to me with a certain weep-inducing force as I stood in a car park in a place called Caledonia State Park looking at a section of map that was simply a blurred smear of whorls, like a poorly taken thumb print. A single con-tour line was interrupted by a printed number in microscopic type. The number said either 1800 or 1200 – it wasn't possible to tell – but it didn't actually matter because there was no scale indicated anywhere, nothing to denote the height interval from one contour line to the next, or whether the packed bands of lines indicated a steep climb or precipitous descent. Not one single thing – not one single thing – within the entire park and for some miles around was denoted. From where I stood, I could be 50 feet or two miles from the Appalachian Trail, in any direction. There was simply no telling.

Foolishly, I had not looked at these maps before setting off from home. I had packed in a hurry, simply noted that I had the correct set, and stuck them in my pack. I looked through them all now with a sense of dismay, as you might a series of com-promising pictures of a loved one. I had known all along that I was never going to walk across Pennsylvania – I had neither the time nor the spirit for it – but I had thought I might find some nice circular walks that would give me something of the challenging flavour of the state without making me endlessly retrace my steps. It was clear now, looking through the complete set, that not only were there no circular hikes to be had, but it was going to be the next thing to pure luck any time I stumbled on the trail at all.

Sighing, I put the maps away and set off through the park on foot looking for the familiar white blazes of the AT. It was a pleasant park in a wooded valley, quite empty on this fine morning. I walked for perhaps an hour along a network of winding paths through trees and over wooden footbridges, but I failed to find the AT, so I returned to the car, and pushed on, along a lonely highway through the dense flying leaves of Michaux State Forest and on to Pine Grove Furnace State Park, a large recreation area built around a nineteenth-century stone kiln, now a picturesque ruin, from which it takes its name. The park had snack huts, picnic tables and a lake with a swimming area, but all were shut and there wasn't a soul about. On the edge of the picnic area was a big dumpster with a sturdy metal lid that had been severely – arrestingly – mangled and dented, and half wrenched from its hinges, presumably by a bear trying to get at park rubbish. I examined it with the deepest respect; I hadn't realized black bears were quite that strong.

Here at least the AT blazes were prominent. They led around the lake and up through steep woods to the summit of Piney Mountain, which wasn't indicated on the map and isn't really a mountain since it barely rises to 1,500 feet. Still, it was challenging enough on a hot summer's day. Just outside the park there is a board marking the traditional, but entirely notional, midpoint of the Appalachian Trail, with 1,080.2 indicated miles of hiking in either direction. (Since no-one can say exactly how long the AT is, the real midpoint could be anywhere within 50 miles or so; in any case, it would change from year to year because of reroutings.) Two-thirds of thru-hikers never see it anyway, because they have dropped out by this point. It must actually be quite a depressing moment – to have slogged through a mountainous wilderness for ten or eleven weeks and to realize that for all that effort you are still but halfway there.

It was also round here that one of the trail's more notorious murders took place, the one at the heart of the book *Eight Bullets*, which I had bought at ATC headquarters the day before. The story is simply told. In May 1988, two young hikers, Rebecca Wight and Claudia Brenner, who were lesbians, excited the attention of a disturbed young man with a rifle, who shot them eight times from a distance as they made love in a leafy clearing beside the trail. Wight was killed. Brenner, seriously wounded, managed to stumble down the mountain to a road and was rescued by some passing teenagers in a pickup truck. The murderer was swiftly caught and convicted.

The next year a young man and woman were killed by a drifter at a shelter just a few miles to the north, which rather gave Pennsylvania a bad reputation for a while, but then there were no murders anywhere along the AT for seven years until the recent deaths of the two young women in Shenandoah National Park. Their deaths brought the official murder toll to nine – quite a large number for any footpath, no matter how you look at it – though in fact there probably have been more. Between 1946 and 1950 three people vanished while hiking through one small area of Vermont, but they aren't included in the tally; whether because it happened so long ago or because it was never conclusively proved they were murdered I couldn't say. I was also told by an acquaintance in New England of an older couple who were killed by a deranged axe murderer in Maine sometime in the 1970s, but again it doesn't appear in any records because, evidently, they were on a side trail when they were attacked.

I had read *Eight Bullets*, Brenner's account of the murder of her friend, overnight, so I was generally acquainted with the circumstances, but I intentionally left the book in the car as it seemed a little morbid to go looking for a death site nearly a decade after the event. I wasn't remotely spooked by the murder, but even so I felt a vague, low-grade unease at being alone in a silent wood so far from home. I missed Katz, missed his puffing and bitching and unflappable fearlessness, hated the thought that if I sat on a rock waiting he would never come. The woods were in full chlorophyll-choked glory now, which made them seem even more pressing and secretive. Often, I couldn't see five feet into the dense foliage on either side of the path. If I did happen on a bear, I would be quite helpless. No Katz would come along after a minute to smack it on the snout for me and say, 'Jesus, Bryson, you cause me a lot of trouble.' No-one at all would come to share the excitement, it appeared. There didn't seem to be another person within 50 miles. The woods belonged to me and whatever else was out there.

So I walked the 3.5 miles to the top of Piney Mountain with a certain purposeful briskness. At the summit, I stood uncertainly, unable to decide whether to go on a bit further or turn back and perhaps try somewhere else, when there was a dry crack of wood and a careless rustle of undergrowth perhaps 50 feet into the woods – something good-sized and unseen. I stopped everything – moving, breathing, thinking – and stood on tiptoe peering into the leafy void. The noise came again, nearer. Whatever it was, it was coming my way! Whimpering quietly but sincerely, I ran a hundred yards, daypack bouncing wildly, glasses jiggling, then turned, heart stopped, and looked back. A deer, resplendently antlered, stepped onto the path, gazed at me for a moment without concern, and sauntered on. I took a long moment to catch my breath and wiped a river of sweat from my brow. I wasn't sure I was cut out for this sort of thing. I returned to the car without further incident.

I stopped the night near Harrisburg, and in the morning drove north and east across the state on back highways, trying to follow the trail as closely as I could by road, and stopping once or twice where possible to sample the trail, but without finding anything that looked remotely rewarding, so mostly I drove. Pennsylvania is not an easy place to characterize, partly because it is big and populous – 400 miles across from east to west; twelve million inhabitants – and partly because it is such a peculiar, patternless mix of ugly, half-dead factory towns, sweet little college communities, rolling farmland, and industrially scarred hillsides – a place equally at home to Rocky Balboa, Dwight Eisenhower, Andrew Carnegie and an Amish farmer. In the space of five miles it can go from hideous to gorgeous to hideous to more hideous to gorgeous again. I know a man who bought an old farmhouse in a remote, storybook vale as a weekend home. He awoke one Sunday to explosive booms and the tinkle of ceiling plaster and discovered that a gravel company was quarrying right up to his property line. He sold the house at a staggering loss, bought another, even more remote property, and awoke there to the sound of a phalanx of bull- dozers preparing the farmland next door for a giant polypropylene plant. So he moved to Virginia. But that's Pennsylvania for you.

I passed through a long tight valley, enclosed by dark hills. Every farm on both sides of the road grew Christmas trees – endless, genetically identical rows of them that presented an infinite variety of straight lines from whatever angle you viewed them. At the end of each drive there was a mailbox with a name neatly lettered on the side, and every name without exception sounded comical and made up – Pritz, Putz, Mootz, Snootz, Schlepple, Klutz, Kuntz, Kunkle – and the scattered towns were just the same but for the addition of a place suffix: Funksville, Crumsville, Kutztown. Then, little by little, the town names began to take on a frank industrial tone – Port Carbon, Minersville, Lehigh Furnace, Slatedale – and I realized I was entering the strange, half-forgotten world of Pennsylvania's Anthracite Region. At Minersville, I turned onto a back highway and headed through a landscape of overgrown slag heaps and rusting machinery towards Centralia, the strangest, saddest town I believe I have ever seen.

Eastern Pennsylvania sits on one of the richest coalbeds on Earth. Almost from the moment Europeans arrived, they realized there was coal out there in quantities almost beyond conception. The trouble was it was virtually all anthracite, a coal so immensely hard – it is 95 per cent carbon – that for a very long time no-one could figure out how to get it to light. It wasn't until 1828 that an enterprising Scot named James Neilson had the simple but effective idea of injecting heated air rather than cold air into an iron furnace by means of a bellows. The process became known as a hot blast and it transformed the coal industry all over the world (Wales, too, had a lot of anthracite), but especially in the United States. By the end of the century America was producing 300 million tons of coal a year, about as much as the rest of the world put together, and the great bulk of it came from Pennsylvania's anthracite belt.

Meanwhile, to its intense gratification, Pennsylvania had also discovered oil – not only discovered it, but devised ways to make it industrially useful. Petroleum – or rock oil – had been a curiosity of western Pennsylvania for years. It emerged in seeps along riverbanks where it was blotted up with blankets to be made into patent medicines esteemed for their value to cure everything from scrofula to diarrhoea. In 1859, a mysterious figure named Colonel Edwin Drake – who wasn't a colonel at all but a retired railway conductor, with no understanding of geology – developed, from goodness knows where, the belief that oil could be extracted from the ground via wells. At Titusville, he bored a hole to a depth of 69 feet and got the world's first gusher. Quickly it was realized that petroleum in volume could be not just used to bind bowels and banish scabby growths, but refined into lucrative products like paraffin and kerosene. Western Pennsylvania boomed inordinately. In three months, as John McPhee notes in *In Suspect Terrain*, the endearingly named Pithole City went from a population of zero to 15,000, and other towns throughout the region sprang up – Oil City, Petroleum Center, Red Hot. John Wilkes Booth came and lost his savings, then went off to kill a president, but others stayed and made a fortune.

For one lively half-century Pennsylvania had a virtual monopoly on one of the most valuable products in the world, oil, and an overwhelmingly dominant role in the production of a second, coal. Because of the proximity of rich supplies of fuel the state became the centre of big, fuel-intensive industries like steelmaking and chemicals. Lots of people became colossally rich.

But not the mineworkers. Mining has of course always been a wretched line of work everywhere, but nowhere more so than in the United States in the second half of the nineteenth century. Thanks to immigration, miners were infinitely expendable. When the Welsh got bolshie, you brought in Irish. When they failed to satisfy, you brought in Italians or Poles or Hungarians. Workers were paid by the ton, which meant not only that they were given an incentive to hack out coal with reckless haste, but also that any labour they expended making their environment safer or more comfortable went uncompensated. Mine shafts were bored through the earth like holes through Swiss cheese, often destabilizing whole valleys. In 1846, at Carbondale, almost 50 acres of mine shafts collapsed simultaneously without warning, claiming hundreds of lives. Explosions and flash fires were common. Mine dust is incredibly volatile – and most of this at a time, remember, when the only illumination was open flames. Between 1870 and the outbreak of the First World War, 50,000 people died in American mines.

The great irony of anthracite is that, tough as it is to light, once you get it lit it's nearly impossible to put out. Stories of uncontrolled mine fires are legion in eastern Pennsylvania. One fire at Lehigh began in 1850 and didn't burn itself out until the Great Depression – eighty years after it started.

And thus we come to Centralia. For a century Centralia was a sturdy little pit community. However difficult life may have been for the early miners, by the second half of the twentieth century Centralia was a reasonably prosperous, snug, hard-working town with a population approaching 2,000. It had a thriving business district with banks and a post office and the normal range of shops and small department stores, a high school, four churches, an Odd Fellows Club, a town hall – in short, a typical, pleasant, contentedly anonymous small American town.

Unfortunately, it also sat on 24 million tons of anthracite. In 1962, a fire in a tip on the edge of town ignited a coal seam. The fire department poured thousands of gallons of water onto the fire, but each time they seemed to have it extinguished it came back, like those trick birthday candles that go out for a moment and then spontaneously reignite. And then, very slowly, the fire began to eat its way along the subterranean seams. Smoke began to rise eerily from the ground over a wide area, like steam off a lake at dawn. On Highway 61, the asphalt grew warm to the touch, then began to crack and settle, rendering the road unusable. The smoking zone passed under the highway and fanned out through a neighbouring woodland and up towards St Ignatius Catholic Church on a knoll above the town.

The US Bureau of Mines brought in experts, who proposed any number of possible remedies – digging a deep trench through the town, deflecting the course of the fire with ex-plosives, flushing the whole thing out hydraulically – but the cheapest proposal would have cost at least $20 million with no guarantee that it would work, and in any case no-one was empowered to spend that kind of money. So the fire slowly burned on.

In 1979, the owner of a petrol station near the centre of town found that the temperature in his underground tanks was registering 172°F. Sensors sunk into the earth showed that the temperature 13 feet under the tanks was almost 1,000 degrees. Elsewhere people were discovering that their cellar walls and floor were hot to the touch. Smoke by now was seeping from the ground all over town, and people were beginning to grow nauseated and faint from the increased levels of carbon dioxide in their homes. In 1981, a twelve-year-old boy was playing in his grandmother's back garden when a plume of smoke suddenly appeared in front of him. As he stared at it, the ground opened around him. He clung to tree roots until someone heard his calls and hauled him out. The hole was found to be 80 feet deep. Within days, similar cave-ins were appearing all over town. It was about then that people started getting serious about the fire.

The federal government came up with $42 million to evacuate the town. As people moved out, their houses were bulldozed and the rubble was neatly, fastidiously, cleared away until there were almost no buildings remaining. So today Centralia isn't really even a ghost town. It's just a big open space with a grid of empty streets still surreally furnished with stop signs and fire hydrants. Every 30 feet or so there is a neat, paved driveway going 15 or 20 yards to nowhere. There are still a few houses scattered around – all of them modest, narrow, woodframed structures stabilized with brick buttresses – and a couple of buildings in what was once the central business district.

I parked outside a building with a faded sign that said, rather grandly, CENTRALIA MINE FIRE PROJECT OFFICE OF THE COLUMBIA RE-DEVELOPMENT AUTHORITY. The building was boarded and all but falling down. Next door was another, in better shape, called Speed Stop Car Parts, overlooking a neatly groomed park with an American flag on a pole beside a bench. The shop appeared to be still in business, but the interior was darkened and there was no-one around. There was no-one anywhere, come to that – no passing traffic, not a sound but the lazy clank of a metal ring knocking against the flagpole. Here and there in the vacant lots were metal cylinders, like oil drums, that had been fixed in the ground and were silently venting smoke.

Up a slight slope, across an expanse of vacant lots, a modern church, quite large, stood in a lazy pall of white smoke – St Ignatius, I assumed. I walked up. The church looked sound and usable – the windows were not boarded and there were no KEEP OUT signs – but it was locked and there was no board announcing services or anything even to indicate its name or denomination. All around it smoke was hovering wispily off the ground, but just behind it great volumes of smoke were billowing from the earth over a large area. I walked over and found myself on the lip of a vast cauldron, perhaps an acre in extent, which was emitting thick, cloudlike, pure white smoke – the kind of smoke you get from burning tyres or old blankets. It was impossible to tell through the stew of smoke how deep the hole was. The ground felt warm and was loosely covered in a fine ash.

I walked back to the front of the church. A heavy metal crash barrier stood across the old road and a new highway curved off down a hillside away from the town. I stepped round the barrier and walked down old Highway 61. Clumps of weedy grass poked through the surface here and there, but it still looked a serviceable road. All around on both sides for a considerable distance the land smoked broodingly, like the aftermath of a forest fire. About 50 yards along, a jagged crack appeared down the centre of the highway and quickly grew into a severe gash several inches across, emitting still more smoke. In places the road on one side of the gash had subsided a foot or more, or slumped into a shallow, bowl-shaped depression. From time to time I peered into the crack, but couldn't gauge anything of its depth for the swirling smoke, which proved to be disagreeably acrid and sulphurous when the breeze pushed it over me.

I walked along for some minutes, gravely examining the scar as if I were some kind of official inspector of highways before

I spread my gaze more generally and it dawned on me that I was in the middle – very much in the middle – of an extensively smoking landscape, on possibly no more than a skin of asphalt, above a fire that had been burning out of control for thirty-four years – not, I'm bound to say, the smartest place in North America to position oneself. Perhaps it was no more than a literally heated imagination, but the ground suddenly seemed distinctly spongy and resilient, as if I were walking across a mattress. I retreated in haste to the car.

It seemed odd on reflection that I, or any other severely foolish person, could drive in and have a look round a place as patently dangerous and unstable as Centralia, and yet there was nothing to stop anyone from venturing anywhere. What was odder still was that the evacuation of Centralia was not total. Those who wanted to stay and live with the possibility of having their houses fall into the earth were allowed to remain, and a few had evidently so chosen. I got back in the car and drove up to a lone house in the centre of town. The house, painted a pale green, was eerily neat and well maintained. A vase of artificial flowers and other modest decorative knick-knacks stood on a windowsill and there was a bed of marigolds by the freshly painted stoop. But there was no car in the drive and no-one answered the bell.

Several of the other houses proved on closer inspection to be unoccupied. Two were boarded and had DANGER – KEEP OUT notices tacked to them. Five or six others, including a clutch of three on the far side of the central park, were still evidently lived in – one, amazingly, even had children's toys in the garden (who on earth would keep children in a place like this?) – but there was no answer at any of the bells I tried. Everyone was either at work or, for all I knew, lying dead on the kitchen floor. It seemed exceedingly odd that people would be permitted to remain here, but then America is a strange country where personal liberty is concerned. At one house I knocked at I fancied I saw a curtain move, but I couldn't be sure. Who knows how crazy these people might be after three decades of living on top of an inferno and breathing head-lightening quantities of CO_2, or how weary they might have grown of outsiders cheerfully poking around and treating their town as a curious diversion? I was privately relieved that no-one answered my knocks because I couldn't for the life of me think what my opening question would be.

It was well past lunchtime, so I drove the five miles or so to Mount Carmel, the nearest town. Mount Carmel was mildly startling after Centralia – a busy little town, nicely old-fashioned, with traffic on Main Street and sidewalks full of shoppers and other townsfolk going about their business. I had lunch at the Academy Luncheonette and Sporting Goods Store – possibly the only place in America where you can gaze at jockstraps while eating a tuna salad sandwich – and was intending then to push on in search of the AT, but on the way back to the car I passed a public library and impulsively popped in to ask if they had any information on Centralia.

They did – three fat files bulging with newspaper and magazine cuttings, most dating from 1979–81 when Centralia briefly attracted national attention, particularly after the little boy, one Todd Dombowski, was nearly swallowed by the earth in his granny's garden.

There was also, quite poignantly now, a slender, casebound history of Centralia, prepared to mark the town's centenary just before the outbreak of the fire. It was full of photographs showing a bustling town not at all unlike the one that stood just outside the library door, but with the difference of thirty-some years. I had forgotten just how distant the 1960s have grown. All the men in the photograph wore hats; the women and girls were in billowy skirts. All, of course, were happily unaware that their pleasant, anonymous town was quite doomed. It was nearly impossible to connect the busy place in the photographs to the empty space from which I had just come.

As I put the things back in their folders, a cutting fluttered to

the floor. It was an article from *Newsweek*. Someone had under-
lined a short paragraph towards the end of the article and put
three exclamation marks in the margin. It was a quote from a
mine fire authority observing that if the rate of burning held
steady there was enough coal under Centralia to burn for a
thousand years.

It happened that a few miles beyond Centralia there was
another scene of unusual devastation that I had heard about
and was keen to investigate – a mountainside in the Lehigh
Valley that had been so lavishly polluted by a zinc mill that it
had been entirely stripped of vegetation. I had heard about it
from John Connolly, who recalled it as being near Palmerton,
so I drove there the following morning. Palmerton was a good-
sized town, grimy and industrial, but not without its finer points
– a couple of solid turn-of-the-century civic buildings that gave
it an air of consequence, a dignified central square, and a business district that was clearly depressed but gamely clinging to
life. The background was dominated everywhere by big, prison-
like factories all of which appeared to be redundant. At one end
of town, I spotted what I had come to find – a steep, broad eminence, perhaps 1,500 feet high and several miles long, which
was almost entirely naked of vegetation. There was a car park
beside the road, and a factory a hundred yards or so beyond. I
pulled into the car park and got out to gawp – it truly was an
arresting sight.

As I stood there, some fat guy in a uniform stepped out of a
security booth and waddled towards me looking cross and
officious.

'The hell you think you're doing?' he barked.

'Pardon me?' I replied, taken aback, and then: 'I'm looking at
that hill.'

'You can't do that.'

'I can't look at a hill?'

'Not here you can't. This is private property.'

'I'm sorry. I didn't know.'

'Well, it's private – like the sign says.' He indicated a post that was in fact signless and looked momentarily struck. 'Well, it's private,' he added.

'I'm sorry. I didn't know,' I said again, not appreciating yet how keenly this man took his responsibilities. I was still marvelling at the hill. 'That's an amazing sight, isn't it?' I said.

'What is?'

'That mountain. There isn't a scrap of vegetation on it.'

'I wouldn't know. I'm not paid to look at hillsides.'

'Well, you should look sometime. I think you'd be surprised. So is that the zinc factory then?' I said, with a nod at the complex of buildings over his left shoulder.

He regarded me suspiciously. 'What do you want to know for?'

I returned his stare. 'I'm out of zinc,' I replied.

He gave me a sideways look as if to say 'Oh, a wise guy, huh?' and said suddenly, decisively, 'I think maybe I'd better take your name.' With difficulty he extracted a notebook and a stubby pencil from a back pocket.

'What, because I asked you if that was a zinc factory?'

'Because you're trespassing on private property.'

'I didn't know I was trespassing. You don't even have a sign up.'

He had his pencil poised. 'Name?'

'Don't be ridiculous.'

'Sir, you are trespassing on private property. Now are you gonna tell me your name?'

'No.'

We went through a little back and forth along these lines for a minute. At last he shook his head regretfully and said, 'Play it your way then.' He dragged out some communication device, pulled up an antenna and got it to operate. Too late I realized that for all his air of exasperation this was a moment he had dreamed of during many long, uneventful shifts in his little glass booth.

'J.D.?' he said into the receiver. 'Luther here. You got the clamps? I got an infractor in Lot A.'

'What are you doing?'

'I'm impounding your vehicle.'

'Don't be ridiculous. I only pulled off the road for a minute. Look, I'm going, OK?'

I got in the car, started the engine and made to go forward, but he blocked the way. I leaned from the window. 'Excuse me,' I called, but he didn't move. He just stood with his back to me and his arms crossed, conspicuously disregarding me. I tooted the horn lightly, but he was not to be shifted. I put my head out of the window and said, 'All right, I'll tell you my name then.'

'It's too late for that.'

'Oh, for God's sake,' I muttered and then, out of the window, 'Please?' and then, whinily, 'Come on, buddy, *please*?' but he had set a course and was not to be deflected. I leaned out once more. 'Tell me, did they specify "asshole" on the job description, or did you go on a course?' Then I breathed a very bad word and sat and steamed.

Thirty seconds later a car pulled up and a man in sunglasses got out. He was wearing the same uniform, but was ten or fifteen years older and a whole lot trimmer. He had the bearing of a drill sergeant.

'Problem here?' he said, looking from one to the other of us.

'Perhaps you can help me,' I said in a tone of sweet reason. 'I'm looking for the Appalachian Trail. This gentleman here tells me I'm trespassing.'

'He was looking at the *hill*, J.D.,' the fat guy protested a little hotly, but J.D. raised a palm to still him, then turned to me.

'You a hiker?'

'Yes, sir.' I indicated the pack on the back seat. 'I just wanted directions and the next thing I know' – I gave a cheerfully dismayed laugh – 'this man's telling me I'm on private property and he's impounding my car.'

'J.D., the man was looking at the hill and asking questions.'
But J.D. held up another calming hand.

'Where you hiking?'

I told him.

He nodded. 'Well, then you want to go up the road about
four miles to Little Gap and take the right for Danielsville. At the
top of the hill you'll see the trail crossing. You can't miss it.'

'Thank you very much.'

'Not a problem. You have a good hike, you hear.'

I thanked him again and drove off. In the rear-view mirror I
noticed with gratification that he was remonstrating quietly but
firmly with Luther – threatening, I very much hoped, to take his
communication device away.

The route went steeply up to a lonesome pass where there
was a dirt car park. I parked, found the AT and walked along it
on a high exposed ridge through the most amazingly devastated
terrain. For miles it was either entirely barren or covered in the
spindly trunks of dead trees, a few still weakly standing but
most toppled. It brought to mind a First World War battlefield
after heavy shelling. The ground was covered in a gritty black
dust, like iron filings.

The walking was uncommonly easy – the ridge was almost
perfectly flat – and the absence of vegetation meant that there
were boundless views. All the other visible hills, including
those facing me across the narrow valley, looked to be in
good health, except where they had been scarred and gouged
by quarrying or strip mining, which was regularly. I walked
for a little over an hour until I came to a sudden, almost
absurdly steep descent to Lehigh Gap – almost a thousand
feet straight down, or of course straight up for those coming
from the other direction – gave small thanks that I didn't have
to do either and trudged back to the car the way I had
come.

It was almost four o'clock when I got back to the car. The
afternoon was as good as shot. I had driven 350 miles to get to

Pennsylvania, had spent four long days in the state and walked a net 11 miles of the Appalachian Trail. Never again, I vowed, would I try to hike the Appalachian Trail with a car.

Still, I did have the deep and lasting satisfaction of having got a fat guy named Luther in trouble. I have had worse trips.

Chapter 15

Once, aeons ago, the Appalachians were of a scale and majesty to rival the Himalayas – piercing, snow-peaked, pushing breath-takingly through the clouds to heights of four miles or more. New Hampshire's Mount Washington is still an imposing presence, but the stony mass that rises above the New England woods today represents, at most, the stubby bottom one-third of what was ten million years ago.

That the Appalachian Mountains present so much more mod-est an aspect today is because they have had so much time in which to wear away. The Appalachians are immensely old – older than the oceans and continents, far, far older than most other mountain chains. When simple plants colonized the land and the first creatures crawled blinking from the sea, the Appalachians were there. They are, in fact, among the oldest landscape features on Earth.

Something over a billion years ago, the continents of Earth were a single mass called Pangaea surrounded by the lonely

Panthalassan Sea. Then some unexplained turmoil within the earth's mantle caused the land to break apart and drift off as vast asymmetrical chunks. From time to time over the ages since – three times at least – the continents have held a kind of grand reunion, floating back to some central spot and bumping together with slow but crushing force. It was during the third of these collisions, starting about 470 million years ago, that the Appalachians were first pushed up (like a rucked carpet, as the analogy nearly always has it). Four hundred and seventy million years is a mind-dulling number, but if you can imagine flying backwards through time at the rate of one year per second, it would take you about sixteen years to cover such a span. It's a long time.

The continents didn't just move in and out from each other in some kind of grand slow-motion square dance, but spun in lazy circles, changed their orientation, went on cruises to the tropics and poles, made friends with smaller landmasses and brought them home. Florida once belonged to Africa. A corner of Staten Island is, geologically, part of Europe. The seaboard from New England up to Canada appears to have originated in Morocco. Parts of Greenland, Ireland, Scotland and Scandinavia have the same rocks as the eastern United States – are, in effect, ruptured outposts of the Appalachians. There are even suggestions that mountains as far south as the Shackleton Range in Antarctica may be fragments of the Appalachian family.

The Appalachians were formed in three long phases, or orogenies as scientists like to call them, known as the Taconic, Acadian and Alleghenian. The first two were essentially responsible for the northern Appalachians, the third for the central and southern Appalachians. As the continents bumped and nudged, sometimes one continental plate would slide over another, pushing ocean floor before it, reworking the landscape for 150 miles or more inland. At other times it would plunge beneath, stirring up the mantle and resulting in long spells of volcanic activity and earthquakes. Sometimes the collisions would interleave layers of rock like shuffled playing cards.

It is tempting to think of this as some kind of giant continent-sized car crash, but of course it happened with imperceptible slowness. The Proto-Atlantic Ocean (sometimes more romantically called Iapetus), which filled the void between continents during one of the early splits, looks in most textbook illustrations like a transitory puddle – there in Fig. 9A; vanished in Fig. 9B, as if the sun had come out for a day or so and dried it up – yet it existed far longer, hundreds of millions of years longer, than our own Atlantic has. So it was with the formation of mountains. If you were to travel back to one of the mountain-building phases of the Appalachians, you wouldn't be aware of anything geologically grand going on, any more than we are sensible now that India is ploughing into Asia like a runaway truck into a snowbank, pushing the Himalayas up by a milli-metre or so a year.

And as soon as the mountains were built, they began, just as ineluctably, to wear away. For all their seeming permanence, mountains are exceedingly transitory features. In *Meditations at 10,000 Feet*, the writer and geologist James Trefil calculates that a typical mountain stream will carry away about 1,000 cubic feet of mountain in a year mostly in the form of sand granules and other suspended particles. That is equivalent to the capacity of an average-sized dump truck – clearly not much at all. Imagine a dump truck arriving once each year at the base of a moun-tain, filling up with a single load and driving off, not to reappear for another twelve months. At such a rate it seems impossible that it could ever cart away a mountain, but in fact given suffi-cient time that is precisely what would happen. Assuming a mountain 5,000 feet high with 500,000 million cubic feet of mass – roughly the size of Mount Washington – a single stream would level it in about 500 million years.

Of course most mountains have several streams and more-over are exposed to a vast range of other reductive factors, from the infinitesimal acidic secretions of lichen (tiny but relentless) to the grinding scrape of ice sheets, so most mountains vanish very much more quickly – in a couple of hundred million years, say. Right now the Appalachians are shrinking on average by 0.03 millimetres per year. They have gone through this cycle at least twice, possibly more – rising to awesome heights, eroding away to nothingness, rising again, each time recycling their component materials in a dazzlingly confused and complex geology.

The detail of all this is theory, you understand. Very little of it is more than generally agreed upon. Some scientists believe the Appalachians experienced a fourth, earlier mountain-building episode, called the Grenville Orogeny, and that there may have been others earlier still. Likewise Pangaea may have split and re-formed not three times but a dozen times, or perhaps a score of times. On top of all this, there are a number of lapses in the theory, chief of which is that there is little direct evidence of continental collisions, which is odd, even inexplicable, if you accept that at least three continents rubbed together with enormous force for a period of at least 150 million years. There ought to be a suture, a layer of scar tissue, stretching up the eastern seaboard of the United States. There isn't.

I am no geologist, God knows. Show me an unusual piece of greywacke or a handsome chunk of gabbro and I will regard it with respect and listen politely to what you have to say, but it won't actually mean anything to me. If you tell me that once it was seafloor ooze and that through some incredible sustained process it was thrust deep into the earth, baked and squeezed for millions of years, then popped back onto the surface, which is what accounts for its magnificent striations, its vitreous crystals and flaky biotite mica, I will say, 'Goodness!' and 'Is that a fact!' but I can't pretend that anything actual will be going on behind my game expression.

Just occasionally am I permitted an appreciative glimpse into the wonder that is geology, and such a place is the Delaware Water Gap. There, above the serene and stately Delaware River, stands Kittatinny Mountain, a wall of rock 1,300 feet high, consisting of resistant quartzite (or so it says here), that was exposed when the river cut a passage through softer rock on its quiet, steady progress to the sea. The result in effect is a cross-section of mountain, which is not a view you get every day, or indeed anywhere else along the Appalachian Trail that I am aware of, and here it is particularly impressive because the exposed quartzite is arrayed in long, wavery bands that lie at such an improbably canted angle – about 45° – as to suggest to even the dullest imagination that something very big, geologically speaking, happened here.

It is a very fine view. A century or so ago people compared it to the Rhine and even (a little ambitiously, I'm bound to say) the Alps. The artist George Innes came and made a famous painting called *Delaware Water Gap*. It shows the river rolling lazily between meadowy fields dotted with trees and farms, against a distant backdrop of sere hills, notched with a V where the river passes through. It looks like a piece of Yorkshire or Cumbria transplanted to the American continent. In the 1850s, a plush 250-room hotel called Kittatinny House rose on the banks of the river, and was such a success that others soon followed. For a generation after the Civil War, the Delaware Water Gap was the place to be in summer. Then, as is always the way with these things, the White Mountains came into fashion, then Niagara Falls, then the Catskills, then the Disneys. Now almost no-one comes to the Water Gap to stay. People still pass through in large numbers, but they park in a lay-by, have a brief appreciative gaze, then get back in their cars and drive off.

Today, alas, you have to squint, and pretty hard at that, to get any notion of the tranquil beauty that attracted Innes. The Water Gap is not only the nearest thing to spectacle in eastern Pennsylvania, but the only usable breach in the Appalachians in the area of the Poconos. In consequence, its narrow shelf of usable land is packed with state and local roads, a railway line,

and an interstate highway with a long, heartbreakingly uninter-
esting concrete bridge carrying streams of humming trucks and
cars between Pennsylvania and New Jersey – the whole sug-
gesting, as John McPhee neatly put it in *In Suspect Terrain*, 'a
convergence of tubes leading to a patient in intensive care'.

Still, Kittatinny Mountain, towering above the river on the
New Jersey side, is a compelling sight and you can't look at it
– at least I couldn't, at least not this day – without wanting to
climb it and see what is up there. I parked at an information
centre at its base and set off into the welcoming green woods.
It was a gorgeous morning – dewy and cool but with the kind
of sunshine and sluggish air that promises a lot of heat later on
– and I was early enough to be able to get a decent day's walk
in. I was gratified to find that I was really looking forward to
this. I was on the edge of several thousand acres of very pretty
woodlands shared jointly by Worthington State Forest and the
Delaware Water Gap National Recreation Area. The path was
well maintained and just steep enough to feel like healthful
exercise rather than some kind of obsessive torture.

And here was a final, joyful bonus: I had excellent maps. I
was now in the cartographically thoughtful hands of the New
York–New Jersey Trail Conference, whose maps are richly
printed in four colours, with green for woodland, blue for
water, red for trails and black for lettering. They are clearly and
generously labelled and sensibly scaled (1:36,000), and they
include in full all connecting roads and side trails. It is as if they
want you to know where you are and to take pleasure in knowing it.

I can't tell you what a satisfaction it is to be able to say, 'Ah,
Dunnfield Creek, I see,' and, 'So that must be Shawnee Island
down there.' If all the AT maps were anything like as good as
this, I would have enjoyed the experience appreciably more –
say 25 per cent more. It occurred to me now that a great part
of my mindless indifference to my surroundings earlier on was
simply that I didn't know where I was, couldn't know where I

was. Now for once I could take my bearings, perceive my future, feel as if I was somehow in touch with a changing and knowable landscape.

And so I walked five thoroughly agreeable miles up Kittatinny to Sunfish Pond, a very comely 41-acre pond surrounded by woods. Along the way, I encountered just two other people – both day hikers – and I thought again what a stretch it is to suggest that the Appalachian Trail is too crowded. Something like 30 million people live within an hour's drive of the Water Gap – New York is just 45 miles to the east, Philadelphia a little bit more to the south – and it was a flawless summer's day, and the whole of these majestic woods belonged to just three of us.

For northbound hikers Sunfish Pond is something of a glorious novelty, since nowhere south of here will you find a body of water on a mountaintop. It is in fact the first glacial feature northbound hikers come across. During the last ice age, this was about as far as the ice sheets got. The furthest advance in New Jersey was about 10 miles south of the Water Gap, though even here, where the climate would let it go no further, it was still at least 2,000 feet thick.

Imagine that! A wall of ice nearly half a mile high, and beyond it for thousands of square miles nothing but more ice, broken only by the peaks of a very few of the loftiest mountains. What a sight that must have been. And here is the thing. We are still in an ice age, only now we experience it for just part of the year. Snow and ice and cold are not really typical features of Planet Earth. Taking the long view, Antarctica is actually a jungle. (It's just having a chilly spell.) At the very peak of the last ice age 20,000 years ago, 30 per cent of Earth was under ice. Today 10 per cent still is.

There have been at least a dozen ice ages in the last two million years, each lasting in the neighbourhood of 100,000 years. The force of them is quite staggering. The most recent intrusion, called the Wisconsinian ice sheet, spread down from the polar regions over much of Europe and North America, growing to depths of up to two miles and advancing at an estimated rate of 200 to 400 feet a year. As it soaked up the Earth's free water, sea levels fell by 450 feet. Then, about 10,000 years ago, not abruptly exactly but near enough, it began to melt back. No-one knows why. What it left in its wake was a landscape utterly transformed. It dumped Long Island, Cape Cod, Nantucket and most of Martha's Vineyard where previously there had just been sea, and it gouged out the Great Lakes, Hudson Bay, and little Sunfish Pond, among much else. Every foot of the landscape from here on north would be scored and scarred with reminders of glaciation – scattered boulders called erratics, drumlins, eskers, V-shaped valleys, high tarns. I was entering a new world.

No-one knows much of anything about Earth's many ice ages – why they came, why they stopped, when they may return. One interesting theory, given our present-day concerns with global warming, is that the ice ages were caused not by falling temperatures but by rising ones. Warm weather would increase precipitation, which would increase cloud cover, which would lead to less snowmelt at higher elevations. You don't need a great deal of bad weather to get an ice age. As Gwen Schultz notes in *Ice Age Lost*, 'It is not necessarily the amount of snow that causes ice sheets, but the fact that snow, however little, lasts.' In terms of precipitation, she observes, Antarctica 'is the driest large area on Earth, drier overall than any large desert'.

Here's another interesting thought. If glaciers started re-forming, they would have a great deal more water now to draw on – Hudson Bay, the Great Lakes, the hundreds of thousands of lakes of Canada, none of which existed to fuel the last ice sheet – so they would grow much more quickly. And if they did start to advance again, what exactly would we do? Blast them with TNT or maybe nuclear warheads? Well, doubtless we would, but consider this. In 1964, the largest earthquake ever recorded in North America rocked Alaska with 200,000 megatons of concentrated might, the equivalent of 2,000 nuclear bombs. Almost 3,000 miles away in Texas water sloshed out of swimming pools. A street in Anchorage fell 20 feet. The quake devastated 24,000 square miles of wilderness, much of it glaciated. And what effect did all this might have on Alaska's glaciers? None.

Just beyond the pond was a side trail, the Garvey Springs Trail, which descended very steeply to an old paved road along the river, just below a spot called Tocks Island, which would take me in a lazy loop back towards the visitor centre where I had left the car. It was four miles and the day was growing warm, but the road was shaded and quiet – I saw only three cars in an hour or so – and so it was a pleasant stroll, with restful views of the river across overgrown meadows.

By American standards, the Delaware is not a particularly imposing waterway, but it has one almost unique characteristic. It is almost the last significant undammed river in the United States. Now this might seem an inestimable virtue – a river that runs as nature planned it. However, one consequence of its unregulated nature is that the Delaware regularly floods. In 1955 there was a flood that even now is remembered as 'the Big One'. In August of that year – ironically at the height of one of the most severe droughts in decades – two hurricanes hit North Carolina one after the other, disrupting and enlivening weather all up and down the east coast. The first dumped ten inches of rain in two days on the Delaware River Valley. Six days later the valley received ten inches in less than twenty-four hours. At a place called Camp Davis, a holiday complex, forty-six people, mostly women and children, took refuge from the rising flood waters in the camp's main building. As the waters rose, they fled first upstairs and then into the attic, but to no avail. Some time in the night a 30-foot wall of water came roaring through the valley and swept the house away. Amazingly, nine people survived.

Elsewhere, bridges were being brushed aside and riverside towns inundated. Before the day was out, the Delaware River would rise 43 feet. By the time the waters finally receded, 400 people were dead and the whole of the Delaware Valley was devastated.

Into this gooey mess stepped the US Army Corps of Engineers, with a plan to build a dam at Tocks Island, very near where I was walking now. The dam, according to the Corps' plan, would not only tame the river but allow the creation of a new national park, at the heart of which would be a re-creational lake almost 40 miles long. Eight thousand residents were moved out. It was all done very clumsily. One of the people evicted was blind. Several farmers had only parts of their land bought, so that they ended up with farmland but no house or a farmhouse but no land. A woman whose family had farmed the same land since the eighteenth century was carried from her house kicking and bellowing, to the delight of newspaper photographers and film crews.

The thing about the Army Corps of Engineers is that they don't build things very well. A dam across the Missouri River in Nebraska silted up so catastrophically that a noisome blobby ooze began to pour into the town of Niobrara, eventually forcing its permanent abandonment. Then a Corps dam in Idaho failed. Fortunately it was in a thinly populated area and there was some warning. Even so, several small towns were washed away and eleven people lost their lives. But these were relatively small dams. Tocks Dam would have held one of the largest artificial reservoirs in the world, with 40 miles of water behind it. Four substantial cities – Trenton, Camden, Wilmington and Philadelphia – and scores of smaller communities stood downstream. A disaster on the Delaware would truly be a disaster.

And here was the nimble Army Corps of Engineers planning to hold back 250 billion gallons of water with notoriously unstable glacial till. Besides that there were all kinds of environmental worries – that salinity levels below the dam would rise catastrophically, for example, devastating the ecology lower down, not least the valuable oyster beds of Delaware Bay.

In 1992, after years of growing protests that spread far beyond the Delaware Valley, the dam plan was finally put on hold, but by this time whole villages and farms had been bull-dozed. A quiet, remote, very beautiful farming valley that had not changed a great deal in 200 years was lost for ever. 'One beneficial result of the [cancelled] project,' notes the *Appalachian Trail Guide to New York and New Jersey*, 'was that the land acquired by the federal government for the national recreation area has provided the Trail with a protected corridor.'

To tell you the truth I was getting seriously tired of this. I know the Appalachian Trail is supposed to be a wilderness experience and I accept that there are many places where it would be a shame for it to be otherwise, but sometimes, as here, the ATC seems to be positively phobic about human con-tact. Personally, I would have been pleased to be walking now through hamlets and past farms rather than through some silent 'protected corridor'.

Doubtless it is all to do with its historic impulse to tame and exploit the wilderness, but America's attitude to nature is, from all sides, very strange if you ask me. I couldn't help comparing my experience now with an experience I'd had three or four years earlier in Luxemburg when I went hiking with my son for a magazine assignment. Luxemburg is a much more delightful place to hike than you might think. It has lots of woods, but also castles and farms and steepled villages and winding river valleys – the whole, as it were, European package. The foot-paths we followed spent a lot of time in the woods, but also emerged at obliging intervals to take us along sunny back roads and over stiles and through farm fields and hamlets. We were always able at some point each day to call in at a bakery or post office, to hear the tinkle of shop bells and eavesdrop on conversations we couldn't understand. Each night we slept in an inn and ate in a restaurant with other people. We experienced the whole of Luxemburg, not just its trees. It was wonderful, and it was wonderful because the whole charmingly diminutive package was seamlessly and effortlessly integrated.

In America, alas, beauty has become something you drive to, and nature an either/or proposition – either you ruthlessly subjugate it, as at Tocks Dam and a million other places, or you deify it, treat it as something holy and remote, a thing apart, as along the Appalachian Trail. Seldom would it occur to anyone on either side that people and nature could coexist to their mutual benefit – that, say, a more graceful bridge across the Delaware River might actually set off the grandeur around it, or that the AT might be more interesting and rewarding if it wasn't *all* wilderness, if from time to time it purposely took you past grazing cows and tilled fields.

I would have much preferred it if the AT guidebook had said: 'Thanks to the Conference's efforts, farming has been restored to the Delaware River Valley, and the footpath rerouted to incorporate 16 miles of riverside walking because, let's face it, you can get too much of trees sometimes.'

Still, we must look on the bright side. If the Army Corps of Engineers had had its foolish way, I'd have been swimming back to my car now, and I was grateful at least to be spared that.

Anyway, it was time to do some real hiking again.

Chapter 16

In 1983, a man walking in the Berkshire Hills of Massachusetts just off the Appalachian Trail saw – or at least swears he saw – a mountain lion cross his path, which was a little unsettling and even more unexpected since mountain lions hadn't been seen in the northeastern United States since 1903, when the last one was shot in New York State.

Soon, however, sightings were being reported all over New England. A man driving a back road of Vermont saw two cubs playing at the roadside. A pair of hikers saw a mother and two cubs cross a meadow in New Hampshire. Every year there were half a dozen or more reports in similar vein, all by credible witnesses. In the late winter of 1994 a farmer in Vermont was walking across his property, taking some seed to a bird feeder, when he saw what appeared to be three mountain lions about 70 feet away. He stared dumbstruck for a minute or two, for mountain lions are swift, fierce creatures and here were three of them looking at him with calm regard, then he hightailed it to a phone and called a state wildlife biologist. The animals were gone by the time the biologist arrived, but he found some fresh scat, which he dutifully bagged up and despatched to a US Fish and Wildlife Laboratory. The lab report came back that it was indeed the scat of *Felis concolor*, the eastern mountain lion, also variously and respectfully known as the panther, cougar, puma and, especially in New England, catamount.

All this was of some interest to me, for I was hiking in about the same spot as that initial mountain lion sighting. I was back on the trail with a new keenness and a new plan. I was going to hike New England, or at least as much of it as I could knock off till Katz came out in seven weeks to walk with me through Maine's Hundred Mile Wilderness. There were almost 700 miles of gorgeously mountainous Appalachian Trail in New England – about a third of the AT's total trail length – enough to keep me occupied till August. To that end, I had my obliging missus drive me to southwestern Massachusetts and drop me on the trail near Stockbridge for a three-day amble through the Berkshires. Thus it was that I was to be found, on a hot morning in mid-June, labouring sweatily up a steep but modest eminence called Becket Mountain, in a haze of repellent-resistant blackflies, and patting my pocket from time to time to check that my knife was still there.

I didn't really expect to encounter a mountain lion, but only the day before I had read an article in the *Boston Globe* about how western mountain lions – which indubitably are not extinct – had recently taken to stalking and killing hikers and joggers in the California woods, and even the odd poor soul standing at a backyard barbecue in an apron and funny hat. It seemed a kind of omen.

It's not entirely beyond the realm of possibility that mountain lions could have survived undetected in New England. Bobcats – admittedly much smaller creatures – are known to exist in considerable numbers and yet are so shy and furtive that you would never guess their existence. Many forest rangers go whole careers without seeing one. And there is certainly ample room in the eastern woods for large cats to roam undisturbed. Massachusetts alone has 250,000 acres of woodland, 100,000 in the Berkshires. From where I was now, I could, given the will and a more or less infinite supply of noodles, walk all the way to Cape Chidley in northern Quebec, 1,800 miles away on the icy Labrador Sea, and scarcely ever have to leave the cover of trees. Even so, it is unlikely that a large cat could survive in sufficient numbers to breed not just in one area but evidently all over New England and escape notice for nine decades. Still, there was that scat. Whatever it was out there, it shat like a mountain lion.

The most plausible explanation was that any lions out there – if lions they were – were released pets, bought in haste and later regretted. It would be just my luck, of course, to be savaged by an animal with a flea collar and a medical history. I imagined lying on my back, being ravaged, reading a dangling silver tag that said: 'My name is Mr Bojangles. If found please call Tanya and Gus at 924-4667.'

Like most large animals, and a good many small ones, the eastern mountain lion was wiped out because it was deemed to be a nuisance. Until the 1940s, many eastern states had well-publicized 'varmint campaigns', often run by state conservation departments, that awarded points to hunters for every predatory creature they killed, which was just about every creature there was – hawks, owls, kingfishers, eagles, and virtually any type of large mammal. West Virginia gave an annual college scholarship to the student who killed the most animals; other states freely distributed bounties and other cash rewards. Rationality didn't often come into it. Pennsylvania one year paid out $90,000 in bounties for the killing of 130,000 owls and hawks in order to save the state's farmers a slightly less than whopping $1,875 in estimated livestock losses. (It is not very often, after all, that an owl carries off a cow.)

As late as 1890 New York State paid bounties on 107

mountain lions, but within a decade they were virtually all gone. (The very last wild eastern mountain lion was killed in the Smokies in the 1920s.) The timberwolf and woodland caribou also disappeared from their last Appalachian fastnesses in the first years of this century, and the black bear very nearly followed them. In 1900, the bear population of New Hampshire – now over 3,000 – had fallen to just fifty.

There is still quite a lot of life out there, but it is mostly very small. According to a wildlife census by an ecologist at the University of Illinois named V. E. Shelford, a typical ten-square-mile block of eastern American forest holds almost 300,000 mammals – 220,000 mice and other small rodents, 63,500 squirrels and chipmunks, 470 deer, 30 foxes, and 5 black bears.

The real loser in the eastern forests has been the songbird. One of the most striking losses was the Carolina parakeet, a lovely, innocuous bird whose numbers in the wild were possibly exceeded only by the unbelievably numerous passenger pigeon. (When the first pilgrims came to America there were an estimated nine billion passenger pigeons – more than twice the number of all birds found in America today.) Both were hunted out of existence – the passenger pigeon for pig feed and the simple joy of blasting volumes of birds from the sky with blind ease, the Carolina parakeet because it ate farmers' fruit and had a striking plumage that made a lovely lady's hat. In 1914, the last surviving members of each species died within weeks of each other in captivity.

A similar unhappy fate awaited the delightful Bachman's warbler. Always rare, it was said to have one of the loveliest songs of all birds. For years it escaped detection, but in 1939 two birders, operating independently in different places, co-incidentally saw a Bachman's warbler within two days of each other. Both shot the birds (nice work, boys) and that, it appears, was that for the Bachman's warbler. But there are almost certainly others that disappeared before anyone much noticed. John James Audubon's paintings include three birds – the small-headed flycatcher, the carbonated warbler and the Blue Mountain warbler – that have not been seen by anyone since. The same is true of Townsend's bunting, of which there is one stuffed specimen in the Smithsonian Institution in Washington.

What is certainly known is that between the 1940s and 1980s the populations of migratory songbirds fell by 50 per cent in the eastern US (in large part because of loss of breeding sites and other vital wintering habitat in Latin America), and by some estimates are continuing to fall by 3 per cent or so a year. Seventy per cent of all eastern bird species have seen population declines since the 1960s.

These days the woods are a pretty quiet place.

Late in the afternoon, I stepped from the trees onto what appeared to be a disused logging road. In the centre of the road stood an older guy with a pack and a distinctly bewildered look, as if he had just woken from a trance and found himself unaccountably in this place. He had, I noticed, a haze of black-flies of his own.

'Which way's the trail go, do you suppose?' he asked me. It was an odd question because the trail clearly and obviously continued on the other side. There was a three-foot gap in the trees directly opposite and, in case there was any possible doubt, a white blaze painted on a stout oak.

I swatted the air before my face for the twelve thousandth time that day and nodded at the opening. 'Just there, I'd say.'

'Oh, yes,' he answered. 'Of course.'

We set off into the woods together and chatted a little about where we had come from that day, where we were headed, and so on. He was a thru-hiker – the first I had seen this far north – and like me was making for Dalton. He had a curious puzzled look all the time, and regarded the trees in a peculiar way, running his gaze slowly up and down their lengths over and over again, as if he had never seen anything like them before.

'So what's your name?' I asked him.

'Well, they call me Chicken John.'

'Chicken John!' Chicken John was famous. I was quite excited. Some people on the trail take on an almost mythic status because of their idiosyncrasies. Early in the trip Katz and I kept hearing about a kid who had equipment so high-tech that no-one had ever seen anything like it. One of his possessions was a self-erecting tent. Apparently he would carefully open a stuff sack and it would fly out, like joke snakes from a tin. He also had a satellite navigation system, and goodness knows what else. The trouble was his pack weighed about 95 pounds and he dropped out before he got to Virginia, so we never did see him. Woodrow Murphy, the walking fat man, had achieved this sort of fame the year before. Mary Ellen would doubtless have attracted a measure of it if she had not dropped out. Chicken John had it now – though I couldn't for the life of me recall why. It had been months before, way back in Georgia, that I had first heard of him.

'So why do they call you Chicken John?' I asked.

'You know, I don't honestly know,' he said, as if for some time he had been wondering that himself.

'When did you start your hike?'

'January the twenty-seventh.'

'January the twenty-seventh?' I said in small astonishment and did a quick private calculation on my fingers. 'That's almost five months.'

'Don't I know it,' he said with a kind of happy ruefulness.

He had been walking for the better part of half a year and he was still only three-quarters of the way to Katahdin.

'What kind of' – I didn't know quite how to put this – 'what kind of miles are you doing, John?'

'Oh, 'bout fourteen or fifteen if all goes well. Trouble is' – he slid me a sheepish look – 'I get lost a lot.'

That was it. Chicken John was forever losing the trail and ending up in the most improbable places. Goodness knows how anyone could manage to lose the Appalachian Trail. It is the most clearly defined, well-blazed footpath imaginable. Usually it is the only thing in the woods that isn't woods. If you can distinguish between trees and a long open corridor through the trees you will have no trouble finding your way along the AT. Where there might be any doubt at all – where a side trail enters or where the AT crosses a road – there are always blazes. Yet people do get lost. The famous Grandma Gatewood, for instance, was forever knocking on doors and asking where the heck she was.

I asked him what was the most lost he had ever been.

'Thirty-seven miles,' he said almost proudly, or if not proudly then fondly. 'I got off the trail on Blood Mountain in Georgia – still don't know how exactly – and spent three days in the woods before I came to a highway. I thought I was a goner that time. I ended up in Tallulah Falls, and even got my picture in the paper. Police gave me a ride back to the trail the next day, and pointed me the right way. They were real nice.'

'Is it true you once walked three days in the wrong direction?'

He nodded happily. 'Two and a half days to be precise. Luckily, I came to a town on the third day, and I said to a feller, "Excuse me, young feller, where is this?" and he said, "Why, it's Damascus, Virginia, sir," and I thought, well, that's mighty strange because I was in a place with the very same name just three days ago. And then I recognized the fire station.'

'How on earth do you—' I decided to rephrase the question. 'How does it happen, John, exactly?'

'Well, if I knew that I wouldn't do it, I suppose,' he said with a kind of chuckle. 'All I know is that from time to time I end up a long way from where I want to be. But it makes life interesting, you know. I've met a lot of nice people, had a *lot* of free meals. Excuse me,' he said abruptly, 'you sure we're going the right way?'

'Positive.'

He nodded. 'I'd hate to get lost today. There's a restaurant in Dalton.' I understood this perfectly. If you're going to get lost, you don't want to do it on a restaurant day.

We walked the last six miles together, but we didn't talk much after that. I was doing a 19-mile day, the longest I would do anywhere on the trail, and even though the grade was generally easy and I was carrying a light pack, I was real tired by late afternoon. John seemed content to have someone to follow, and in any case had his hands full scrutinizing the trees.

It was after six when we reached Dalton. John had the name of a man on Depot Street who let hikers camp in his back garden and use his shower, so I went with him to a gas station while he asked directions. When we emerged he started off in precisely the wrong direction.

'It's that way, John,' I said.

'Of course it is,' he agreed. 'And the name's Bernard, by the way. I don't know where they got that Chicken John from.'

I nodded and told him I would look for him the next day, but I never did see him again.

I spent the night in a motel, and the next day hiked on to Cheshire. It was only nine miles over easy terrain, but the black-fly made it a torment. I have never seen a scientific name for these tiny, vile, winged specks, so I don't know what they are other than a hovering mass that goes with you wherever you go and are forever in your ears and mouth and nostrils. Human sweat transports them to a realm of orgasmic ecstasy, and insect repellent only seems to excite them further. They are particularly relentless when you stop to rest or take a drink – so relentless that eventually you don't stop to rest and you drink while moving, and then spit out a tongueful of them. It's a kind of living hell. So it was with some relief that I stepped from their woodland domain in early afternoon and strolled into the sunny, dozing straggle that was the little community of Cheshire.

Cheshire had a free hostel for hikers in a church on the main street – Massachusetts people do a lot for hikers, it seems; elsewhere I had seen houses with signs inviting people to help themselves to water or pick apples from trees – but I didn't fancy a night in a bunkhouse, still less a long afternoon sitting around with nothing to do, so I pushed on to Adams, four miles away up a baking highway, but with at least the prospect of a night in a motel and a choice of restaurants.

Adams had just one motel, a dumpy place on the edge of town. I took a room and passed the rest of the afternoon strolling around, idly looking in store windows and browsing through boxes of books in a thrift shop, though of course there was nothing but Reader's Digest volumes and those strange books you only ever see in thrift shops with titles like *Home Drainage Encyclopedia: Volume One* and *Nod If You Can Hear Me: Living with a Human Vegetable*, and afterwards wandered out into the country to look at Mount Greylock, my destination for the next day. Greylock is the highest eminence in Massachusetts, and the first hill over 3,000 feet since Virginia for northbound hikers. It's just 3,491 feet to the top, but, surrounded as it is by much smaller hills, it looks considerably bigger. It has in any case a certain imposing majesty that beckons. I was looking forward to it.

And so early the next morning, before the day's heat had a chance to get properly under way – and a scorcher was forecast – I stopped in town for a can of pop and a sandwich for my lunch, and set off on a wandering dirt road towards the Gould Trail, a side trail leading steeply up to the AT and on to Greylock.

Greylock is certainly the most literary of Appalachian mountains. Herman Melville, living on a farm called Arrowhead on its western side, stared at it from his study window while he wrote *Moby-Dick,* and, according to Maggie Stier and Ron McAdow in their excellent *Into the Mountains,* a history of New England's peaks, claimed that its profile reminded him of a whale. When the book was finished, he and a group of friends hiked to the top and partied there till dawn. Nathaniel Hawthorne and Edith

Wharton also lived nearby and set works there, and there was scarcely a literary figure associated with New England from the 1850s to 1920s who didn't at some time hike or ride up to admire the view.

Ironically, at the height of its fame, Greylock lacked much of the green-cloaked majesty it enjoys today. Its sides were mangy with the scars of logging, and the lower slopes gouged with holes for slate and marble quarries. Big, ramshackle sheds and sawhouses poked into every view. All that healed and grew over, and then in the 1960s, with the enthusiastic support of state officials in Boston, plans were drawn up to turn Greylock into a ski resort, with an aerial tram, a network of chairlifts, and a summit complex consisting of a hotel, shops and restaurants – all in 1960s Jetsons-style architecture – but luckily nothing ever came of it. Today Greylock sits on 11,600 acres of preserved land. It's a beauty.

The hike to the top was steep, hot, and seemingly endless, but worth the effort. The open, sunny, fresh-aired summit of Greylock is crowned with a large, handsome stone building called Bascom Lodge, built in the 1930s by the tireless and ubiquitous cadres of the Civilian Conservation Corps. It now offers overnight accommodation to hikers and a restaurant. Also on the summit is a wonderful, wildly incongruous lighthouse (Greylock is 140 miles from the sea), which serves as the Massachusetts memorial for soldiers killed in the First World War. It was originally planned to stand in Boston Harbor, but for some reason ended up here.

I ate my lunch, treated myself to a wee and a wash in the lodge, and then hurried on, for I still had eight miles to go and I had a rendezvous arranged with my wife at four in Williamstown. For the next three miles, the walk was mostly along a lofty ridgeline connecting Greylock to Mount Williams. The views were sensational, across lazy hills to the Adirondacks half a dozen miles to the west, but really hot. Even up here the air was heavy and listless. And then it was a very steep descent

– 3,000 feet in three miles – through dense, cool woods to a back road that led through exquisitely pretty open countryside.

Out of the woods it was sweltering. It was two miles along a road totally without shade and so hot I could feel the heat through the soles of my boots. When at last I reached Williamstown a sign on a bank announced a temperature of 97°. No wonder I was hot. I crossed the street and stepped into a Burger King, our agreed rendezvous. If there is a greater reason for being grateful to live in the twentieth century than the joy of stepping from the dog's breath air of a really hot summer's day into the crisp, clean, surgical chill of an air-conditioned establishment, then I can't think of it.

I bought a bucket-sized Coke and sat in a booth by the window, feeling very pleased. I had done 17 miles over a reasonably challenging mountain in hot weather. I was grubby, sweatstreaked, comprehensively knackered and rank enough to turn heads. I was a walker again.

In 1850, New England was 70 per cent open farmland and 30 per cent woods. Today the proportions are exactly reversed. Probably no area in the developed world has undergone a more profound change in just a century or so, at least not in a contrary direction to the normal course of progress.

If you were going to be a farmer, you could hardly choose a worse place than New England. (Well, the middle of Lake Erie maybe, but you know what I mean.) The soil is rocky, the terrain steep, and the weather so bad that people take actual pride in it. A year in Vermont, according to an old saw, is 'nine months of winter followed by three months of very poor sledding'.

But until the middle of the nineteenth century farmers survived in New England because they had proximity to the coastal cities like Boston and Portland and because, I suppose, they didn't know any better. Then two things happened: the invention of the McCormick reaper, which was ideally suited to the big, rolling farms of the Middle West but no good at all for the cramped, stony fields of New England, and the development of the railroads, which allowed the Midwestern farmers to get their produce to the East in a timely fashion. The New England farmers couldn't compete, and so they became Midwestern farmers, too. By 1860, nearly half of Vermont-born people – 200,000 out of 450,000 – were living elsewhere.

In 1840, during the presidential election campaign, Daniel Webster gave an address to 20,000 people on Stratton Mountain in Vermont. Had he tried the same thing twenty years later (which admittedly would have been a good trick as he had died in the meantime) he would have been lucky to get an audience of fifty.

Today Stratton Mountain is pretty much all forest, though if you look carefully you can still see old cellar holes and the straggly remnants of apple orchards clinging glumly to life in the shady understorey beneath younger, more assertive birches, maples and hickories. Everywhere throughout New England you find old, tumbledown field walls, often in the middle of the deepest, most settled-looking woods – a reminder of just how swiftly nature reclaims the land in America.

And so I walked up Stratton Mountain on an overcast, mercifully cool June day. It was four steep miles to the summit at just under 4,000 feet. For a little over a hundred miles through Vermont the AT coexists with the Long Trail, which threads its way up and over the biggest and most famous peaks of the Green Mountains all the way to Canada. The Long Trail is actually older than the AT – it was opened in 1921, the year the AT was proposed – and I'm told that there are Long Trail devotees even yet who look down on the AT as a rather vulgar and over-ambitious upstart. In any case, Stratton Mountain is usually cited as the spiritual birthplace of both trails, for it was here that James P. Taylor and Benton MacKaye claimed to have received the inspiration that led to the creation of their wilderness ways – Taylor in 1909, MacKaye sometime afterwards.

Stratton was a perfectly fine mountain, with good views across to several other well-known peaks – Equinox, Ascutney, Snow and Monadnock – but I couldn't say that it was a summit that would have inspired me to grab a hatchet and start clearing a route to Georgia or Quebec. Perhaps it was just the dull, heavy skies and bleak light, which gave everything a flat, washed-out feel. Eight or nine other people were scattered around the summit, but there was one youngish, rather podgy man on his own in a very new and expensive-looking windcheater. He had some kind of hand-held electronic device with which he was taking mysterious readings of the sky or landscape.

He noticed me watching and said, in a tone that suggested he was hoping someone would take an interest, 'It's an Enviro Monitor.'

'Oh, yes?' I responded politely.

'Measures eighty values – temperature, UV index, dew point, you name it.' He tilted the screen so I could see it. 'That's heat stress.' It was some meaningless number that ended in two decimal places. 'It does solar radiation,' he went on, 'barometric pressure, wind chill, rainfall, humidity – ambient and active – even estimated burn time adjusted for skin type.'

'Does it bake cookies?' I asked.

He didn't like this. 'There are times when it could save your life, believe me,' he said, a little stoutly. I tried to imagine a situation in which I might find myself dangerously imperilled by a rising dew point, and could not. But I didn't want to upset the man, so I said: 'What's that?' and pointed at a blinking figure in the upper left-hand corner of the screen.

'Ah, I'm not sure what that is. But this' – he stabbed the console of buttons – 'now this is solar radiation.' It was another meaningless figure, to three decimal places. 'It's very low today,' he said and angled the machine to take another reading. 'Yeah, very low today.' Somehow I knew this already. In fact, although I couldn't attest any of it to three decimal places, I had a pretty good notion of the weather conditions generally, on account of I was out in them. The interesting thing about the man was that he had no pack, and so no waterproofs, and was wearing shorts and trainers. If the weather did swiftly deteriorate, and in New England it most assuredly can, he would probably die, but at least he had a machine that would tell him when and let him know his final dew point.

Call me a tiresome old fogey, but I hate all this technology on the trail. Some AT hikers, I had read, now carry laptop computers and modems, so that they can file daily reports to their family and friends. (If you are considering doing this yourself, here's a tip. Nobody cares that much. I'm sorry, that's not true. Nobody cares at all.) And now increasingly you find people with electronic gizmos like the Enviro Monitor or wearing sensors attached by wires to their pulse points so that they look as if they've come to the trail straight from some sleep clinic.

In 1996 the *Wall Street Journal* ran a splendid article on the nuisance of satellite navigation devices, cellphones and other such appliances in the wilderness. All this high-tech equipment, it appears, is drawing up into the mountains people who perhaps shouldn't be there. At Baxter State Park in Maine, the *Journal* reported, one hiker called up a National Guard Unit and asked them to send a helicopter to airlift him off Mount Katahdin because he was tired. On Mount Washington, meanwhile, 'two very demanding women', according to an official there, called the mountain patrol HQ and said they couldn't manage the last mile and a half to the summit even though there were still four hours of daylight left. They asked for a rescue team to come and carry them back to their car. The request was refused. A few minutes later, they called again and demanded in that case that a rescue team bring them some torches. That request was refused also. A few days later, another hiker called and requested a helicopter because he was a day behind schedule and was afraid he would miss an important business meeting. The article also described several people who had got lost with satellite navigation devices. They were able to report their positions as 36.2° north by 17.48° west or whatever, but unfortunately didn't have the faintest idea what that meant as they hadn't brought maps or compasses or, evidently, brains.

My new friend on Stratton, I believe, could have joined their club. I asked him whether he felt it was safe for me to make a descent with solar radiation showing 18.574.

'Oh, yeah,' he said quite earnestly. 'Solar radiationwise, today is very low risk.'

'Thank goodness,' I said, quite earnestly, too, and took my leave of him and the mountain.

And so I proceeded across Vermont, in a series of pleasant day hikes, without anything electronic but with some very nice packed lunches that my wife made for me each night before retiring and left in precisely the same spot on the top shelf in the fridge. Each morning I would rise at dawn, put my lunch in my pack, and drive off to Vermont. I would park the car and walk up a big mountain or across a series of rolling green hills.

At some point in the day when it pleased me, usually about 11 a.m., I would sit on a rock or a log, take out my packed lunch and examine the contents. I would go, as appropriate, 'Peanut butter cookies – my favourite!' or, 'Oh, hum, luncheon meat again,' and eat in a zestful chewy silence, thinking of all the mountaintops I had sat on with Katz where we would have killed for this. Then I would pack up everything very neatly, drop it in my pack and hike again till it was time to clock off and go home. And so passed late June and the first part of July.

I did Stratton Mountain and Bromley Mountain, Prospect Rock and Spruce Peak, Baker Peak and Griffith Lake, White Rocks Mountain, Button Hill, Killington Peak, Gifford Woods State Park, Quimby Mountain, Thistle Hill and finally concluded with a gentle 11-mile amble from West Hartford to Norwich. This took me past Happy Hill Cabin, the oldest shelter on the AT and possibly the most sweetly picturesque – it was torn down soon after by some foolishly unsentimental trail officials. The town of Norwich is notable for three things: for being pronounced 'Nor-witch' (it used to be 'Norritch' before it got taken over by outsiders in the 1950s), for being the town that inspired the Bob Newhart Show on television (the one where he ran an inn and all the locals were charmingly imbecilic) and for being the home of the great Alden Partridge, of whom no-one has ever heard, though of course you are about to.

Partridge was born in Norwich in 1755 and was a demon walker – possibly the first person on the whole planet who walked long distances for the pleasure of it. In 1785, he became superintendent of West Point at the unprecedentedly youthful age of thirty, then had some kind of falling out there, moved back to Norwich and set up a rival institution, the American Literary, Scientific and Military Academy. There he coined the term 'physical education' and took his appalled young charges on brisk rambles of 35 or 40 miles over the neighbouring mountains. In between times he went off on more ambitious hikes of his own. On a typical trip he strode 110 miles over the mountains from Norwich to Williamstown, Massachusetts – essentially the route I had just completed in gentle stages – trotted up Mount Greylock and came back home the same way. The trip there and back took him just four days – and this at a time, remember, when there were no maintained footpaths or helpful blazes. He did this sort of thing with virtually every peak in New England. There ought to be a plaque to him somewhere in Norwich to inspire the few hardy hikers still heading north at this point, but sadly there is none.

From Norwich, it is about a mile to the Connecticut River and a pleasant, unassuming 1930s bridge leading to the state of New Hampshire and the town of Hanover on the opposite bank. Once the road that led from Norwich to Hanover was a leafy, gently sinuous two-lane affair – the sort of tranquil, alluring byway you would hope to find connecting two old New

England towns a mile apart. Then some highway official or other decided that what would be a really good idea would be to build a big, fast road between the two towns. That way people could drive the one mile from Norwich to Hanover perhaps as much as eight seconds faster and not have to suffer paroxysms of anguish if somebody ahead wanted to turn onto a side road because now there would be turning lanes everywhere – turning lanes big enough for a truck pulling a titan missile to manoeuvre through without rolling over a kerb or disrupting the vital flow of traffic.

So they built a broad, straight highway, six lanes wide in places, with concrete dividers down the middle and outsized sodium street lamps that light the night sky for miles around. Unfortunately, this had the effect of making the bridge into a bottleneck where the road narrowed back to two lanes. Sometimes two cars would arrive simultaneously at the bridge and one of them would have to give way – well, imagine! – so, as I write, they are replacing that uselessly attractive old bridge with something much grander and in keeping with the Age of Concrete. For good measure they are widening the street that leads up a short hill to the centre of Hanover. Of course, that means chopping down trees all along the street and drastically foreshortening most of the front gardens with concrete retaining walls, and even a highway official would have to admit that the result is not exactly a picture, not something you would want to put on a calendar called 'Beautiful New England', but it will shave a further four seconds off that daunting trek from Norwich, and that's the main thing.

All this is of some significance to me partly because I live in Hanover, but mostly, I believe, because I live in the late twentieth century. Luckily I have a good imagination, so as I strode from Norwich to Hanover I imagined not a lively mini-expressway, but a country lane shaded with trees, bounded with hedges and wild flowers, and graced with a stately line of modestly scaled lamp-posts, from each of which was suspended, upside down, a highway official, and I felt much better.

Chapter 17

Of all the catastrophic fates that can befall you in the out of doors, perhaps none is more eerily unpredictable than hypothermia. There is scarcely an instance of hypothermic death that isn't in some measure mysterious and improbable. Consider a small story related by David Quammen in his book *Natural Acts.*

   In the late summer of 1982, four youths and two men were on a canoeing holiday in Banff National Park when they failed to return to their base camp at the end of the day. The next morning a search party went out looking for them. They found the missing canoeists floating dead in their lifejackets in a lake. All were face-up and composed. Nothing about them indicated distress or panic. One of the men was still wearing his hat and glasses. Their canoes, drifting nearby, were sound, and the weather overnight had been calm and mild. For some unknowable reason, the six had carefully left their canoes and lowered themselves fully dressed into the cold water of the lake, where they had peacefully perished. In the words of one witness it was 'like they had just gone to sleep'. In a sense they had.

Popular impressions to the contrary, relatively few victims of hypothermia die in extreme conditions, stumbling through blizzards or fighting the bite of arctic winds. To begin with, relatively few people go out in that kind of weather and those that do are generally prepared. Most victims of hypothermia die in a much more dopey kind of way, in temperate seasons and with the air temperature nowhere near freezing. Typically, they are caught by an unforeseen change of conditions or combination of changes – a sudden drop in temperature, a cold pelting rain, the realization that they are lost – for which they are emotionally or physically under-equipped. Nearly always they compound the problem by doing something foolhardy – leaving a well-marked path in search of a short cut, blundering deeper into the woods when they would have been better off staying put, fording streams that only get them wetter and colder.

Such was the unfortunate fate of Richard Salinas. In 1990 Salinas went hiking with a friend in Pisgah National Forest in North Carolina. Caught by fading light, they headed back to their car, but somehow became separated. Salinas was an experienced hiker and all he had to do was follow a well-defined trail down a mountain to a car park. He never made it. Three days later, his jacket and knapsack were found abandoned on the ground miles into the woods. His body was discovered two months later snagged on branches in the little Linville River. As far as anyone can surmise, he had left the trail in search of a short cut, got lost, plunged deep into the woods, panicked and plunged deeper still, until at last hypothermia fatally robbed him of his senses. Hypothermia is a gradual and insidious sort of trauma. It overtakes you literally by degrees as your body temperature falls and your natural responses grow sluggish and disordered. In such a state, Salinas had abandoned his possessions, and soon after made the desperate and irrational decision

to try to cross the rain-swollen river, which in normal circumstances he would have realized could only take him further
away from his goal. On the night he got lost, the weather was
dry and the temperature in the forties. Had he kept his jacket
and stayed out of the water, he would have had an uncomfort-
ably chilly night and a story to tell. Instead, he died.

A person suffering hypothermia experiences several progres-
sive stages beginning, as you would expect, with mild and then
increasingly violent shivering as the body tries to warm itself
with muscular contractions, and proceeding on to profound
weariness, heaviness of movement, a distorted sense of time
and distance, and increasingly helpless confusion resulting in a
tendency to make imprudent or illogical decisions and a failure
to observe the obvious. Gradually the sufferer grows thoroughly
disoriented and subject to increasingly dangerous hallucinations
– including the decidedly cruel misconception that he is not
freezing but burning up. Many victims tear off clothing, fling
away their gloves or crawl out of their sleeping bags. The
annals of trail deaths are full of stories of hikers found half
naked lying in snowbanks just outside their tents. When this
stage is reached, shivering ceases as the body just gives up and
apathy takes over. The heart rate falls and brainwaves begin to
look like a drive across the prairies. By this time, even if the
victim is found the shock of revival may be more than his body
can bear.

This was neatly illustrated by an incident reported in the
January 1997 issue of *Outside* magazine. In 1980, according to
the article, sixteen Danish seamen issued a mayday call, donned
lifejackets and jumped into the North Sea as their vessel sank
beneath them. There they bobbed for ninety minutes before a
rescue ship was able to lift them from the water. Even in
summer the North Sea is so perishingly cold that it can kill a
person immersed in it in as little as thirty minutes, so the sur-
vival of all sixteen was a cause of some jubilation. They were
wrapped in blankets and guided below, where they were given

a hot drink, and abruptly dropped dead – all sixteen of them.

But enough of arresting anecdote. Let's toy with this fascinating malady ourselves.

I was in New Hampshire now, which pleased me, because we had recently moved to the state, so I was naturally interested to explore it. Vermont and New Hampshire are so snugly proximate and so similiar in size, climate, accent and livelihoods (principally skiing and tourism) that they are often bracketed as twins, but in fact they have quite different characters. Vermont is Volvos and antique shops and country inns with cutely contrived names like Quail Hollow Lodge and Fiddlehead Farm Inn. New Hampshire is guys in hunting caps and pickup trucks with number plates bearing the feisty slogan 'Live Free or Die.' The landscape too differs crucially. Vermont's mountains are comparatively soft and rolling and its profusion of dairy farms gives it a more welcoming and inhabited feel. New Hampshire is one big forest. Of the state's 9,304 square miles of territory, some 85 per cent – or an area somewhat larger than Wales – is woods, and nearly all the rest is either lakes or above treeline. So apart from the very occasional town or ski resort, New Hampshire is primarily, sometimes rather dauntingly, wilderness. And its hills are loftier, craggier, more difficult and forbidding.

In *The Thru-Hiker's Handbook* – the one indispensable guide to the AT, I might just say here – the great Dan 'Wingfoot' Bruce notes that when the northbound hiker leaves Vermont he has completed 80 per cent of the miles, but just 50 per cent of the effort. The New Hampshire portion alone, running 162 miles through the White Mountains, has thirty-five peaks over 3,000 feet. If Ben Nevis were on the Appalachian Trail in New Hampshire, it would just squeak into the top ten. Snowdon would be swallowed without trace. New Hampshire is hard.

I had heard so much about the ardours and dangers of the White Mountains that I was mildly uneasy about venturing into them alone – not terrified exactly, but prepared to be if I heard just one more bear-chase story – so you may conceive my quiet joy when a friend and neighbour named Bill Abdu offered to accompany me on some day hikes. Bill is a very nice fellow, amiable and full of knowledge, experienced on mountain trails, and with the inestimable bonus that he is a gifted orthopaedic surgeon – just what you want in a dangerous wilderness. I didn't suppose he'd be able to do much useful surgery up there, but if I fell and broke my back at least I'd know the Latin names for what was wrong with me.

We decided to start with Mount Lafayette, and to that end set off by car one clear July dawn and drove the two hours to Franconia Notch State Park – a notch in New Hampshire parlance is a mountain pass – a famous beauty spot at repose beneath commanding summits in the heart of the 700,000-acre White Mountain National Forest. Lafayette is 5,249 feet of steep, heartless granite. An 1870s account, quoted in *Into the Mountains*, observes: 'Mount Lafayette is . . . a true alp, with peaks and crags on which lightnings play, its sides brown with scars and deep with gorges.' All true. It's a beast. Only nearby Mount Washington exceeds it for both heft and popularity as a hiking destination in the White Mountains.

From the valley floor we had 3,700 feet of climb, 2,000 feet of it in the first two miles, and three smaller peaks en route – Mount Liberty, Little Haystack and Mount Lincoln – but it was a splendid morning, with mild but abundant sunshine and that invigorating minty-clean air you only get in northern mountains. It had the makings of a flawless day. We walked for perhaps three hours, talking little because of the steepness of the climb, but enjoying being out and keeping a good pace.

Every guidebook, every experienced hiker, every sign-board beside every trailhead car park warns you that the weather in the White Mountains can change in an instant. Stories of campers who go for a stroll along sunny heights in shorts and sneakers only to find themselves, three or four hours later, stumbling to unhappy deaths in freezing fog are the stuff of every campfire, but they are also true. It happened to us when we were a few hundred feet shy of the summit of Little Haystack Mountain. The sunshine abruptly vanished, and from out of nowhere a swirling mist rolled into the trees. With it came a sudden fall in temperature, as if we had stepped into a cold store. Within minutes the forest was settled in a great foggy stillness, chill and damp. Timberline in the White Mountains occurs as low as 4,800 feet, about half the height in most other ranges, because the weather is so much more severe, and I began to see why. As we emerged from a zone of krummholz, the stunted trees that mark the last gasp of forest at treeline, and stepped onto the barren roof of Little Haystack we were met by a stiff, sudden wind – the kind that would snatch a hat from your head and fling it a hundred yards before you could raise a hand – which the mountain had deflected over us on the sheltered western slopes but which here was flying unopposed across the open summit. We stopped in the lee of some boulders to put on waterproofs, for the extra warmth as much anything, for I was already quite damp from the sweat of effort and the moist air – a clearly foolish state to be in with the temperature falling and the wind whisking away any body heat. I opened my pack, rooted through the contents and then looked up with that confounded expression that comes with the discovery of a reversal. I didn't have my waterproofs. I rooted again, but there was hardly anything in the pack – a map, a light jumper, a water bottle, and a packed lunch. I thought for a moment and with a small inward sigh remembered pulling the waterproofs out some days before and spreading them out in the basement to air. I hadn't remembered to put them back.

Bill, tightening a drawstring on his windcheater hood, looked over. 'Something wrong?'

I told him. He made a grave expression. 'Do you want to turn back?'

'Oh, no.' I genuinely didn't want to. Besides, it wasn't that bad. There wasn't any rain and I was only a little chilly. I put the jumper on and felt immediately better. Together we looked at his map. We had done almost all the height and it was only a mile and a half along a ridgeline to Lafayette, at which point we would descend steeply 1,200 feet to Greenleaf Hut, a mountain lodge with a cafeteria. If I did need to warm up, we would reach the hut a lot faster than if we went five miles back down the mountain to the car.

'You sure you don't want to turn back?'

'No,' I insisted. 'We'll be there in half an hour.'

So we set off again into the galloping wind and depthless grey murk. We cleared Mount Lincoln, at 5,100 feet, then descended slightly to a very narrow ridgeline. Visibility was no more than 15 feet and the winds were razor-sharp. Air temperature falls by about 2.5°F with every thousand feet of elevation, so it would have been chillier at this height anyway, but now it was positively uncomfortable. I watched with alarm as my jumper accumulated hundreds of tiny beads of moisture, which gradually began to penetrate the fabric and join the dampness of the shirt beneath. Before we had gone a quarter of a mile the jumper was wet through and hanging heavily on my arms and shoulders.

To make things worse, I was wearing blue jeans. Everyone will tell you that blue jeans are the most foolish item of clothing you can wear on a hike. I had contrarily become something of a devotee because they are tough and give good protection against thorns, ticks, insects and poison ivy – perfect for the woods. However, I freely concede they are completely useless in cold and wet. The cotton jumper was something I had packed as a formality, as you might pack anti-snakebite medicine or splints. It was July, for goodness' sake. I hadn't expected to need any kind of outerwear beyond possibly my trusty waterproofs, which of course I didn't have either. In short, I was dangerously misattired and all but asking to suffer and die. I certainly suffered.

I was lucky to escape with that. The wind was whooshing

along noisily and steadily at a brisk 25 miles an hour, but gusting to at least double that, and from ever-shifting directions. At times, when the wind was head-on, we would take two steps forward and one back. When it came from an angle, it gave us a stiff shove towards the edge of the ridge. There was no telling in the fog how far the fall would be on either side, but it looked awfully steep, and we were after all a mile up in the clouds. If conditions had deteriorated just a little – if the fog had completely obscured our footing or the gusts had gathered just enough bump to knock a grown man over – we would have been pinned down up there, with me pretty well soaked through. Forty minutes before we had been whistling in sunshine. I understood now how people die in the White Mountains even in summer.

As it was, I was in a state of mild distress. I was shivering foolishly and feeling oddly lightheaded. There didn't seem to be any call to panic just yet, but I was clearly in bother. The ridge seemed to run on for ever, and there was no guessing in the milky void how long it would be till the form of Lafayette would rise to meet us. I glanced at my watch – it was two minutes to eleven; just right for lunch when and if we ever got to the godforsaken lodge – and took some comfort from the thought that at least I still had my wits about me. Or at least I felt as if I did. Presumably a confused person would be too addled to recognize that he was confused. Ergo if you know that you are not confused then you are not confused. Unless, it suddenly occurred to me – and here was an arresting notion – *unless* persuading yourself that you are not confused is merely a cruel, early symptom of confusion. Or even an advanced symptom. Who could tell? For all I knew I could be stumbling into some kind of helpless pre-confusional state characterized by the fear on the part of the sufferer that he may be stumbling into some kind of helpless pre-confusional state. That's the trouble with losing your mind; by the time it's gone, it's too late to get it back.

I glanced at my watch again and discovered with horror that it was still only two minutes to eleven. My sense of time was going! I might not be able to reliably assess my faltering brain, but here was proof on my wrist. How long would it be till I was dancing around half naked and trying to beat out flames, or seized with the brilliant notion that the best way out of this mess would be to glide to the valley floor on a magic, invisible parachute? I whimpered a little and scooted on, waited a good full minute and stole a glance at my watch again. Still two minutes to eleven! I was definitely in trouble.

Bill, who seemed serenely impervious to cold and of course had no idea that we were doing anything but proceeding along a high ridge in an unseasonal breeze, looked back from time to time to ask how I was doing.

'Great!' I'd say, for I was too embarrassed to admit that I was in fact losing my mind preparatory to stepping over the edge with a private smile and a cry of 'See you on the other side, old friend!' I don't suppose he had ever lost a patient on a mountaintop and I didn't wish to alarm him. Besides, I wasn't entirely convinced I was losing my grip; just severely uncomfortable.

I've no idea how long it took us to reach the windy summit of Lafayette other than that it was a double eternity. A hundred years ago there was a hotel on this bleak, forbidding spot and its windworn foundations are still a landmark – I have seen it in photographs – but I have no recollection of it now. My focus was entirely on descending the side trail to Greenleaf Hut. It led through a vast talus field and then, a mile or so further on, into woods. Almost as soon as we left the summit, the wind dropped and within 500 feet the world was quite calm, eerily so, and the dense fog was nothing more than straggly drifting shreds. Suddenly we could see the world below and how high up we were, which was a considerable distance, though all the nearby summits were wreathed in clouds. To my surprise and gratification, I felt much better. I stood up straight, with a sense of novelty, and realized that I had been walking in a severe hunch for some time. Yes, I definitely felt much better: hardly cold at all and agreeably clear-headed.

'Well, that wasn't so bad,' I said to Bill with a mountain man chuckle and pressed on to the hut.

Greenleaf Hut is one of ten picturesque and, in this case, brilliantly handy stone lodges built and maintained in the White Mountains by the venerable Appalachian Mountain Club. The AMC, founded over 120 years ago, is not only the oldest hiking club in America, but the oldest conservation group of any type. It charges a decidedly ambitious $50 a night for a bunk, dinner and breakfast, and consequently is known to thru-hikers as the Appalachian Money Club. Plus you have to make reservations days or sometimes weeks in advance. It doesn't really give the impression of being the thru-hiker's friend – more a hiking club for Cape Cod types. Still, to its credit, the AMC maintains 1,400 miles of trails in the Whites, runs an excellent visitor centre at Pinkham Notch, publishes worthwhile books and does let you come into its huts to use the toilets, get water or just warm up, which is what we gratefully did now.

We purchased cups of warming coffee and took them to a set of refectory tables, where we sat with a sprinkling of other steamy hikers and ate our packed lunches. The lodge was very congenial in a basic and rustic sort of way, with a high ceiling and plenty of room to move around. When we'd finished I was beginning to stiffen up, so I got up to move around and looked in on one of the two dormitories. It was a large room, packed with built-in bunks stacked four high. It was clean and airy, but startlingly basic, and presumably would be like an army barracks at night when it was full of hikers and their equipment. It didn't look remotely appealing to me. Benton MacKaye had nothing to do with these huts, but they were absolutely in accord with his vision – spare, rustic, wholesomely communal – and I realized with a kind of dull shock that if his dreams of a string of trailside hostels had been realized this is precisely how they would have been. My fantasy of a relaxed and cosy refuge with a porchful of rockers would actually have been rather more like a spell at boot camp – and an expensive one at that if the AMC's fees were anything to go by.

I did a quick calculation. Assuming $50 as the standard price, it would have cost the average thru-hiker somewhere between $6,000 and $7,500 to stay in a lodge each night along the trail. Clearly, it would never have worked. Perhaps it was better that things were as they were.

The sun was shining weakly when we emerged from the hut and set off back down the mountain on a side trail to Franconia Notch, and as we descended it gathered strength until we were back in a nice July day, with the air lazy and mild and the trees fetchingly speckled with sunlight and birdsong. By the time we reached the car, in late afternoon, I was almost completely dry, and my passing fright on Lafayette – now basking in hearty sunshine against a backdrop of vivid blue sky – seemed a remote memory.

As we climbed in, I glanced at my watch. It said two minutes to eleven. I gave it a shake and watched with interest as the second hand kicked back into motion.

Chapter 18

On the afternoon of 12 April 1934, Salvatore Pagliuca, a meteor-
ologist at the summit weather observatory on Mount
Washington, had an experience no-one else has had before or
since.

Mount Washington sometimes gets a little gusty, to put it
mildly, and this was a particularly breezy day. In the previous
twenty-four hours the wind speed had not fallen below 107
miles an hour, and often gusted much higher. When it came
time for Pagliuca to take the afternoon readings, the wind was
so strong that he tied a rope round his waist and had two
colleagues take hold of the other end. As it was, the men had
difficulty just getting the weather station door open and needed
all their strength to keep Pagliuca from becoming a kind of
human kite. How Pagliuca managed to reach his weather instruments and take readings is not known, nor are his words when
he finally tumbled back in, though 'Jeeeeeeee*sus*!' would seem
an apt possibility.

What is certain is that Pagliuca had just experienced a surface wind speed of 231 miles an hour. Nothing approaching that velocity has ever been recorded elsewhere.

In *The Worst Weather on Earth: A History of the Mount Washington Observatory*, William Lowell Putnam drily notes: 'There may be worse weather, from time to time, at some forbidding place on Planet Earth, but it has yet to be reliably recorded.' Among the Mount Washington weather station's many other records are: most weather instruments destroyed, most wind in twenty-four hours (nearly 3,100 miles of it), and lowest wind chill (a combination of 100 mph winds and a temperature of −47°F, a severity unmatched even in Antarctica).

Washington owes its curiously extreme weather not so much to height or latitude, though both are factors, as to its position at the precise point where high altitude weather systems from Canada and the Great Lakes pile into moist, comparatively warm air from the Atlantic or southern US. In consequence it receives 246 inches of snow a year and snowpacks of 20 feet. In one memorable storm in 1969, 98 inches of snow – that's eight feet – fell on the summit in three days. Wind is a particular feature; on average it blows at hurricane force (over 75 mph) on two winter days in three and on 40 per cent of days overall. Because of the length and bitterness of its winters, the average mean annual temperature at the summit is a meagre 27°F. The summer average is 52°F – a good 25°F lower than at its base. It is a brutal mountain, and yet people go up there – or at least try to – even in winter.

In *Into the Mountains*, Maggie Stier and Ron McAdow record how two University of New Hampshire students, Derek Tinkham and Jeremy Haas, decided to hike the entire Presidential Range – seven summits, including Washington, all named for US Presidents – in January 1994. Although they were experienced winter hikers and were well equipped, they couldn't have imagined what they were letting themselves in for. On their second night, the winds rose to 90 miles an hour and the temperature plummeted to –32°F. I have experienced –25°F in calm conditions and can tell you that even well wrapped and with the benefit of residual heat from indoors it becomes distinctly uncomfortable within a couple of minutes. Somehow the two survived the night, but the next day Haas announced he could go no further. Tinkham helped him into a sleeping bag, then stumbled on to the weather observatory a little over two miles away. He made it, just, though he was gravely frostbitten. His friend was found the next day, 'half out of his sleeping bag and frozen solid'.

Scores of others have perished in far less taxing conditions on Washington. One of the earliest and most famous deaths was that of a young woman named Lizzie Bourne who in 1855, not long after Mount Washington began to attract tourists, decided to amble up in the company of two male companions on a summery September afternoon. As you will have guessed already, the weather turned and they found themselves lost in fog. Somehow they got separated. The men made it after nightfall to a hotel on the summit. Lizzie was found the next day just 150 feet from the front door, but quite dead.

Altogether 122 people have lost their lives on Washington. Until recently, when it was overtaken by Mount Denali in Alaska, it was the most murderous mountain in North America. So when the fearless Dr Abdu and I pulled up at its base a few days later for the second of our grand ascents I had brought enough backup clothes to cross the Arctic – waterproofs, woollen jumper, jacket, gloves, spare trousers and long underwear. Never again would I be chilled at height.

Washington, the highest peak north of the Smokies and east of the Rockies at a solidly respectable 6,288 feet, gets few clear days and this was a clear day, so the crowds were out in force. I counted over seventy cars at the Pinkham Notch Visitor Center car park at 8.10 in the morning when we arrived, and more pouring in every minute. Mount Washington is the most popular summit in the White Mountains and the Tuckerman Ravine

Trail, our chosen route, is the most popular trail up Mount
Washington. Some 60,000 hikers a year take to the Tuckerman
route, though a good many of them get a lift to the top of the
mountain and walk down, so the figures are perhaps a trifle
skewed. In any case, it was no more than moderately busy on
a good, hot, blue-skied, gorgeously promising morning in late
July.

The walk up was much easier than I had dared hope. Even
now, I could not quite get used to the novelty of walking big
hills without a large pack. It makes such a difference. I won't
say we bounded up, but considering that we had almost 4,500
feet of climb in a little over three miles, we walked at a pretty
steady clip. It took us two hours and forty minutes (Bill's hiking
guide to the White Mountains suggested a walking time of four
hours and fifteen minutes), so we were pretty proud.

There may be more demanding and exciting summits to
reach along the Appalachian Trail than Mount Washington but
none can be more startling. You labour up the last steep stretch
of rocky slope to what is after all a considerable eminence and
pop your head over the edge and there you are greeted by, of
all things, a vast terraced car park, full of automobiles gleaming
hotly in the sun. Beyond stands a scattered complex of buildings among which move crowds of people in shorts and
baseball caps. It has the air of a world fair bizarrely transferred
to a mountaintop. You get so used along the AT to sharing
summits with only a few other people, all of whom have
worked as hard as you to get there, that this was positively dazzling. On Washington, visitors can arrive by car on a winding
toll road or on a cog railway from the other side, and hundreds
of people – hundreds and hundeds of them, it seemed – had
availed themselves of these options. They were everywhere,
basking in the sunshine, draped over the railings on the viewing terraces, wandering between various shops and food places.
I felt for some minutes like a visitor from another planet. I loved
it. It was a nightmare, of course, and a desecration of the

highest mountain in the northeast, but I was delighted it existed in one place. It made the rest of the trail seem perfect.

The epicentre of activity was a monstrously ugly concrete building, the Summit Information Center, with big windows, broad viewing platforms and an exceedingly lively cafeteria. Just inside the door was a large list of all the people who had died on the mountain and the causes, beginning with one Frederick Strickland of Bridlington, Yorkshire, who lost his way while hiking in an October storm in 1849, and ran on through a quite breathtaking array of mishaps before concluding with the deaths of two hikers in an avalanche just three months earlier. Already six people had died on Washington's slopes in 1996, with the year barely half over – quite a sobering statistic – and there was plenty of room on the board for more.

In the basement was a small museum with displays on Washington's climate, geology, and distinctive plant life, but what particularly captivated me was a comical short video called *Breakfast of Champions*, which I presume the meteorologists had made for their own amusement. It was filmed with a fixed camera on one of the summit terraces and showed a man sitting at a table, as if at an open-air restaurant, during one of its famous blows. While the man holds down the table with his arms, a waiter approaches against the wind with great and obvious difficulty, like someone wingwalking at 30,000 feet. He tries to pour the customer a bowl of cereal, and it all flies horizontally from the box. Then he adds milk, but this goes the same way (mostly over the customer – a particularly gratifying moment). Then the bowl flies away and the cutlery, as I recall, and then the table starts to go, and then the film ends. It was so good I watched it twice, then went off to find Bill so he could see it, but I couldn't spot him in the restless throngs, so I went outside onto the viewing platform and watched the cog railway train chuffing up the mountain, pouring out clouds of black smoke as it came. It stopped at the summit station and hundreds more happy tourists tumbled off.

Tourism goes back a long way on Mount Washington. As early as 1852 there was a restaurant at the summit and the proprietors were serving about a hundred meals a day. In 1853, a small stone hotel called Tip-Top House was built atop the mountain and was a huge and immediate success. Then in 1869 a local entrepreneur named Sylvester March built the cog railway, the first in the world. Everyone thought he was mad and that even if he succeeded in building the railway, which was doubtful, there wouldn't be any demand for it. In fact, as the disgorging throngs below me demonstrated now, people haven't tired of it yet.

Five years after the railway opened the old Tip-Top was succeeded by a much grander Summit House Hotel, and that was followed by a 40-foot tower with a multi-coloured searchlight, which could be seen all over New England and far out to sea. By late in the century a daily newspaper was being published on the summit as a summer novelty and American Express had opened a branch office.

Meanwhile back at ground level, things were also booming. The modern tourist industry, in the sense of people travelling en masse to a congenial spot and finding lots of diversions awaiting them when they get there, is essentially a White Mountains invention. Massive hotels, with up to 250 rooms, sprang up in every glen. Built in a jaunty domestic style, like cottages blown up to the scale of hospitals or sanatoria, these were exceedingly ornate and elaborate structures, among the largest and most complicated ever built of wood, with wandering rooflines robustly punctuated with towers and turrets and every other mark of architectural busyness the Victorian mind could devise. They had winter gardens and salons, dining rooms that could seat 200, and verandas like the promenade decks of ocean liners from which guests could drink in the wholesome air and survey nature's craggy splendour.

The finer hotels were very fine indeed. The Profile House at Franconia Notch had its own private railway line to Bethlehem

Junction eight miles away; its grounds held twenty-one cottages, each with up to twelve bedrooms. The Maplewood had its own casino. Guests at the Crawford House could choose among nine daily newspapers from New York or Boston, shipped in specially. Whatever was new and exciting – lifts, gas lighting, swimming pools, golf courses – the White Mountain hotels were in the vanguard. By the 1890s, there were 200 hotels scattered through the White Mountains. There has never been a collection of hotels of comparable grandeur anywhere, certainly not in a mountain setting. And now they are virtually all gone.

In 1902, the grandest of them all, the Mount Washington Hotel, opened at Bretton Woods, in an open, meadowy setting against the backdrop of the Presidential Range. Built in a commanding style described optimistically by the architect as 'Spanish Renaissance', it was the pinnacle of grace and opulence, with 2,600 acres of cultivated grounds, 235 guestrooms and every detail of finery that heaps of money could buy. For the plasterwork alone, the developers brought in 250 Italian artisans. But already it was something of an anachronism.

Fashion was moving on. American holidaymakers were discovering the seaside. The White Mountain hotels were a little too dull, a little too remote and expensive, for modern tastes. Worse, they had begun to attract the wrong sort of people – parvenus from Boston and New York. Finally, and above all, there was the automobile. The hotels were built on the assumption that visitors would come for a fortnight at least, but the motor car gave tourists a fickle mobility. In the 1924 edition of *New England Highways and Byways from a Motor Car*, the author gushed about the unrivalled splendour of the White Mountains – the tumbling cataracts of Franconia, the alabaster might of Washington, the secret charm of the little towns like Lincoln and Bethlehem – and encouraged visitors to give the mountains a full day and night. America was entering the age not just of the automobile but of the retarded attention span.

One by one the hotels closed down, became derelict or, more often, burned to the ground (often, miraculously, almost the only thing to survive was the insurance policy), and their grounds slowly returned to forest. Once I could have seen perhaps twenty large hotels from the summit. Today there is just one, the Mount Washington, still imposing and festive with its perky red roof, but inescapably forlorn in its solitary grandeur. (And even it has staggered along the edge of bankruptcy several times.) Elsewhere across the spacious valley far below, where once had proudly stood the Fabyan, the Mount Pleasant, the Crawford House and many others, today there was only forest, highways and motels.

From beginning to end the great age of the resort hotels in the White Mountains lasted just fifty years. Once again, I offer you the Appalachian Trail as a symbol of venerability. And with that in mind, I went off to find my friend Bill and complete our walk.

Chapter 19

'I've had a brilliant idea,' said Stephen Katz. We were in the living room of my house in Hanover. It was two weeks later. We were leaving for Maine in the morning.

'Oh yeah?' I said, trying not to sound too wary, for ideas are not Katz's strongest suit.

'You know how awful it is carrying a full pack?'

I nodded. Of course I did.

'Well, I was thinking about it the other day. In fact I've been thinking about it a lot because to tell you the truth, Bryson, the idea of putting that pack on again filled me with' – he lowered his voice a tone – 'fucking dread.' He nodded with solemnity and repeated the two key words. 'And then I had a great idea. An alternative. Close your eyes.'

'What for?'

'I want to surprise you.'

I hate having to close my eyes for a surprise, always have, but I did it.

I could hear him rooting in his army surplus duffel bag. ' "Who carries a lot of weight all the time?" ' he continued. 'That was the question I asked myself. "Who carries a lot of weight day in and day out?" Hey, don't look yet. And then it occurred to me.' He was silent a moment, as if making some crucial adjustment that would assure a perfect impression. 'OK, now you can look.'

I uncovered my eyes. Katz, beaming immoderately, was wearing a *Des Moines Register* newspaper delivery bag – the kind of bright yellow pouch that paper boys in America traditionally sling over their shoulders before climbing on their bikes and riding off to do their rounds.

'You can't be serious,' I said quietly.

'Never been more serious in my life, my old mountain friend. I brought you one too.' He handed me one from his duffel bag, still pristinely folded and in a transparent wrapper.

'Stephen, you can't walk across the Maine wilderness with a newspaper delivery bag.'

'Why not? It's comfortable, it's waterproof – near enough – it's *capacious*, and it weighs all of about four ounces. It is the Perfect Hiking Accessory. Let me ask you this. When was the last time you saw a paper boy with a hernia?' He nodded sagely, as if he had foxed me with that one.

I made some tentative, preparatory shapes with my mouth prior to saying something, but Katz raced on before I could get a thought in order.

'Here's the plan,' he continued. 'We cut our load down to the bare minimum – no stoves, no gas bottles, no noodles, no coffee, no tents, no stuff sacks, no sleeping bags. We hike and camp like mountain men. Did Daniel Boone have a three-season fibre-fill sleeping bag? I don't think so. All we take is cold food, water bottles, maybe one change of clothes. I figure we can get the load down to five pounds. And' – he waggled his hand delightedly in the empty newspaper bag – 'we put it *all in here*.' His expression begged me to drape him with plaudits.

'Have you given any thought to how ridiculous you would look?'

'Yup. Don't care.'

'Have you considered what a source of uncontained mirth you would be to every person you met between here and Katahdin?'

'Don't give the tiniest shit.'

'Well, has it occurred to you what a ranger would say if he found you setting off into the Hundred Mile Wilderness with a newspaper delivery bag? Do you know they have the power to detain anyone they think is not mentally or physically fit?' This was actually a lie, but it brought a promising hint of frown to his brow. 'Also, has it also occurred to you that maybe the reason newspaper boys don't get hernias is that they only carry the bag for an hour or so a day – that maybe it might not be so comfortable lugging it for ten hours at a stretch over mountains – that maybe it would bang endlessly against your legs and rub your shoulders raw? Look how it's chafing against your neck already.'

His eyes slid stealthily down to the strap. The one positive thing about Katz and his notions was that it was never very hard to talk him out of them. He took the bag off over his head. 'OK,' he agreed, 'screw the bags. But we pack light.'

I was happy with that. In fact, it seemed a perfectly sensible proposal. We packed more than Katz wanted – I insisted on sleeping bags, warm clothes and our tents on the grounds that this could be a good deal more demanding than Katz appreciated – but I agreed to leave behind the stove, gas bottles and pots and pans. We would eat cold stuff – principally Snickers, raisins, and an indestructible type of salami product called Slim Jims. It wouldn't kill us for a fortnight. Besides, I couldn't face another bowl of noodles. Altogether we saved perhaps five pounds of weight each – hardly anything really – but Katz seemed disproportionately happy. It wasn't often he got his way even in part.

And so the next day, my wife drove us deep into the boundless woods of northern Maine for our trek through the Hundred Mile Wilderness. Maine is deceptive. It is the twelfth smallest state, but it has more uninhabited forest – 10 million acres – than any other state but Alaska. In photographs it looks serene and beckoning, almost park-like, with hundreds of cool, deep lakes, and hazy, tranquil miles of undulating mountains. Only Katahdin, with its rocky upper slopes and startling muscularity, offers anything that looks faintly intimidating. In fact, it is all hard.

The trail maintainers in Maine have a certain hale devotion to seeking out the rockiest climbs and most forbidding slopes, and of these Maine has a breathtaking plenitude. In its 283 miles, the Appalachian Trail in Maine presents the northbound hiker with almost 100,000 feet of climb, the equivalent of three Everests. And at the heart of it all lies the famous Hundred Mile Wilderness – 99.7 miles of boreal forest trail without a shop, house or paved road, running from the village of Monson to a public campground at Abol Bridge, just below Katahdin. It is the remotest section of the entire AT. If something goes wrong in the Hundred Mile Wilderness, you are on your own. You could die of an infected blood blister out there.

It takes a week to ten days for most people to cross this fabled expanse. Because we had a fortnight, we had my wife drop us at Caratunk, a remote village on the Kennebec River, 38 miles short of Monson and the official start of the Wilderness. We would have three days of limbering up, and a chance to resupply at Monson before plunging irreversibly into the deepest woods. I had already done a little hiking to the west around Rangeley and Flagstaff Lakes, in the week before Katz came, as a kind of reconnoitre, so I felt as if I knew the terrain. Even so it was a shock.

It was the first time in almost four months that I had hoisted a pack with a full load. I couldn't believe the weight, couldn't believe that there had ever been a time when I could believe the weight. The strain was immediate and discouraging. But at least I had been hiking. Katz, it was quickly evident, was starting from square one – actually, several score pancake breakfasts to the wrong side of square one. From Caratunk it was a long, gently upward haul of five miles to a big lake called Pleasant Pond, hardly taxing at all, but I noticed right away that he was moving with incredible deliberativeness, breathing very hard, and wearing a kind of shocked 'Where am I?' expression.

All he would utter was 'Man!' in an amazed tone when I asked him how he was, and a single heartfelt 'Fuhhhhhhhhck' – breathy and protracted, like the noise of a plumped cushion when someone sits on it – when he let his pack fall from his back at the first rest stop after forty-five minutes. It was a muggy afternoon and Katz was a river of sweat. He took a water bottle and downed nearly half of it. Then he looked at me with quietly desperate eyes, put his pack back on and wordlessly returned to his duty.

Pleasant Pond was a holiday spot – we could hear the happy shrieks of children splashing and swimming perhaps a hundred yards away, though we couldn't see anything of the lake through the trees. Indeed without their gaiety we wouldn't have known it was there, a sobering reminder of how suffocating the woods can be. Beyond rose Middle Mountain, just 2,500 feet high, but acutely angled and an entirely different experience on a hot day with a cumbersome pack sagging down on tender shoulders. I plodded joylessly on to the top of the mountain. Katz was soon far behind and moving with shuffling slowness.

It was after six o'clock when I reached the base of the mountain on the other side and found a decent campsite beside a grassy, little-used logging road at a place called Baker Stream. I waited a few minutes for Katz, then put up my tent. When he still hadn't come after twenty minutes, I went looking for him. He was almost an hour behind me when I finally found him, and his expression was glassy-eyed.

I took his pack from him and sighed at the discovery that it was light.

'What's happened to your pack?'

'Aw, I threw some stuff,' he said unhappily.

'What?'

'Oh, clothes and stuff.' He seemed uncertain whether to be ashamed or belligerent. He decided to try belligerence. 'That stupid sweater for one thing.' We had disputed mildly over the need for woollens.

'But it could get cold. It's very changeable in the mountains.'

'Yeah, right. It's August, Bryson. I don't know if you noticed.'

There didn't seem much point in trying to reason with him. When we reached the camp and he was putting up his tent I looked into his pack. He had thrown away nearly all his spare clothes and, it appeared, a good deal of the food.

'Where's the peanuts?' I said. 'Where's all your Slim Jims?'

'We didn't need all that shit. It's only three days to Monson.'

'Most of that food was for the Hundred Mile Wilderness, Stephen. We don't know what kind of supplies there'll be in Monson.'

'Oh.' He looked struck and contrite. 'I *thought* it was a lot for three days.'

I looked despairingly in the pack and then looked round. 'Where's your other water bottle?'

He looked at me sheepishly. 'I threw it.'

'You threw a water bottle?' This was truly staggering. If there is one thing you need on the trail in August, it is lots of water.

'It was heavy.'

'Of course it's heavy. Water's always heavy. But it is also kind of vital, wouldn't you say?'

He gave me a helpless look. 'I just had to get rid of some weight. I was desperate.'

'No, you were stupid.'

'Yeah, that too,' he agreed.

'Stephen, I wish you wouldn't do these things.'

'I know,' he said and looked sincerely repentant.

While he finished putting up his tent, I went off to filter water for the morning. Baker Stream was really a river – broad, clear and shallow – and very beautiful in the glow of a summery evening, with a backdrop of overhanging trees and the last rays of sunlight sparkling its surface. As I knelt by the water, I became curiously aware of something – some *thing* – in the woods beyond my left shoulder, which caused me to straighten up and peer through the clutter of foliage at the water's edge. Goodness knows what impelled me to look because I couldn't have heard anything over the musical tumult of water, but there about 15 feet away in the dusky undergrowth, staring at me with a baleful expression, was a moose – full-grown and female, or so I presumed since it had no antlers. It had evidently been on its way to the water for a drink when it was brought up short by my presence, and now clearly was undecided what to do next.

It is an extraordinary experience to find yourself face to face in the woods with a wild animal that is very much larger than you. You know these things are out there, of course, but you never expect at any particular moment to encounter one, certainly not up close – and this one was close enough for me to see the flea-like insects floating in circles about its head. We stared at each other for a good minute, neither of us sure what to do. There was a certain obvious and gratifying tang of adventure in this, but also something much more low-key and elemental – a kind of respectful mutual acknowledgement that comes with sustained eye contact. It was this that was unexpectedly thrilling – the sense that there was in some small measure a salute in our cautious mutual appraisal. Very slowly, so as not to alarm it, I crept off to get Katz.

When we returned, the moose had advanced to the water and was drinking about 25 feet upstream. 'Wow,' Katz breathed. He was thrilled, too, I was pleased to note. The moose looked up at us, decided we meant her no harm and went back to drinking. We watched her for perhaps five minutes, but the mosquitoes were chewing us up, so we withdrew and returned to our camp feeling considerably elated. It seemed a kind of confirmation – we *were* in the wilderness now – and an agreeable reward for a day of hard toil.

We ate a dinner of Slim Jims, raisins and Snickers, and retired to our tents to escape the endless assault of mosquitoes. As we lay there, Katz said, quite brightly: 'Hard day today. I'm beat.' It was unlike him to be chatty at tent time.

I grunted in agreement.

'I'd forgotten how hard it is.'

'Yeah, me, too.'

'First days are always hard, though, aren't they?'

'Yeah.'

He gave a settling-down sigh and yawned melodiously. 'It'll be better tomorrow,' he said, still yawning. By this he meant, I supposed, that he wouldn't fling anything foolish away. 'Well, good night,' he added.

I stared at the wall of my tent in the direction from which his voice had come. In all the weeks of camping together, it was the first time he had wished me a good night.

'Good night,' I said.

I rolled over on my side. He was right, of course. First days are always bad. Tomorrow would be better. We were both asleep in minutes.

Well, we were both wrong. The next day started well enough, with a sunny dawn that promised another hot day. It was the first time along the trail that we had woken to warmth and we enjoyed the novelty of it. We packed up our tents, breakfasted on raisins and Snickers, and set off into the deep woods.

By nine o'clock the sun was already high and blazing. Even on hot days, the woods are normally cool, but here the air was heavy and listless and steamy, almost tropical. About two hours after setting off, we came to a lagoon, about two acres in size,

I would guess, and filled with papery reeds, fallen trees and the bleached torsos of dead trees that were still standing. Dragonflies danced across the surface. Beyond, waiting, rose a titanic heap called Moxie Bald Mountain. But what was of immediate note was that the trail ended, abruptly and puzzlingly, at the water's edge. Katz and I looked at each other: something wrong here surely. For the first time since Georgia, we wondered if we had lost the trail. (God knows what Chicken John would have made of it.) We retraced our steps a considerable distance, studied our map and trail guide, tried to find an alternative way round the pond through the hot and impenetrable undergrowth on every side, and finally concluded that we were intended to ford it. On the far shore, perhaps 80 yards away, Katz spied a white AT blaze. Clearly we had to wade across.

Katz led the way, barefoot and in boxer shorts, using a long stick like a punting pole to try to pick his way across on a jumble of submerged or half-submerged logs. I followed in a similar manner, but staying far enough back not to put my weight on a log he was using. They were covered in a slick moss and tended to bob or rotate alarmingly when stepped on. Twice he nearly toppled over. Finally, about 25 yards out, he lost it altogether and plunged with wheeling arms and an unhappy wail into the murky water. He went completely under, came up, went under again, and came up flailing and floundering with such wildness that for a few sincerely mortifying moments I thought he was drowning. The weight of his pack was clearly dragging him backwards and keeping him from gaining an upright position or even successfully keeping his head above water. I was about to drop my pack and plunge in to help when he managed to catch hold of a log and pull himself to a standing position. The water was up to his chest. He clung to the log and heaved visibly with the effort of catching his breath and calming himself down. He had obviously had a fright.

'You all right?' I said.

'Oh, peachy,' he replied. 'Just peachy. I don't know why they couldn't have put some crocodiles in here and made a real adventure of it.'

I crept on and an instant later I tumbled in, too. I had a few surreal, slow-motion moments of observing the world from the unusual perspective of the waterline or just below while my hand reached helplessly for a log that was just beyond my grasp – all this in a curious bubbly silence – before Katz sloshed to my assistance, firmly grabbed my shirt and thrust me back into a world of light and noise, and set me on my feet. He was surprisingly strong.

'Thank you,' I gasped.

'Don't mention it.'

We waded heavily to the far shore, taking it in turns to stumble and help each other up, and sloshed up onto the muddy bank trailing strands of half-rotted vegetation and draining huge volumes of water from our packs. We dumped our loads and sat on the ground, bedraggled and spent, and stared at the lagoon as if it had just played a terrible practical joke on us. I could not remember feeling this exhausted this early in the day anywhere along the trail. As we sat there, there were voices and two young hikers, hippyish and very fit, emerged from the woods behind us. They nodded hellos and looked appraisingly at the water.

'Afraid you gotta wade this one,' Katz said.

One of the hikers looked at him in a not unkindly way. 'This your first time hiking up here?' he said.

We nodded.

'Well, I don't want to discourage you, but mister you've only just *started* to get wet.'

With that he and his partner hoisted their packs above their heads, wished us luck and walked into the water. They waded skilfully across in perhaps thirty seconds – Katz and I had taken as many minutes – and stepped out on the other side, as if from a foot bath, put their dry packs back on, gave a small wave and disappeared.

Katz took a big thoughtful breath, partly sigh, partly just experimenting with the ability to breathe again. 'Bryson, I'm not trying to be negative – I swear to God I'm not – but I'm not sure I'm cut out for this. Could you lift your pack over your head like that?'

'No.'

And on that premonitory note, we strapped up and set squelchily off up Moxie Bald Mountain.

The Appalachian Trail was the hardest thing I have ever done, and the Maine portion was the hardest part of the Appalachian Trail, and by a factor I couldn't begin to compute. Partly it was the heat. Maine, that most moderate of states, was having a killer heatwave. In the baking sun, the shadeless granite pavements of Moxie Bald radiated an oven-like heat, but even in the woods the air was oppressive and close, as if the trees and foliage were breathing on us with a hot, vegetative breath. We sweated helplessly, copiously, and drank unusual quantities of water, but could never stop being thirsty. Water was sometimes plentiful, but more often non-existent for long stretches so that we were never sure how much we could prudently swallow without leaving ourselves short later on. Even fully stocked, we were short now thanks to Katz's dumping a bottle. Finally, there were the insects, which were relentless, the strangely unsettling sense of isolation, and the ever-taxing terrain.

Katz responded to this in a way that I had never seen. He showed a kind of fixated resolve, as if the only way to deal with this problem was to bull through it and get it over with.

The next morning we came very early to the first of several rivers we would have to ford. It was called Bald Mountain Stream, but in fact it was a river – broad, lively, strewn with boulders. It was exceedingly fetching – it glittered with dancing spangles in the early morning sun and was gorgeously clear – but the current seemed strong and there was no telling from the shore how deep it might be in the middle. Several large streams in the area, my *Appalachian Trail Guide to Maine* noted blithely, 'can be difficult or dangerous to cross in high water'. I decided not to share this with Katz.

We took off our shoes and socks, rolled up our trousers, and stepped gingerly out into the frigid water. The stones on the bottom were all shapes and sizes – flat, egg-shaped, domed – very hard on the feet, and covered with a filmy green slime that was ludicrously slippery. I hadn't gone three steps when my feet skated and I fell painfully on my ass. I struggled halfway to my feet, but slipped and fell again; struggled up, staggered side-ways a yard or two and pitched helplessly forward, breaking my fall with my hands and ending up in the water doggie-style. As I landed, my pack slid forward and my boots, tied to its frame by their laces, were hurled into a kind of contained orbit; they flew round the side of the pack in a long, rather pretty trajectory, and came to a halt against my head, then plunked into the water where they dangled in the current. As I crouched there, breathing evenly and telling myself that one day this would be a memory, two young guys – clones almost of the two we had seen the day before – strode past with confident, splashing steps, packs above their heads.

'Fall down?' said one brightly.

'No, I just wanted a closer look at the water.' You moronic fit twit.

I went back to the riverbank, pulled on my soaked boots, and discovered that it was infinitely easier crossing with them on. I got a tolerable grip and the rocks didn't hurt as they had on my bare feet. I crossed cautiously, alarmed at the force of the current in the centre – each time I lifted a leg the current tried to reposition it downstream, as if it belonged to a gateleg table – but the water was never more than about three feet deep, and I reached the other side without falling.

Katz, meantime, had discovered a way across using boulders as stepping stones, but ended up stranded on the edge of a noisy torrent of what looked like deep water. He stood there covered with frowns. I couldn't for the life of me figure out how he had got up there – his boulder seemed isolated in an expanse of dangerously streaming water from all sides, and clearly he didn't know what to do now. He tried to ease himself into the water to wade the last ten yards to shore, and was instantly whisked away like a feather. For the second time in two days I sincerely thought he was drowning – he was certainly helpless – but the current carried him to a shallow bar of gleaming pebbles 20 feet further on, where he came up sputtering on his hands and knees, struggled up onto the bank, and continued on into the woods without a backward glance, as if this were the most normal thing in the world.

And so we pressed on to Monson, over hard trail and more rivers, collecting bruises and scratches and insect bites that turned our backs into relief maps. On the third day, forest-dazed and grubby, we stepped onto a sunny road, the first since Caratunk, and followed it on a hot ambulation into the forgotten hamlet of Monson. Near the centre of town was an old clapboard house with a painted wooden cut-out of a bearded hiker standing on the lawn bearing the message WELCOME AT SHAW'S.

Shaw's is the most famous guesthouse on the AT, partly because it's the last comfort stop for anyone going into the Hundred Mile Wilderness and the first for anyone coming out, but also because it's very friendly and good value. For $28 each we got a room, dinner and breakfast, and free use of the shower, laundry and guest lounge. The place was run by Keith and Pat Shaw, who started the business more or less by accident twenty years ago when Keith brought home a hungry hiker off the trail and the hiker passed on the word of how well he had been treated. Just a few weeks earlier, Keith told me proudly as we signed in, they had registered their 20,000th hiker.

We had an hour till dinner. Katz borrowed $5 – for pop, I presumed – and vanished to his room. I had a shower, put a load of washing in the machine and wandered out to the front lawn where there were a couple of Adirondack chairs on which I intended to park my weary butt, smoke my pipe and savour the blissful ease of late afternoon and the pleasant anticipation of a dinner earned. From a screened window nearby came the sounds of sizzling food and the clatter of pans. It smelled good, whatever it was.

After a minute, Keith came out and sat with me. He was an old guy, comfortably into his sixties, with almost no teeth and a body that looked as if it had put up with all kinds of tough stuff in its day. He was real friendly.

'You didn't try to pet the dog, did ya?' he said.

'No.' I had seen it from the window: an ugly, vicious mongrel that was tied up behind the house and got stupidly and disproportionately worked up by any noise or movement within a hundred yards.

'You don't wanna try to pet the dog. Take it from me: you do not wanna pet that dog. Some hiker petted him last week when I told him not to and it bit him in the balls.'

'Really?'

He nodded. 'Wouldn't let go neither. You shoulda heard that feller wail.'

'Really?'

'Had to hit the damn dog with a *rake* to get him to let go. Meanest damn dog I ever seen in my life. You don't wanna get near him, believe me.'

'How was the hiker?'

'Well, it didn't exactly make his day, I tell you that.' He scratched his neck contemplatively, as if he were thinking of having a shave one of these days. 'Thru-hiker, he was. Come all the way from Georgia. Long way to come to get your *balls* nipped.' Then he went off to check on dinner.

Dinner was at a big dining room table that was generously covered in platters of meat, bowls of mashed potatoes and corn on the cob, a teetering plate of bread, a tub of butter. Katz arrived a few moments after me, looking freshly showered and

very happy. He seemed unusually, almost exaggeratedly, ener-
gized, and gave me an impetuous tickle from behind as he
passed, which was out of character.

'You all right?' I said.

'Never been better, my old mountain companion, never been
better.'

We were joined by two others, a sweetly hesitant and
wholesome-looking young couple, both tanned and fit and also
very clean. Katz and I welcomed them with smiles, and started
to pitch in, then paused and put back the bowls when we realized the couple were mumbling grace. This seemed to go on for
ever. Then we pitched in again.

The food was terrific. Keith acted as waiter and was most
insistent that we eat plenty. 'Dog'll eat it if you don't,' he said.
I was happy to let the dog starve.

The young couple were thru-hikers, from Indiana. They had
started at Springer on 28 March – a date that seemed impossibly
snow-flecked and distant now in the full heat of an August
evening – and had hiked continuously for 141 days. They had
completed 2045.5 miles. They had 114.9 miles to go.

'So you've nearly done it, huh?' I said, a trifle inanely, but just
trying to make conversation.

'Yes,' said the girl. She said it slowly, as two syllables, as if it
hadn't previously occurred to her. There was something
serenely mindless in her manner.

'Did you ever feel like giving up?'

The girl thought for a moment. 'No,' she said simply.

'Really?' I found this amazing. 'Did you never think, "Jeez, this
is too much. I don't know that I want to go through with this"?'

She thought again, with an air of encroaching panic. These
were obviously questions that had never penetrated her skull.

Her partner came to her rescue. 'We had a couple of low
moments in the early phases,' he said, 'but we put our faith in
the Lord and His will prevailed.'

'Praise Jesus,' whispered the girl, almost inaudibly.

'Ah,' I said, and made a mental note to lock my door when I went to bed.

'And God bless Allah for the mashed potatoes!' said Katz happily and reached for the bowl for the third time.

After dinner, Katz and I strolled to a general store up the road to get supplies for the Hundred Mile Wilderness, which we would start in the morning. He seemed odd in the grocery store – cheerful enough, but distracted and inattentive. We were supposed to be stocking up for ten days in the wilds – a fairly serious business – but he seemed unwilling to focus, and kept wandering off or picking up inappropriate things like chilli sauce and tin openers.

'Hey, let's get a sixpack,' he said suddenly, in a party voice.

'Come on, Stephen, get serious,' I said. I was looking at cheeses.

'I am serious.'

'Do you want cheddar or colby?'

'Whatever.' He wandered off to the beer cooler and came back carrying a sixpack of Budweiser.

'Hey, whaddaya say to a sixpack, bud – a sixpack of Bud, bud?' He nudged me in the ribs to emphasize the joke.

I pulled away from the nudge in distraction. 'Come on, Stephen, stop dicking around.' I had moved on to the chocolate bars and biscuits and was trying to figure out what might last us ten days without melting into a disgusting ooze or bouncing into a bag of crumbs. 'Do you want Snickers or do you want to try something different?' I asked.

'I want Budweiser.' He grinned, then, seeing this had passed me by, adopted a sudden, solemn, jokeless tone. 'Please, Bryson, can I borrow' – he looked at the price – 'four dollars and seventy-nine cents. I'm broke.'

'Stephen, I don't know what's come over you. Put the beer back. Anyway, what happened to that five dollars I gave you?'

'Spent it.'

'What on?' And then it occurred to me. 'You've been drinking already, haven't you?'

'No,' he said robustly, as if dismissing a preposterous and possibly slanderous allegation.

But he was drunk – or at least half drunk. 'You have,' I said in amazement.

He sighed and rolled his eyes slightly. 'Two quarts of Michelob. Big deal.'

'You've been drinking.' I was appalled. 'When did you start drinking again?'

'In Des Moines. Just a little. You know, a couple of beers after work. Nothing to get in a panic about.'

'Stephen, you know you can't drink.'

He didn't want to hear this. He looked like a fourteen-year-old who had just been told to clean up his room. 'I don't need a lecture, Bryson.'

'I'm not going to buy you beer,' I said evenly.

He grinned as if I were being unaccountably priggish. 'Just a sixpack. Come on.'

'*No!*'

I was furious, livid – more furious than I had been about anything in years. I couldn't believe he was drinking again. It seemed such a deep, foolish betrayal of everything – of himself, me, what we were doing out here.

Katz was still wearing half a grin, but it didn't belong to his emotions any longer. 'So you're not going to buy me a couple of lousy beers after all I've done for you?'

This seemed a low blow. 'No.'

'Then fuck you,' he said and turned on his heel and walked out.

Chapter 20

Well, that rather coloured things, as you can imagine. We never said another word about it. It just hung there. At breakfast, we exchanged good mornings, more or less as normal, but didn't speak beyond that and afterwards, as we waited by Keith's van for a promised lift to the trailhead, we stood in an awkward silence, like adversaries in a property dispute waiting to be summoned into the judge's chambers.

At the edge of the woods when we alighted there was a sign announcing that this was the start of the Hundred Mile Wilderness, with a long soberly phrased warning to the effect that what lay beyond was not like other stretches of the trail, and that you shouldn't proceed if you didn't have at least ten days' worth of food and weren't feeling pretty tip-top.

It gave the woods a more ominous, vaguely moody feel. They were unquestionably different from woods further south – darker, more shadowy, inclining more to black than green. There were different trees, too – more conifers at low levels and many more birches – and scattered through the undergrowth were large, rounded black boulders, like sleeping animals, which lent the still recesses a certain eeriness. When Walt Disney decided to make *Bambi*, he despatched his artists to the Maine woods to make sketches, but this was palpably not a Disney wood of roomy glades and cuddlesome creatures. This brought to mind the woods in *The Wizard of Oz*, where the trees have ugly faces and malign intent, and every step seems a gamble. This was a wood for looming bears, dangling snakes, wolves with laser-red eyes. I understood at once why the velvet-jacketed Henry David Thoreau shat himself here.

As ever, the trail was well blazed, but in places almost overgrown, with ferns and other low foliage almost meeting in the middle over the path. Since only 10 per cent of thru-hikers make it this far, and it is much too distant for most day hikers, the trail in Maine is more thinly used. Above all, what set the trail apart was the terrain. In profile, the topography of the AT over the 18-mile section from Monson to Barren Mountain looks reasonably undemanding, rolling along at a more or less steady 1,200 feet with just a few steep rises and falls. In fact, it was hell.

Within half an hour we had come to a wall of rock, the first of many, perhaps 400 feet high. The trail ran up its face along a slight depression, like a lift shaft. It was as near perpendicular as a slope can get without actually being a rock climb. Slowly and laboriously we picked our way between and over boulders, using our hands as much as our feet. Combined with our exertion, the cloying heat was almost unbearable. I found I had to stop every ten or twelve yards to draw breath and wipe burning sweat from my eyes. I was swimming in heat, bathed in heat, swaddled in it. I don't believe I have ever been so warm or sweated so freely. I drank three-quarters of a bottle of water on the way up and used much of the rest to wet a bandanna and try to cool my throbbing head. I felt dangerously overheated and faint. I began to rest more frequently and for longer periods, to try to cool down a little, but each time I set off again

the heat came flooding back. I had never had to work so hard
or so tiringly to clear an Appalachian impediment, and this was
just the first of a series.

The top of the climb brought several hundred yards of bare,
gently sloping granite, like walking along a whale's back. From
each summit the panorama was sensational – for as far as the
eye could see, nothing but heavy green woods, denim-blue
lakes, and undulant mountains. Many of the lakes were
immense – as big as Windermere at least – and nearly all of
them had probably never felt so much as a human toe. There
was a certain captivating sense of having penetrated into a
secret corner of the world, but in the murderous sun it was
impossible to linger.

Then came a difficult and unnerving descent down a rocky
cliff face on the other side, a short walk through a dark, water-
less valley, and delivery to the foot of another wall of rock. And
so the day went, with monumental climbs and the hope of
water over the next hill the principal thing drawing us on. Katz
was soon out of water altogether. I gave him a drink of mine
and he accepted it gratefully, with a look that asked for a truce.
There was, however, still a kind of odour between us, an
unhappy sense that things had changed and would not be the
same again.

It was doubtless my fault. I pushed on further and longer
than we would have normally, and without consulting him,
unsubtly punishing him for having unbalanced the equilibrium
that had existed between us, and Katz bore it silently as his due.
We did 14 miles, an exceedingly worthy distance in the circumstances, and might have gone further, but at half past six we
came to a broad ford called Wilber Brook and stopped. We
were too tired to cross – that is to say, I was too tired – and it
would be folly to get wet so near sundown. We made camp and
shared out our cheerless rations with a kind of strained polite-
ness. Even if we had not been at odds, we would scarcely have
spoken. We were too tired. It had been a long day – the hardest

of the trip – and the thought that hung over us was that we had 85 more miles of this before we got to the camp store at Abol Bridge, 100 miles till we reached the difficult summit of Katahdin.

Even then we had no prospect of real comfort. Katahdin is in Baxter State Park, which takes a certain hearty pride in its devotion to ruggedness and deprivation. There are no restaurants and lodges, no gift shops and hamburger stands, not even any paved roads. The park itself is in the middle of nowhere, a two-day hike from Millinocket, the nearest town. It could be ten or eleven days before we had a proper meal or slept in a bed. It seemed a long way off.

In the morning we silently forded the stream – we were getting pretty good at it now – and started up the long, slow climb to the roof of the Barren–Chairback Range, 15 miles of ragged summits that we had to cross before descending to a more tranquil spell in the valley of the Pleasant River. The map showed just three tarns in those mountains, glacial leftovers, all off the trail, but otherwise no indication of water at all. With less than four litres of water capacity between us and the day already warm, the long haul between water sources promised to be at the very least uncomfortable.

Barren Mountain was a strenuous slog, much of it straight up and all of it hot, though we seemed to be getting stronger. Even Katz was moving with a comparative lightness. The weather remained sultry. It took us nearly all the morning to hike the four and a half miles up. I reached the top some time ahead of Katz. The summit was sun-warmed granite, hot to the touch, but there was a wisp of breeze – the first in days – and I found a shady spot beneath a disused fire tower. It was the first time in what seemed like weeks that I had sat anywhere in relative comfort. I leaned back and felt as if I could sleep for a month. Katz arrived ten minutes later, puffing hard but pleased to be at the top. He took a seat on a boulder beside mine. I had about two inches of water left, and passed him the bottle. He took a very modest sip and made to hand it back.

'Go on,' I said, 'you must be thirsty.'

'Thanks.' He took a slightly less modest sip and put the bottle down. He sat for a minute, then got out a Snickers, broke it in two and extended half to me. It was a somewhat odd thing to do because I had Snickers of my own and he knew that, but he had nothing else to give.

'Thanks,' I said.

He gnawed off a bite of Snickers, ate for a minute and said from out of nowhere: 'Girlfriend and boyfriend are talking. The girlfriend says to the boyfriend, "Jimmy, how do you spell *paedophilia*?" The boyfriend looks at her in amazement. "Gosh, honey," he says "that's an *awfully* big word for an eight-year-old."'

I laughed.

'I'm sorry about the other night,' Katz said.

'Me too.'

'I just got a little . . . I don't know.'

'I know.'

'It's kind of hard for me sometimes,' he went on. 'I try, Bryson, I really do, but.' He stopped there and shrugged reflectively, a little helplessly. 'There's just this kind of hole in my life where drinking used to be.' He was staring at the view – the usual verdant infinity of woods and lakes, shimmering slightly in a heat haze. There was something in his gaze – a miles-away fixedness – that made me think for a minute he had stopped altogether, but he went on: 'When I went back to Des Moines after Virginia and got that job building houses, at the end of the day all the crew would go off to this tavern across the street. They'd always invite me, but I'd say' – he lifted two hands and put on a deep, righteous voice – '"No, boys, I'm reformed." And I'd go home to my little apartment and heat a TV dinner, and feel all virtuous, like I'm supposed to. But really, you know, when you do that night after night it's kind of hard to persuade yourself you're leading a rich and thrilling existence. I mean, if you had a Fun-o-Meter, the needle wouldn't exactly be jumping into the orgasmic zone because you've got your own TV dinner. You know what I'm saying?'

He glanced over, to see me nod.

'So anyway one day after work, they invited me for about the hundredth time and I thought, "Oh, what the hell. No law that says I can't go in a tavern like anybody else." So I went and had a Diet Coke and it was OK. I mean, it was nice just to be out. But you know how good a beer is at the end of a long day. And there was this *jerk* named *Dwayne* who kept saying, "Go on, have a beer. You *know* you want one. One little beer's not gonna hurt ya. You haven't had a drink for three years. You can handle it."' He looked at me again. 'You know?'

I nodded.

'Caught me when I was vulnerable,' Katz said with a hard, ironic smile. 'You know, when I was still breathing. I never had more than three, I swear to God. I know what you're going to say – believe me, everybody's said it already. I know I can't drink. I know I can't have just a couple of beers like a normal person, that pretty soon the number will creep up and up and spin out of control. I know that. But.' He stopped there again, shaking his head. 'But I love to drink. I can't help it. I mean, I *love* it, Bryson – love the taste, love that buzz you get when you've had a couple, love the smell and feel of taverns. I miss dirty stories and the click of pool balls in the background, and that kind of bluish, underlit glow of a bar at night.' He was quiet again for a minute, lost in a little reverie for a lifetime's drinking. 'And I can't have it any more. I know that.' He breathed out heavily through his nostrils. 'It's just that. It's just that sometimes all I see ahead of me is TV dinners – a sort of endless line of them dancing towards me like in a cartoon. You ever eat TV dinners?'

'Not for years and years.'

'Well, they're shit, believe me. And, I don't know, it's just kind of hard . . .' He trailed off. 'Actually, it's *real* hard.' He looked at me, on the edge of emotion, his expression frank and humble. 'Makes me kind of an asshole sometimes,' he said quietly but sincerely.

I gave him a smile. 'Makes you more of an asshole,' I said.

He grunted a laugh. 'Yeah, I guess.'

I reached over and gave him a stupidly affectionate jab on the shoulder. He received it with a flicker of appreciation.

'And do you know what the fuck of it is?' he said in a sudden pull-yourself-together voice. 'I could kill for a TV dinner right now. I really could.'

We laughed.

'Hungry Man Turkey Dinner with plastic giblets and forty-weight gravy. Hmmmm-mmmm. I'd leave your scrawny ass up here for just a *sniff* of that.' Then he brushed at a corner of his eye, said, 'Hoo, fuck,' and went to have a pee over the cliff edge.

I watched him go, looking old and tired, and wondered for a minute what on earth we were doing up here. We weren't boys any more.

I looked at the map. We were practically out of water, but it was less than a mile to Cloud Pond, where we could refill. We split the last half-inch, and I told Katz I would go on ahead to the pond, filter the water and have it waiting for him when he arrived.

It was an easy twenty-minute walk along a grassy ridgeline. Cloud Pond was down a steep side trail, about a quarter of a mile off the AT. I left my pack propped against a rock at the trailside, and went with our water bottles and the filter down to the pond edge and filled up.

It took me perhaps twenty minutes to walk down, fill the three bottles and walk back, so when I returned to the AT it had been about forty minutes since I had seen Katz. Even if he had tarried on the mountaintop, and even allowing for his modest walking speed, he should have reached here by now. Besides, it was an easy walk and I knew he was thirsty, so it was odd that he wasn't here more promptly. I waited fifteen minutes and then twenty and twenty-five, and finally I left my pack and went back to look for him. It was well over an hour since I had seen him when I reached the mountaintop, and he wasn't there. I stood confounded on the spot where we had last been together. His stuff was gone. He had obviously moved on, but if he wasn't on Barren Mountain and wasn't at Cloud Pond and was nowhere in between, then where was he? The only possible explanations were that he had gone back the other way, which was out of the question – Katz would never have left me without explanation; never – or that he had somehow fallen off the ridgeline. It was an absurd notion – there wasn't anything remotely challenging or dangerous about the ridgeline – but you never know. John Connolly had told us weeks before of a friend of his who had fainted in the heat and tumbled a few feet off a safe, level trail; he had lain unnoticed for hours in blazing sunshine and slowly baked to death. All the way back to the Cloud Pond turnoff I carefully surveyed the trail-edge brush for signs of disturbance and peered at intervals over the lip of the ridge, fearful of seeing Katz spread-eagled on a rock. I called his name several times, and got nothing in return but my own fading voice.

By the time I reached the turnoff it had been nearly two hours since I had seen him. This was becoming worryingly inexplicable. The only remaining possibility was that he had walked past the turnoff while I was down at the pond filtering water, but this seemed manifestly improbable. There was a prominent arrowed sign by the trail saying CLOUD POND and my pack had been clearly visible beside the trail. Even if he had somehow failed to notice these things, he knew that Cloud Pond was only a mile from Barren Mountain. When you have hiked the AT as much as we had, you get so you can judge a mile with considerable accuracy. He couldn't have gone too far beyond without realizing his mistake and coming back. This just didn't make sense.

All I knew was that Katz was alone in a wilderness with no water, no map, no clear idea of what terrain lay ahead, presumably no idea of what had become of me, and a worrying lack of sense. If there was ever one person who would decide while lost on the AT to leave the trail and try for a short cut, it was Katz. I began to feel extremely uneasy. I left a note on my pack and went off down the trail. A half-mile further on, the trail descended very steeply, almost perpendicularly, more than 600 feet to a deep, nameless valley. He had to have realized by this point, surely, that he had gone wrong. I had told him Cloud Pond was a level stroll.

Calling his name at intervals, I picked my way slowly along the path down the cliff face, fearing the worst at the bottom – for this was a precipice one could easily fall down, especially with a big ungainly pack and a preoccupied mind – but there was no sign of him. I followed the trail two miles through the valley and up onto the summit of a high pinnacle called Fourth Mountain. The view from the top was expansive in every direction; the wilderness had never looked so big. I called his name long and hard, and got nothing in return.

It was getting on for late afternoon by this time. He had been at least four hours without water. I had no idea how long a person could survive without water in this heat, but I knew from experience that you couldn't go for more than half an hour without experiencing considerable discomfort. It occurred to me with a sinking feeling that he might have seen another pond – there were half a dozen to choose from scattered across the valley 2,000 feet below – and decided in his perplexity that perhaps that was it, and tried to reach it cross country. Even if he wasn't confused, he might simply have been driven by thirst to try to reach one of those ponds. They looked wonderfully cool and refreshing. The nearest was only about two miles away, but there was no trail to it and it was down a perilous slope through the woods. Once you were in the woods and bereft of bearings, you could easily miss it by a mile. Conversely, you could be within 50 yards of it and not know, as we had seen at Pleasant Pond a few days before. And once you were lost in these immense woods, you would die. It was as simple as that. No-one could save you. No helicopter could spot you through the cover of trees. No rescue teams could find you. None, I suspected, would even try. There would be bears down there, too – bears that had possibly never seen a human. All the possibilities made my head hurt.

I hiked back to the Cloud Pond turnoff, hoping more than anything I had hoped for in a long time that he would be sitting on the pack, and that there would be some amusing, unconsidered explanation – that we had kept just missing each other, like in a stage farce: him waiting bewildered at my pack, then going off to look for me; me arriving a moment later, waiting in puzzlement and going off – but I knew he wouldn't be there, and he wasn't. It was nearly dusk when I got back. I wrote a fresh note and left it under a rock in the middle of the AT, just in case, hoisted my pack and went down to the pond, where there was a shelter.

The irony was that this was the nicest campsite I experienced anywhere along the AT, and it was the one place I camped without Katz. Cloud Pond was a couple of hundred acres of exquisitely peaceful water surrounded by dark coniferous forest, the treetops pointy black silhouettes against a pale blue evening sky. The shelter, which I had to myself, was on a level area 30 or 40 yards back from the pond and slightly above it. It was practically new and spotless. There was a privy nearby. It was nearly perfect. I dumped my stuff on the wooden sleeping platform and went down to the water's edge to filter water, so I wouldn't have to do it in the morning, then stripped to my boxers and waded a couple of feet into the dark water to have a wash with a bandanna. If Katz had been there, I'd have had a swim. I tried not to think about him – certainly not to visualize him lost and bewildered. There was, after all, nothing I could do now.

Instead, I sat on a rock and watched the sunset. The pond was almost painfully beautiful. The long rays of the setting sun made the water shimmer golden. Offshore, two loons cruised, as if out for a spin after supper. I watched them for a long time, and thought about something I had seen on a BBC nature programme some time before.

Loons, according to the programme, are not social creatures. But towards the end of summer, just before they fly back to the North Atlantic, where they pass the winter bobbing on stormy waves, they host a series of get-togethers. A dozen or more loons from all the neighbouring ponds fly in, and they all swim around together for a couple of hours for no discernible reason other than the pleasure of being together. The host loon leads the guests on a proud but low-key tour of his territory – first to his favourite little cove, say, then perhaps over to an interesting fallen log, then on to a patch of lily pads. 'This is where I like to fish in the mornings,' he seems to be saying. 'And here's where we're thinking of moving our nesting site next year.' All the other loons follow him around with diligence and polite interest. No-one knows why they do this (but then no-one knows why one human being would want to show another his converted bathroom) or how they arrange their rendezvous, but they all show up each night at the right lake at the right time as certainly as if they had been sent a card that said: 'We're Having a Party!' I think that's wonderful. I would have enjoyed it more if I hadn't kept thinking of Katz stumbling and gasping and searching for a lake by moonlight.

Oh, and by the way, the loons are disappearing everywhere because their lakes are dying from acid rain.

I had a rotten night, of course, and was up before five and back on the trail at first light. I continued on north in the direction I guessed Katz had gone, but with the nagging thought that I was plunging ever further into the Hundred Mile Wilderness – not perhaps the best direction to go if he was somewhere nearby and in trouble. There was a certain incidental disquiet at the thought that I was on my own in the middle of nowhere – a disquiet briefly but vividly heightened when I stumbled in my haste on the return descent to the deep, nameless valley and came within a trice of falling 50 long feet, with a messy bounce at the bottom. I hoped I was doing the right thing.

Even flat out it would take me three days, perhaps four, to reach Abol Bridge and the campground. By the time I alerted authorities, Katz would have been missing for four or five days. On the other hand, if I turned now and went back the way we had come, I could be in Monson by the following afternoon. What I really needed was to meet somebody coming south who could tell me if they had seen Katz, but there was no-one out on the trail. I looked at my watch. Of course there wasn't. It was only a little after six in the morning. There was a shelter at Chairback Gap, six miles further on. I would reach it by eight or so. With luck, there might still be someone there. I pressed on with more care and a queasy uncertainty.

I clambered back over the pinnacle of Fourth Mountain – much harder with a pack – and into another wooded valley beyond. Four miles after leaving Cloud Pond, I came to a tiny stream, barely worthy of the term – really just a slick of moist mud. Speared to a branch beside the trail, in an intentionally prominent place, was an empty pack of Old Gold cigarettes. Katz didn't really smoke, but he always carried a pack of Old Golds. In the mud by a fallen log were three cigarette butts. He had obviously waited here. So he was alive and hadn't left the trail, and clearly had come this way. I felt immeasurably better. At least I was going in the right direction. As long as he stayed on the trail, I was bound eventually to overtake him.

I found him four hours after setting off, sitting on a rock by the turnoff for West Chairback Pond, head inclined to the sun as if working on his tan. He was extensively scratched and muddy, and wildly bedraggled, but otherwise looked OK. He was of course delighted to see me.

'Bryson, you old mountain man, you're a welcome sight. Where have you been?'

'I was wondering the same about you.'

'Guess I missed the last watering hole?'

I nodded.

He nodded, too. 'Knew I had, of course. Soon as I got down to the bottom of that big cliff, I thought, "Shit, this can't be right."'

'Why didn't you come back?'

'I don't know. I got it in mind somehow that you must have pushed on. I was real thirsty. I think I might have been a little confused – a little addled, as you might say. I was real thirsty.'

'So what did you do?'

'Well, I pushed on and kept thinking I had to come to water sooner or later, and eventually I came to a mud slick—'

'Where you left the cigarette pack?'

'You saw it? I'm so proud. Yeah, well, I soaked up some water there with my bandanna, because I remembered that's what Fess Parker did once on the Davy Crockett Show.'

'How very enterprising.'

He accepted the compliment with a nod. 'That took about an hour, and then I waited another hour for you and had a couple of smokes, and then it was getting dark so I put my tent up, ate a Slim Jim and went to bed. Then this morning I sponged up a little more water with my bandanna and I came on here. There's a real nice pond just down there, so I thought I'd wait here where there was water and hope that you'd come along eventually. I didn't think you'd leave me up here on purpose, but you're such a walking daydream I could just imagine you getting all the way to Katahdin before you noticed I wasn't with you.' He put on a poncey accent. ' "Oh, I say, *delight*ful view – don't you agree, Stephen? Stephen? Stephen? Now where the *deuce* has he got to?"' He gave me a familiar smile. 'So I'm real glad to see you.'

'How'd you get so scratched up?'

He looked at his arm, which was covered in a zig-zag of dried blood. 'Oh that? It's nothing.'

'What do you mean it's nothing? It looks like you've been doing surgery on yourself.'

'Well, I didn't want to alarm you, but I also got kind of lost.'
'How?'

'Well, between losing you and coming upon the mud slick, I tried to get to a lake I saw from the mountain.'

'Oh, Stephen, you didn't.'

'Well, I was real thirsty, you know, and it didn't look too far. So I plunged off into the woods. Not real smart, right?'
'No.'

'Yeah, well, I learned that real fast because I hadn't gone more than half a mile before I was totally lost. I mean totally lost. It's weird, you know, because you're thinking all you've got to do is go downhill to the water and come back the same way, and that shouldn't be too tough as long as you pay attention. But the thing is, Bryson, there's nothing to pay attention to out there. It's just one big wood. So when I realized I didn't have the faintest idea where I was I thought, "OK, well, I got lost by going downhill, so I'd better go back up." But suddenly there's a *lot* of uphills, and a lot of downhills too, and it's real confusing. So I went up and up and up until I *knew* I'd gone a lot further than I'd come, and then I thought, "Well, Stephen, you stupid piece of shit" – 'cause I was getting a little cross with myself by this time, to tell you the truth – I thought, "you must have gone too far, you jackass," so I went back down a ways, and *that* didn't work, so then I tried going sideways for a while, and – well, you get the picture.'

'You should never leave the trail, Stephen.'

'Oh, now there's a timely piece of advice, Bryson. Thank you so much. That's like telling somebody who's died in a crash, "Drive safely now."'

'Sorry.'

'Forget it. I think maybe I'm still a little, you know, unsettled.

I thought I was done for. Lost, no water – and you with the chocolate chip cookies.'

'So how did you get back to the trail?'

'It was a miracle, I swear to God. Just when I was about to lie down and give myself to the wolves and bobcats, I look up and there's a white blaze on a tree and I look down and I'm *standing* on the AT. At the mud slick, as a matter of fact. I sat down and had three smokes one after the other, just to calm myself down, and then I thought, "Shit, I bet Bryson's walked by here while I've been blundering around in the woods, and he'll never come back because he's already checked this section of trail." And then I began to worry that I never would see you again. So I really *was* glad when you turned up. To tell you the truth, I've never been so glad to see another person in my whole life, and that includes some naked women.'

There was something in his look.

'You want to go home?' I asked.

He thought for a moment. 'Yeah. I do.'

'Me, too.'

So we decided to leave the endless trail and stop pretending we were mountain men because we weren't. At the bottom of Chairback Mountain, four miles further on, there was a dirt logging road. We didn't know where it went other than that it must go somewhere. An arrow on the edge of the map pointed south to Katahdin Iron Works, site of an improbable nineteenth-century factory in the woods and now a state historical monument. According to my Trail Guide there was public parking at the old iron works, so there must be a road out. At the bottom of the mountain, we watered up at a brook that ran past, and then started off along the logging road. We hadn't been walking more than three or four minutes when there was a noise in the near distance. We turned to see a cloud of dust heading our way led by an ancient pickup truck moving at great speed. As it approached I instinctively put my thumb out, and to my astonishment it stopped about 50 feet past us.

We ran up to the driver's window. There were two guys in the cab, both in hard hats and dirty from work – loggers obviously.

'Where you going?' asked the driver.

'Anywhere,' I said. 'Anywhere but here.'

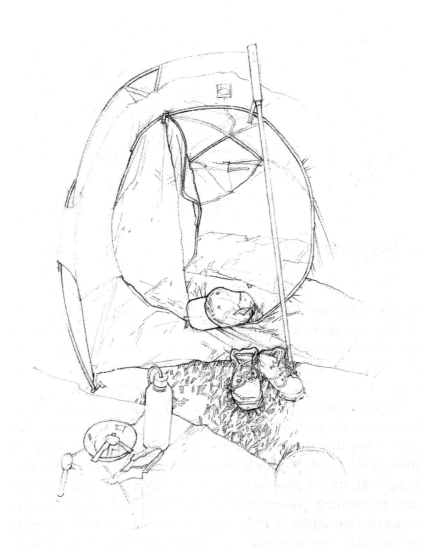

Chapter 21

So we didn't see Katahdin. We didn't even see Katahdin Iron Works, except as a glimpsed blur, because we shot past it at about 70 miles an hour on the bounciest, most terrifyingly hasty ride I ever hope to have in the back of a pickup truck on a dirt road.

We held on for dear life in the open back, lifting our feet to let chainsaws and other destructive-looking implements slide past – first this way, then that – while the driver propelled us through the flying woods with reckless zest, bouncing over potholes with such vigour as to throw us a foot or two into the air, and negotiating curves as if in startled afterthought. In consequence we alighted at the little community of Milo, 20 miles to the south, on unsteady legs and blinking at the suddenness with which our circumstances had changed. One moment we were in the heart of the wilderness, facing at least a two-day hike to civilization, and now we were in the forecourt of a gas station on the edge of a remote little town. We watched the pickup truck depart, then took our bearings.

'You want to get a Coke?' I said to Katz. There was a machine by the gas station door.

He looked at it. 'No,' he said. 'Maybe later.'

It was unlike Katz not to fall upon soft drinks and junk food with exuberant lust when the opportunity presented itself, but I believed I understood. There is always a measure of shock when you leave the trail and find yourself parachuted into a world of comfort and choice, but it was different this time. This time it was permanent. We were hanging up our hiking boots. From now on, there would *always* be Coke, and soft beds and showers and whatever else we wanted. There was no urgency now. It was a strangely subduing notion.

Milo had no motel, but we were directed to a place called Bishop's Boarding-house. It was a large old white house on a handsome street of substantial old houses, the kind where the garages were originally carriage houses with quarters upstairs for the servants.

We were received with warmth and bustling kindliness by the proprietor, Joan Bishop, a cheery, snowy-haired lady with a hearty Down East accent who came to the door wringing floury hands on an apron and waved us and our grubby packs into the spotless interior without a flicker of dismay.

The house smelled wholesomely of fresh-baked pastry, garden tomatoes, and air nobly unmodified by fans or air conditioners – old-fashioned summer smells. She called us 'you boys', and acted as if she had been expecting us for days, possibly years.

'Goodness me, just look at you boys!' she clucked in astonishment and delight. 'You look as if you've been wrestling bears!'

I suppose we must have looked a sight. Katz was liberally covered in blood from his fraught stumble through the woods, and there was tiredness all over us, even in our eyes.

'You boys go up and get yourselves cleaned up and come

down to the porch afterwards and I'll have a nice jug of iced tea waiting for you. Or would you rather have lemonade? Never mind, I'll make both. Now go on!' And off she bustled.

'Thanks, Mom,' we muttered in a dazzled and grateful unison.

Katz was instantly transformed – so much so that he felt perhaps a trifle too much at home. I was wearily taking some things from my pack when he suddenly appeared in my room without knocking and hastily shut the door behind him, looking flummoxed. Only a towel, clutched not quite adequately around his waist, preserved his hefty modesty.

'Little old lady,' he said in amazement.

'Pardon?'

'Little old lady in the hallway,' he said again.

'It is a guesthouse, Stephen.'

'Yeah, I hadn't thought of that,' he said. He peeked round the door and disappeared without elaboration.

When we had showered and changed, we joined Mrs Bishop on the screened porch, where we slumped heavily and gratefully in the big old porch chairs, legs thrust out, the way you do when it's hot and you're tired. I was hoping that Mrs Bishop would tell us that she was forever putting up hikers who had been foiled by the Hundred Mile Wilderness, but in fact we were the first she could recall in that category.

'I read in the paper the other day that a man from Portland hiked Katahdin to celebrate his seventy-eighth birthday,' she said conversationally.

That made me feel immensely better, as you can imagine.

'I expect I'll be ready to try again by then,' Katz said, running a finger along the line of scratch on his forearm.

'Well, it'll still be there, boys, when you're ready for it,' she said. She was right, of course.

We dined in town at a popular restaurant, and afterwards, with the evening warm and congenial, went for a stroll. Milo was a sweetly hopeless town – commercially forlorn, far from anywhere and barely alive, but curiously likeable. Perhaps it was just that it was our last night away from home.

'So do you feel bad about leaving the trail?' Katz asked after a time.

I thought for a moment, unsure. I had come to realize that I didn't have any feelings towards the AT that weren't thoroughly contradictory. I was weary of the trail, but captivated by it; found the endless slog increasingly exhausting but ever invigorating; grew tired of the boundless woods but admired their boundlessness; enjoyed the escape from civilization and ached for its comforts. All of this together, all at once, every moment, on the trail or off.

'I don't know,' I said. 'Yes and no, I guess. What about you?'

He nodded. 'Yes and no.'

We walked along for some minutes, lost in small thoughts.

'Anyway, we did it,' Katz said at last, looking up. He noted my quizzical expression. 'Hiked Maine, I mean.'

I looked at him. 'Stephen, we didn't even see Mount Katahdin.'

He dismissed this as a petty quibble. 'Another mountain,' he said. 'How many do you need to see, Bryson?'

I gave a small laugh. 'Well, that's one way of looking at it.'

'It's the *only* way of looking at it,' Katz went on and quite earnestly. 'As far as I'm concerned, I hiked the Appalachian Trail. I hiked it in snow and I hiked it in heat. I hiked it in the South and I hiked it in the North. I hiked it till my feet bled. I *hiked* the Appalachian Trail, Bryson.'

'We missed out a lot of it, you know.'

'Details,' Katz sniffed.

I shrugged, not unhappily. 'Maybe you're right.'

'Of course I'm right,' he said, as if he were seldom otherwise.

We had reached the edge of town, by the little gas station/ grocery store where the lumberjacks had dropped us. It was still open.

'So what do you say to some cream soda?' Katz said brightly. 'I'll buy.'

I looked at him with deepened interest. 'You don't have any money.'

'I know. I'll buy it with your money.'

I grinned and handed him a five-dollar bill from my wallet.

'*X Files* tonight,' Katz said happily – very, very happily – and disappeared into the store. I watched him go, shaking my head, and wondered how he always knew.

So that, I'm afraid, is how it ended for me and Katz – with a six-pack of cream soda in Milo, Maine.

I continued to hike, on and off, in a modest way, through the rest of summer and into autumn. In early November, when winter was blowing in and the hiking season was clearly at an end, I finally sat down at the kitchen table with my trail log and a calculator and totted up the miles I had done. I checked the numbers through twice, then looked up with an expression not unlike the one Katz and I had shared months before in Gatlinburg when we realized we were never going to hike the Appalachian Trail.

I had done 870 miles, considerably less than half, not a huge amount more than one-third. All that effort and sweat and disgusting grubbiness, all of those endless plodding days, the nights on hard ground – all that added up to just 39.5 per cent of the trail. Goodness knows how anyone ever completes the whole thing. I am filled with admiration and incredulity for those who see it through. But, hey and excuse me, 870 is still a lot of miles.

Stephen Katz returned to Des Moines, to a life of devoted sobriety. He calls from time to time and talks about coming out sometime to try the Hundred Mile Wilderness again, though I don't suppose he ever will.

I won't say that the experience changed our lives, and I can't speak for Katz, but I certainly gained an appreciation and respect for woods and wilderness and the colossal scale of

America. I lost a lot of weight and for a time was remarkably fit.

Best of all, these days when I see a mountain, I look at it slowly and appraisingly, with a narrow, knowing gaze, and eyes of chipped granite.